THE DYNAMICS OF SPIRITUAL WARFARE TEACHING SERIES
VOLUME II

The Authority of the Believer

Advanced Volume
With Chart Study Guide

By
Dr. T.C. Maxwell

THE DYNAMICS OF SPIRITUAL WARFARE TEACHING SERIES
VOLUME II, THE AUTHORITY OF THE BELIEVER

ISBN: 1-59352-087-5

Published by:
Christian Services Network
1975 Janich Ranch Ct.
El Cajon, CA 92019
Toll Free: 1-866-484-6184

Printed in the United States of America

THIS IS A WARNING!
(10 pointers on how to handle this book)

1. Please study this book with an open spirit. It's like eating fish-enjoy the meat and spit out the bones. *Ignite the Warfare* was good, but this book will be great.

2. You may not agree with every point and that's alright.

3. There are some areas I'm short on information. I'm learning spiritual warfare according to Scripture, and some areas I went all out, too much information. At least to me I am doing my best.

4. This book isn't meant to be used as a Bible replacement, but as a Bible aide. It is only a Scriptural support at best. These teachings are based upon my testamonies, revelations, and actual events.

5. It will take you several readings and long hours of study to understand certain pointes of view mentioned herein. This book is for the slow reader as well as the swift.

6. We're not trying to re-invent the wheel, but understand how to make it roll better.

7. Is there enough solid information in this book to defeat Satan? Yes, as long as you stand on the Word and listen to the Holy Spirit. Obedience is the key to success.

8. If you're going to preach or teach from this book, you can plan on souls being delivered; please give God the glory and write, e-mail, or call us. It will encourage us to hear testimonies.

9. I tend to get a little tough at times, so let us be in prayer for our leaders, the legal system and others; I highly respect our government. I want a city, state, nation and world wide revival.

10. If at best this book is used only as a prop for the coffee table or decoration for the kitchen counter, let me inform you thal I have a few more coming very soon-or just pass it along to your worst enemy!

THIS IS ONLY A WARNING!!!!!!! I'M TOO YOUNG TOO RECEIVE HATE MAIL!

Before You Start To Read This Book, You Must Read *Ignite the Warfare. Volume 1*

While you're reading and studying this book, call for information on the workbook to both Volumes I & II and the tape library.

ABOUT THE AUTHOR

Dr. T.C. Maxwell was born in Stucky Still, a subdivision of Groveland, Florida. The son of Oliver and Shirley Maxwell, the fourth of eight children, he was thought to be a peculiar little boy. He didn't talk much and often played alone. His parents wondered what life had to offer him. At a tender age he had his first spiritual encounter and when he was a teenager he received Jesus Christ as his personal Lord and Savior. January 13, 1974 God called him to preach the Gospel some months later. After some basic training, and years of being a good Sunday school student, he began to fulfill that call.

After high school and community college, he received a Bachelor's degree from Evangel Center for Religious Training. He has also received a Masters in Religious Education and a Doctorate of Humanities from Canon Bible College and Seminary. He has also received various awards, certificates, religious and non-religious accolades throughout his 28-plus years of preaching, pastoring and mentoring.

T.C. is the husband of one wife, Audrey Maxwell. They have been married twenty wonderful years. He is the father of two beautiful and intelligent daughters who love God, Teri Renee and Precious Jewel Maxwell. T.C.'s calling is that of an Apostle. He's also the Bishop of several churches and mentors to many young pastors nationally as well as in foreign countries. At the present he's traveling with his wife conducting revivals, seminars and doing workshops. They now reside in Boca Raton, Florida.

Dr. T.C. Maxwell lives a life of spiritual warfare in his daily walk with God. In these pages he has given you just a portion of the insight that God has dealt unto him. There will be other books, tapes, videos and national crusades on the subject of "warfare not welfare" coming your way soon.

PREFACE
Finding Strength in the Struggle!

This testimony from my wife made such an impact in *Ignite the Warfare* that I had to bring it back.

Dr. T.C. Maxwell

It seems like only yesterday that the Lord permitted us to go through an intense time of trials and suffering. Our first daughter was only one year old (she's now 21), and we were young pastors with a small congregation. During this time, it seemed as if our natural life began to come apart at the seams. My husband was self-employed in the landscaping business with only a few commercial accounts. Due to the economic condition of the congregation, most-and sometimes all-of our personal income was used to take care of the financial obligations of the church. Of course this meant that home and family felt the pain and suffering of this sacrifice. We were being tested by the trials of ministry as it speaks of in 2 Corinthians 4:8-11, (KJV).

> *We are troubled on every side, yet not distressed, we are perplexed, but not in despair; persecuted, but not forsaken; cast down, but not destroyed; always bearing about in the body the dying of the Lord Jesus, that the life also of Jesus might be made manifest in our body. For we which live are always delivered unto death for Jesus' sake, that the life also of Jesus might be made manifest in our mortal flesh.*

After being forced to give up all we owned we moved in with a friend. I was working at the time for a temporary service, had a newborn infant, and my husband was building a business. The pressure was so great I was brought to what seemed to me to be the end of my rope. My husband was doing all he could to make provisions, to no avail. Through it all we kept the faith-at least that's all I heard my husband speak out of his mouth. I began to give up. For me, the suffering was not the problem. My baby was not able to have some necessities of life and for me that was unbearable. I found myself rocking my baby, crying, and apologizing to her. One day my husband walked in on me praying to God and asking that He take me home to be with Him in heaven. My husband held me in his arms and asked me not to pray that prayer. He didn't want to be left here without me. He held me as he began to encourage and pray for me. He prayed with such faith and power that I began to feel the compassion of the warmth of the Holy Ghost. At that moment, I made a quality decision to reach beyond battle fatigue and to fight the enemy alongside my husband and my family.

By this time, we had been forced to close our small storefront church and return to fellowship with my husband's former Bishop and the congregation we had left one year earlier. We had no transportation for a long season. We had preached spiritual warfare before, and even fought spiritual battles, but nothing like this. I decided to do not only what I had been taught, but also what I had taught others. I prayed, making my needs known to God; I turned my plate over and began to fast. I said to God, "I won't eat until You bless us." After several days of fasting, God blessed us.

My husband secured a management position over a Southern Bell building, where he supervised twenty-five people. A short time later, as he was walking across the parking lot of our building, he met a young man whose father owned the apartment complex we lived in. My husband and this young man talked, (my husband was totally unaware of who he was). The young man never revealed that his father owned the complex and went back and told his father about the young man he had met. They were seeking a property manager for the large complex, which would entail a rent-free, two-bedroom apartment and other perks.

The next day a memo was placed over the mailboxes of each building. While on my knees praying and still fasting, my husband went out to check the mail and found the memo. He removed it from the wall, hurried into the house and interrupted my prayer to read the memo. I read it, and then bowed my head in prayer because I was now able to pray more specifically that my husband be chosen for this position. He immediately went to apply. When he walked into the downtown office, God had gone before him and given him favor. He handed the completed application to the secretary and when she saw his name she said, "The owner's son already said that you would be a good person for the position." My husband was hired immediately.

The present manager had not moved out and was delaying the move. I ended the fast and said, "Lord I want to move into our apartment before Easter," which was only about three weeks away. As you may have guessed; we moved in a few days before Easter. That was years ago.

T.C. Maxwell, my friend, my love, my husband, and my trainer, was able to teach me *The Dynamics of Spiritual Warfare* because he had fought in it before me and with me. For this I am grateful. He is such a prayer warrior that for many his congregation of warriors have called him "Drill Sergeant." They have been taught-and to this day-demonstrate that the weapons of our warfare are not carnal, but are mighty through God to the pulling down of strongholds. He has led many out of the "welfare" mentality and into the "warfare" mentality.

The Dynamics of Spiritual Warfare is such a reality that you must read these volumes with the desire to possess all that our Heavenly Father has promised. You must desire to understand that Jesus the Christ suffered, died, and rose on the morning of the third day with all power in his hand. He gave that power to us, the elect of God. Please dive in and let *The Authority of the Believer* bless and encourage you to continue to fight the good fight of faith.

> *To be not conformed to this world, but rather transformed*
> *by the renewing of your mind that you may prove what is*
> *that good, and acceptable, and perfect will of God*
> (Romans 12:2)

This is my prayer.

Audrey R. Maxwell
Prophetess

TABLE OF CONTENTS

CHAPTER ONE

The Start of Warfare

On a hot summer day in South Florida, I was at football practice with the Junior Varsity team. There I was weighing every bit of one hundred thirty-three pounds, standing 5'8" tall. I was the split-end/cornerback, and I didn't need to be much heavier for my position. I also had good speed. Many days the coach would have the whole team race, and I would come in first or second (not bragging). But I learned personally that speed isn't everything. There was a particular drill we did that was necessary to prepare us for the season, but I avoided it as much as possible, because the drill requirement had little to do with speed...it was for strength, stamina and endurance. I believe I had those qualities, but I hated to be challenged in those areas, because it took physical contact, and I hated to be sore and bruised.

We had a fullback on the team nicknamed Big Nate. The word on the streets was Nate was a twin and he came out a single. We believe Nate ate his twin and he became double the size (joke). That day the coach for whatever reason (maybe he had a sun stroke) put me (T.C.) at 133 lbs. up against Big Nate (220 lbs and 6'2"). If this was a foot race, no problem, but this was strength against stamina contest. The team makes a circle and the coach gives you or your opponent the football. The other individual must tackle the ball carrier as many times as possible in five minutes.

I got the ball first and had quick feet. Big Nate suffered a little and ran out of breath due to low stamina, (well, he got me

3

once or twice). But after a two-minute break, Big Nate retrieved the ball, with a revengeful attitude and coach told the team to tighten the circle. My first ten attempts to tackle this mountain were disastrous. I attacked him at his strongest points, which were his chest and big arms and oh my God! Big Nate ran me over, sat on me, fell on me and embarrassed the pride out of me. In the background I could hear the team saying, "You're getting your butt kicked real good." It was because I had only been paying attention to my position and I didn't watch others practice in the circle. That day I decided to become a team player. The coach was screaming at me "What's wrong Maxwell? Can't you take down one man?" Because of the lack of team participation, I didn't have the strength or technique to handle my opponent.

It was only two-minutes into the drill, and I began to listen to my teammates, especially those that played on the line of scrimmage. They were slow compared to the split ends, cornerbacks and running backs, but they knew their job. One of them said to go for the ankles. Nothing else I did worked, so what did I have to lose? I was also tired of getting my butt kicked all over the circle. Big Nate came up to run me over for the 11th time and I got aim at him chest level, he dropped to his waist and Big Nate flipped and hit the ground. I turned around, and he was laid out flat. A light was turned on in my head. Thank You Jesus! I received the revelation. The last two minutes of the drill I ignited the warfare.

It's not by speed, nor by might, but by the revelation of information. This story happened almost 30 years ago. Thank you coach, thank you Nate, and especially the guys who worked on the line of scrimmage. You don't get much credit, but you're very important to winning in the trenches. Wars sometimes don't keep to our schedules, but all battles must be fought, ready or not. My battle didn't start in the circle that day. It started when I joined the team in the beginning. The circle revealed my progress.

How we respond to adversity may be the difference of life and death. It only takes seconds, minutes or hours to give the proper response. The training may take years or a lifetime. You may not have years to learn the lesson of a lifetime, so I'll share some of my experiences and adventures to assist you in your warfare. I don't expect you to understand everything, but what you get will bless you tremendously. We will pull back the curtains of the Spirit realm. Some things are only spiritual and have no natural explanation; others can be understood by using types, examples and shadows. We don't proclaim perfection because we know in part, understand in part and are willing to share the good, the bad and the ugly.

Please do us a favor and pray, study and try to understand these teachings. There is a real world all around, above and out of our sight. We will use a chart to explore their occupants, the role and function in each heaven. This is only a speck of all the multi-trillion events of activities. We are going to use stories, illustrations, and charts to make plain the things that seem a mystery.

THE THRONE OF GOD

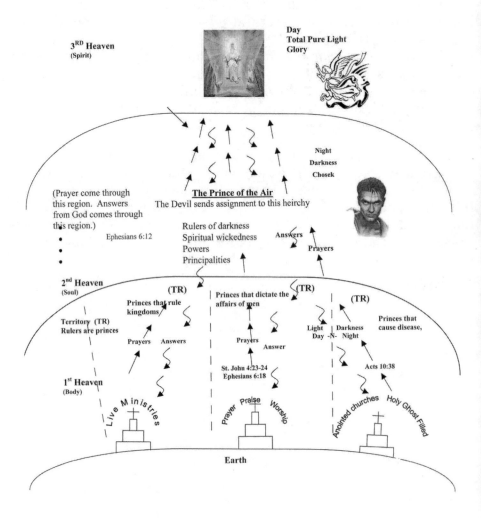

3RD Heaven
(Spirit)

Day
Total Pure Light
Glory

Night
Darkness
Chosek

(Prayer come through this region. Answers from God comes through this region.)

• Ephesians 6:12
•
•

The Prince of the Air
The Devil sends assignment to this heirchy

Rulers of darkness
Spiritual wickedness
Powers
Principalities

Answers

Prayers

2nd Heaven
(Soul)

(TR)

Territory (TR)
Rulers are princes

Princes that rule
kingdoms

Princes that dictate the
affairs of men

(TR)

(TR)

Princes that
cause disease,

Prayers   Answers

Prayers

Answer

Light | Darkness
Day -N- Night

1st Heaven
(Body)

Live Ministries

St. John 4:23-24
Ephesians 6:18

Prayer Praise Worship

Acts 10:38

Anointed churches   Holy Ghost Filled

Earth

It is time to walk in the spirit world and allow me to explain the charts.

3RD HEAVEN

I
N
H
A
B
I
T
A
N
S

- Father
- Son
- The Holy Spirit is at work in the Church on earth
- Ruling angels is Eph. 1:21;3:10; Col. 1:16; 2:10; 1 Peter 3:22
- Seraphim–Isa. 6:1-7
- Cherubim–Gen. 3:24; Ex. 25:18-20; Eze. 1:4-28; 10:1-22
- Warrior Archangels–Isa. 14:14; Daniel 10:13,21; 12:1; Jude 9; Rev. 12:7
- Messenger Archangels–Daniel 8:16; 9:21; Luke 1:19
- Living Creature–Rev. 4:6-9; 5:8; 6:1,3,5,7
- Guardian Angels–St. Matthew 18:10; Heb. 1:14
- Redeem Patriots and Saints–St. Matthew 27:52-53; St. Luke 23:43

The center of heaven is the throne of God. Which is God's dwelling place. In spiritual warfare we know God is everywhere at all times. The throne room is the meeting place established not only for infinite man to focus on, but all of the Hosts of Heaven (1st, 2nd, 3rd). There are perpetual praises around the throne, thunder, lightning and loud noises. There are angels singing, 24 Elders playing harps and the seraphim and cherubim, are rejoicing. The 3rd Heaven isn't a quiet place.

The glory of God and the host of heaven rejoice every time a sinner accepts Jesus as Lord and Savior. There are prayers of the saints that come through the 2nd heaven as a sweet smelling savor. Angels are on the alert watching the little ones that love God. Warrior angels are escorting messenger angels with answered prayer requests. Saints from the 1st heaven are given access while in prayer to the throne of God. They come boldly and leave with strength goodness and mercy following them. New arrivals are saints who have died, and there are angels that

7

bring them into the presence of God. In St. Luke 16:22, Jesus is seated at the right hand talking to God about us, covering our faults and washing us with His Word.

We have all of these activities happening on our behalf 24 hours a day, 7 days a week. God is saying to us that all of this is for our authority as believers in Him. The heavens are busy establishing order for the authority of the saints.

The 3rd Heaven gets visits from the accuser of the brethren which is Satan who is constantly bringing accusation against us. But remember, we have an advocate with the Father. And we are bought with a price by the precious blood of Jesus. Every time Satan reminds God of our past, Jesus reminds him of His future which allows us to focus on the occupants of the 3rd Heaven, (some not mentioned on the charts).

THE THRONE OF GOD
(where the Father and Son are presently seated).

3rd Heaven is where the Throne of God, the Father, Son and the Holy Ghost rules as one God.

The Father:

The Lord is in His holy temple, the Lord's throne is in Heaven: His eyes behold, His eyelids try, the children of men.

(Psalm 11:4)

The Lord hath prepared His throne in the heavens; and His kingdom ruleth over all.

(Psalm 103:19)

Because God is so awesome His Name is to be honored, worshiped and praised continually in Heaven and on Earth.

After this manner therefore pray ye: Our Father which art in heaven, hallowed be thy name.

(St. Matthew 6:9)

God the Father, Son and Holy Spirit created the heavens and from His throne He rules in the affairs of men. God controls the activities of angels, demons and Satan. A sparrow doesn't fall to the ground and die without His foreknowledge. Studying spiritual warfare, you must know who's in charge. Why is this so important to know? Because the Heavens do rule (Daniel 4:26). God established and rules all the Heavens. We must pray that His will be done on earth, as it is in Heaven.

The Son:

The wisdom and power of God, counted equal with God the Father. The express image of God the Father: The express image of God.

And if I go and prepare a place for you, I will come again, and receive you unto myself; that where I am, there ye may be also.
(St John 14:3)

A little while, and ye shall not see me: and again a little while, and ye shall see me, because I go to the Father.
(St John 16:16)

The Son must return to the Father God, because His mission was fulfilled on Calvary as a ransom for sin.

I came forth from the Father, and am come into the world: again, I leave the world, and go to the Father.
(St. John 16:28)

Because of Jesus the perfect sin offering for mankind, no one can condemn us because of our past, because, God justifies us.

Who is he that condemneth? It is Christ that died, ye rather, that is risen again, who is even at the right hand God, who also maketh intercession for us.
(Roman 8:34)

The Holy Spirit:

The third person in the trinity is the Holy Ghost. He is the

Spirit of God who reigns in the Church on Earth, but also controls access to heavenly places.

> *But he, being full of the Holy Ghost looked up steadfastly into Heaven and saw the glory of God, and Jesus standing on the right hand of God. And said, " Behold, I see the Heavens opened, and the Son of man standing on the right hand of God.*
>
> (Acts 7:55-56)

The Holy Ghost is the authority to the believers.

The Holy Ghost confirms the testimony of Jesus that He is the Son of God, and being equal with God is seated on the right hand of Authority. Because the Holy Ghost is the authority of the believer; He allows a spirit-filled believer to look from Earth to the 3rd Heaven. We will not spend much time writing on the Holy Spirit in this chapter, but understand this; He is in charge of the Church, the saints and controls all spiritual activities dealing with the heavenlies. Don't try to fight any warfare without the Holy Spirit. The 5 fold gifts, the fruit of the spirit, the nine gifts all operated by the Holy Spirit.

The Angels:

> *The Host of Heaven, the ministers, that does his pleasure.*
> (Psalm 103:20-21)

> *Now there was a day when the Sons of God came to present themselves before the Lord.*
> (Job 1:6)

I believe angels are on assignment hearkening to the voice of the Lord. They come and go throughout the Heavenlies. They have business meetings with God as well as worship services.

> *Again there was a day when the Sons of God came to present themselves before the Lord.*
> (Job 2:1)

Angels have assignments to watch over and protect the saints of God they also report on 2nd heaven activities and Satanic assaults on earth.

10

Take heed that ye despise not one for these little ones; for I say unto you, that in heaven their angels do always behold the face of my father, which is in heaven.

(St. Matthew 18:10)

And he said, " Hear thou therefore the word of the Lord: I saw the Lord sitting on His throne, and all the hosts of heaven standing by him on his right hand and on His left.

(1 Kings 22:19)

There are times when Satan comes to angelic meetings to accuse and get permission to attack the saints of God. Satan can no longer dwell in the 3rd Heaven, only visit to accuse. I don't think he would want to stay because there is too much praise and worship to God going on, and praise and worship is what bounds and controls him. When praises go up, blessings come down. When accusations go up, trouble comes down.

The revelation of Jesus Christ, which God gave unto him, to show unto his servants things which must shortly come to pass; and he sent and signified it by His angel unto His servant John.

(Revelation 1:1)

Jesus used angels to share the Revelation of the end time with the believers.

The Remaining Hosts:

There are more angels, beasts, cherubim, seraphim, and living creatures mentioned in the Old and New Testaments:

And the four and twenty elders and the four beasts fell down and worshipped God that sat on the throne saying Amen; Alleluia.

(Revelation 19:4)

All the worship and praises go to God but heaven has earth on its mind. God doesn't take His eyes off of mankind.

And when he had taken the book the four beasts and four and twenty elders fell down before the lamb, having every

11

one of them harps and golden vials full of odours, which are the prayers of the saints.

(Revelation 5:8)

Every need of the believer is important to God. Our prayers are presented to Him as an anointed odor as a gift is given to a king.

And all the angels stood round about the throne, and about the elders and the four beasts, and fell before the throne on their faces and worshipped God.

(Revelation 7:11)

Also note that there are the seven spirits of God sent forth into the Earth from Heaven. These seven spirits stood before the throne of God. These are the charismatic gifts: the spirit of wisdom, understanding, counsel, strength, knowledge, and the fear of the Lord, the Spirit of the Lord.

Saints:

Let us therefore come boldly unto the throne of grace that we may obtain mercy, and find grace to help in time of need.

(Hebrew 4:16)

And hath raised up together, and made us sit together in heavenly places in Christ Jesus.

(Ephesians 2:6)

Not everyone that saith unto me Lord, Lord, shall enter into the Kingdom of heaven: but he that doeth the will of my Father, which is in heaven.

(St Matthew 7:21)

And I say unto you, that many shall come from the east and west, and shall sit down with Abraham, and Isaac, and Jacob, in the kingdom of heaven.

(St Matthew 8:11)

And Enoch walked with God: and he was not; for God took him.

(Genesis 5:24)

And it came to pass, that the beggar died, and was carried by the angels into Abraham's bosom...

(St. Luke 16:22)

And Jesus said unto him, Verily I say unto thee, today shalt thou be with me in paradise.

(St. Luke 23:43)

And when he had opened the fifth seal, I saw under the altar the souls of them that were slain for the word of God and for the testimony which they held:

(Revelation 6:9)

And I said unto him, Sir, thou, knowest. And he said to me, these are they which came out of great tribulation, and have washed their robes and made them white in the blood of the Lamb. Therefore they are before the throne of God, and serve Him day and night in his temple: and he that sitteth on the throne shall dwell among them.

(Revelation 7:14-15)

2ND HEAVEN:
The Sphere or Space between the Throne of God (Heaven) and the Inhabitation of Man (Earth).

The devil wants to keep you out of the 3rd Heaven. Having previously lived there, he hates the idea of the saints dwelling with God forever. Satan set up his kingdom between the throne of God (3rd Heaven) and man's home on Earth. He will offer you the kingdom of this world (1st Heaven) and the glory of men, if you fall down and worship him. He doesn't want you to worship God on His throne.

- Lucifer (light bearer, shining one) Isa. 14:12
- Satan (adversary) 2 Cor. 2:11; 1 Peter 5:8

- Beelzebub (prince of demons) Matt .12:24
- Apollyon (destroyer) Rev. 9:11
- Belial (vileness, ruthlessness) 2 Cor. 6:15
- The Prince of the Air–Eph. 2:2
- Ruler of darkness–Eph. 6:12
- The dragon–Rev. 12:7
- The Accuser of the brethren–Rev. 12:10
- The liar–St. John 8:44
- The enemy–St. Luke 10:19
- The God of this age–2 Cor. 4:4
- The Fallen Angels–Rev. 12:7

The 2nd Heaven is Satan's throne and temporary kingdom; he lost his position with God. Now as he is seated in the 2nd heaven, he attempts to cause mankind to lose fellowship with God. Satan has limitations. He can't destroy you without God's permission. He can't persecute you more than you can bear. He cannot stand before you, when you submit to God, especially when there's praise in your mouth. Satan is already defeated and judged.

There are demons, imps, and other fallen creatures that work under Satan's control. His kingdom is divided but still effective on planet Earth because all of mankind has not accepted Jesus as their Savior. These spirits rule over territory and regions because of ignorance. They cause sickness, disease, crimes, hatred and every vile act outside of true holiness. They despise revelation knowledge. When one is cast out, it goes and gets several others to regain old territory but can only come into an empty vessel.

They talk and live in any individual that will open up to them. They find open gates through T.V. programs, music, ungodly fellowships, occult books and false religions that do not preach and proclaim Jesus Christ as Lord. They control presidents, senators, congressmen, preachers, movie stars, athletes and anyone who doesn't submit to Jesus. Wicked demons will not always manifest themselves; some just want to dwell anywhere. They want private control, even if it's in swine.

We know from Scripture that others lived in animals like snakes, pigs, etc. We also know that others lived in false apostles, prophets and children. They caused men to lose their minds and run naked in graveyards, cutting themselves. Satan once made a child jump into a burning fire, He also made a young girl to dance for the head of John the Baptist. He made men stone Stephen and whip Paul. But his biggest act was crucifying Jesus on the cross. Scripture says if he knew what this was to cause him, he would have left Him alone. At the crucifixion they thought they killed Jesus and that death could hold Him in the grave. He met them in the 2nd Heaven, took their authority, then paraded their chief throughout the 1st, 2nd, and 3rd Heavens. Jesus gathered their spoils and gave authority back to man. Jesus also gave spiritual gifts unto men: that of Apostle, Prophet, Evangelist, Pastor, Teacher, Miracles, Healings, Helps, Government, and Diversities of tongues to establish the Church and His Kingdom on Earth. The believer must know that Satan works through ignorance and he's trying to keep the gifts out of the Church. A church without operating gifts is void of God's presence. This is why so many ministries have an issue with the gifts of Apostle and Prophet. They're the foundation of the New Testament Church, and if you leave out the foundation, then the house can't stand against the changes of life.

1ST HEAVEN:
The Inhabitation of Man

In the 3rd heaven Satan rebelled against God and was kicked out, (Isaiah 14:12). He lost his beauty (Ezekiel 28). In the 2nd heaven two thousand years ago, Jesus dethroned Satan and rose on the third day with all power in heaven and in earth. In the first heaven according to the book of the Revelation 12th chapter, Satan again is defeated by Michael and his angels. They had cast him out of the 2nd heaven into Earth (1st heaven) and the saints defeated and overcame him by the blood of the Lamb and the words of their testimony. Jesus and the angels came to Earth to do a clean-up job on Satan in the 19th and 20th chapters of Revelation. Satan will be bound eternally, never to rise again.

We must submit to the control of the Holy Ghost, which is the spirit of truth. Many of the events in this book will expose, explain and bring to light events that have happened, those that are presently happening and those that will happen in the future dealing with the 1st heaven.

MY PERSONAL TRI-HEAVEN EXPERIENCE
The Night Raids

I can recall a vision I had a few years ago while fasting and praying to break a stronghold. During this time in my life, the Holy Spirit was pressing me to walk in His authority and not to back down. I had been through several midnight raids by demons (A midnight raid is an attack or ambush when you don't expect it.). For whatever reason, the hierarchy of Satan must have been on spiritual patrol in the 1st heaven. At night I would have tremendous battles. Many times I woke up sweating and tired. I knew the demon's assignment was to take me out, eradicate me immediately.

One day I was praying and walking around my home and I saw a vision of Satan hovering like a blimp over my home with his sword drawn in a striking position. I believe he was evaluating assignments and monitoring progress. I began to pray to God more earnestly and rebuked Satan with authority. I said, "Satan, the Lord rebuke thee in the Name of Jesus." Satan appeared in the vision, looking like the traditional devil with horns. But instead of a pitchfork, he had a sword (Maybe the pitchfork is for those that he controls already and the sword is for those he needs to attack.). Please be advised that though I have cast out demons and saw satanic manifestations on many occasions, I never saw the devil himself so plainly before. Sometimes demons scream and act violent when they manifest themselves. I've seen this happen in and out of the Church. When God exposes the devil, it's not to scare you, but to let you know the devil is a defeated foe. I remember in my vision that the devil was not big and intimidating. He had been down-sized. Maybe the fasting, praying and studying of the Word affected the size of Satan's manifestation. After this vision, I got a clear view of the enemy.

Thank God I've learned spiritual warfare instead of welfare. That night, the demons lost and Satan's midnight raiders were cast out and defeated on their next raids. They came in to attack one way, but left screaming seven ways. Revelation causes us to defeat our enemy and put fear in them. This situation which looked bad and helpless, God turned around in a flash.

DANIEL'S SIMILAR EXPERIENCE

In the third year of Cyrus, king of Persia, a thing was revealed unto Daniel, whose name was called Belteshazzar; and the thing was true, but the time appointed was long: and he understood the thing, and had understanding of the vision.

(Daniel 10:1)

One of the most important lessons you can learn in the book of Daniel is about vision and that the heavens do rule. It happens in the heavenlies before earth gets an e-mail.

Nebuchadnezzar dreamed of an image with the head of gold. The secret and interpretation was revealed from heaven by God. "Then was the secret revealed unto Daniel in a night vision."

Then Daniel blessed the God of heaven.

He revealeth the deep and secret things. He knoweth what is in darkness, and the light dwelleth with him. Daniel answered in the presence of the king, and said, The secret which the king hath demanded cannot the wise men, the astrologers, the magicians, the soothsayers, show unto the king: But there is a God in heaven that revealeth secrets and maketh known the king Nebuchadnezzar what shall be in the latter days. Thy dream, and the vision of thy head upon the bed are these.

(Daniel 2:19,22,27-28)

And Daniel goes on to reveal the vision of the image. This image represents the five dispensations of secular dynasties and their final demise... the stone that smote the image became a great mountain and filled the whole earth. This stone was cut out without hands. It was Christ's Kingdom a heaven-sent, heaven-ruled Kingdom that destroyed the toes of the image.

> *And whereas thou sawest the feet and toes, part of potter's clay and part of iron, the kingdom shall be divided; but there shall be in it of the strength of the iron, for as much as thou sawest the iron mixed with miry clay. And as the toes of the feet were part iron, and part of clay, so the kingdom shall be partly strong, and partly broken. And whereas thou sawest iron mixed with miry clay, they shall mingle themselves with these of men: but they shall not cleave one to another, even as iron is not mixed with clay.*
>
> (Daniel 2:41-43)

The rulers of this federation will not seek God but associate themselves with what pleases men. When they turn from God, the last secular kingdom will be destroyed because the heavens do rule. Remember the events of mankind are established in the spirit world then the physical world. Always remember, it's spiritual first, then physical.

This is why the revelation of Daniel the 2nd and 10th chapters and the events that lead to and follow are so profound. Daniel was mourning and seeking the face of God concerning an issue of great importance. Daniel had an excellent, Godly mindset and though God spoke to him many times in dreams and visions, this occasion was different from the others.

Daniel prayed and God answered him the first time, but Satan was allowed to hinder the answer. Why? Maybe the behind-the-scene activities that we take for granted needed to be revealed. There are forces at work, good and evil. The average person never fathoms how busy the heavenlies are at work.

I once listened to two air-traffic controllers talk about how much activity goes on at major airports. They say the airways are just as busy as major city interstates at 8 a.m. and 5 p.m. But in the air you can't afford any fender-benders. There are control towers with radars to monitor all activity.

God was going to deliver him, but Satan wanted to keep them in ignorance. Daniel was praying and demons were scrambling to hinder his prayers! There was so much going on until God sent an angel to inform Daniel about the prayer he first prayed 21 days go. Then said he unto me,

> *Fear not, Daniel: for from the first day that thou didst set thine heart to understand and to chasten thyself before thy God thy words were heard, and I am come for thy words.*
>
> (Daniel 10:12)

This is a breakthrough. A breakthrough is an act or instance of breaking through an abstraction or defensive line. The devil believes this is his world and when the saints pray it causes a heaven–quake. The heavenlies start to cave in on the earth (as in heaven, so on earth).

In Acts 4:37, Paul and Silas are singing and praying. Satan has set up force-shields to prevent earth-to-heaven activities. Also, he fights heaven-to-earth activities. A part of spiritual warfare includes territory, principalities, rulers of darkness and light. Spiritual wickedness sometimes advances, and hinders and at other times retreats. But when God sent His angels on assignment, Satan tried to guard and control the same territory.

> *The angel said, "But the prince of the kingdom of Persia withstood me one and twenty days: but lo, Michael, one of the chief princes, came to help me; and I remained there with the kings of Persia."*
>
> (Daniel 10:13)

This chapter also speaks about Cyrus, king of Persia. But in verse 13, it mentions the T.R. demons because Israel, God's chosen, was in the clutches of his control. Through spiritual warfare we can better understand Israel's history and struggles. In Bible history, Cyrus the natural king, was to decree liberation for the Jews and rebuild Jerusalem (2 Chronicles 36:22-23, Ezra 1:1-8, Isaiah 44:28; 45:14). This was spoken 175 years before he was born. Scripture even mentions his name. Satan of course can read, and he knew God was setting up a breakthrough. The angel said the Prince (T.R. demon), not Cyrus, withstood him for 21 days. The angel spoke of what happened in the spiritual realm. It got so bad that Michael the war angel had to intervene.

Michael is the Warrior Archangel. His assignment is to protect messenger angels and fight for Israel. I believe lately, he's been very busy. The angel said, *"Now I am come to make thee understand what shall befall thy people in the latter days: for yet the vision is for many days."* The devil doesn't want the people of God to know their future. Satan is already defeated. As long as he can keep you in the "closet" (dark) about anything, he has the advantage. God doesn't permit Satan in every battle to operate this way.

Many times, because of opposition people don't endure and they forfeit their blessing. What if Daniel had said the Lord wasn't answering his prayers and walked away from God? Our uninformed or misinformed spiritual intelligence doesn't stop what happens in the heavenlies because the heavens do rule. Satan would have still lost in the heavenlies but won in the life of Israel. God forbid. I wonder how many miracles have happened but the prayer warrior stopped interceding before the manifestation. This is warfare. There is no set time for victories. They don't just come in church events, revivals and conferences. God is not bound by mandates, schedules and deadlines. He's omnipotent.

God, for whatever reason, allows Satan to hinder, scramble and tie-up things. This doesn't affect who God is, but it causes us to trust in Him more, rather than in things. When God allows all of these things to happen, He's still God Almighty, the Alpha and Omega, the First before nothing and the Last after everything. God is sovereign.

Then the angel said, *"Knowest thou wherefore I come unto thee? And now will I return to fight with prince of Persia: and when I am gone forth, lo, the price of Grecia shall come."* Daniel even got a word on who would be the next power broker in Israel's future affairs. The Grecian Empire a few years later would rule—Alexander the Great, a mighty ruler in world history.

But he would conquer most of the known world and rule over great kingdoms by the age of 32. Later he would die from mosquito bites and drinking bad swamp water (Malaria). Remember, the heavens do rule. Kings, princes, generals, presidents, etc. are all controlled by someone or something.

That's why we pray for leaders that they be righteous.

> *When the righteous are in authority, the people rejoice,*
> *but when the wicked beareth rule, the people mourn.*
> (Proverbs 29:2)

Why was Daniel mourning for Israel? Because of their sin. They were placed under the charge of another nation. God is so good that in time he rose up a Cyrus and a Daniel.

> *Delight thyself in the Lord; and he shall give thee the*
> *desires of thine heart.*
> (Psalm 37:4)

Delight means "to take great pleasure, to satisfy greatly, to please." Sometimes our deliverance comes through people who act as angels. This kind of good is authorized by God. He causes men to bless the believer's heart.

David's Desire

The desire of an authorized believer is so important to God that He sends angels to fight for them to satisfy their thirst. Look at the story of a warrior to be king. David longed for something and his (angels) warriors set out to get it. In actuality, they broke through the enemy occupied territory and took it. They fought going in to defeat the enemy and fought coming out. I believe they didn't waste a drop of water because this was for their leader. I wonder today how believers would fight for their leader.

> *Now three of the thirty captains went down to the rock to*
> *David, into the cave of Adullam; and the host of the*
> *Philistines encamped in the valley of Rephaim. And*

David was then in the hold, and the Philistines garrison was then at Bethlehem. And David longed, and said, oh that one would give me drink of the water of the well of Bethlehem, that is by the gate.

(1 Chronicles 11:15-17)

The three break through the host of the Philistines, and draw water out of the well of Bethlehem, that was by the gate, and took it, and brought it to David.

But David would not drink of it but poured it out to the Lord and said,

My God forbid it me that I should do this thing: shall I drink of the blood of these men that have their lives in jeopardy? For with the jeopardy of their lives they brought it. Therefore he would not drink it. These things did these three mighties.

(1 Chronicles 11:18-19)

Messengers and warriors are both important in getting a breakthrough. When the messenger encounters trouble in his path, he will need a warrior to lead the way. Remember the guys in the trenches who don't mind getting dirty and know to cut the enemy down. Then the messenger will return and help the warrior to double team the enemy to serve notice upon him for the next battle.

We will take a closer look at the three mighties:

(1st) Adino the Eznite, the chief of the mighty, who killed 8900 men in one battle. *Adino* means "ornament." He was Tachmonite, the name of his family. (2nd) Eleazor son of Bodo, his name means "God is helper." He arose and smote the Philistines until his hand was weary *and his hand clave unto the sword; and the Lord wrought a great victory that day and the people returned after him only to spoil.* (3rd) Shammah (the son of Agee, the Haratire). He defended the grounds after everyone fled and slew the Philistines and the Lord wrought a great victory.

2 Samuel 23:8-17 gives also the story of the 3 mighties. When

you delight yourself in the Lord, and please the Lord, then He will give you the desires of your heart. What is in your heart comes from the Lord, when you search for Him and seek to please Him. God also gives us the mighties, His angels charge concerning thee, to encamp around about thee, to minister to thee, and to listen for the voice of God that speaks from your desire (heart). They're equipped to battle in every region for the authorized believer.

Whether spiritual, physical or financial, we need help. The forces that bind us must be destroyed, the strongholds must be pulled down.

What brings a breakthrough? I believe it is submission to God, a righteous prayer life, seeking the kingdom and denying the works of the flesh to operate. Sounds easy and simple? You can have the wisdom of men, the riches of King Solomon and still need a breakthrough. The Lord appeared to Solomon by night and said, *"If my people, which are called by my name shall humble themselves, and pray, and seek my face, and turn from their wicked ways; then will I hear from heaven and will forgive their sin and will heal their land."* (2 Chronicles 7:14). A breakthrough, is caused by: (1) humbling yourself, (2) praying and (3) seeking the Kingdom (His face), (4) turning from your wicked ways.

Then God in the 3rd heaven will send to the 1st heaven (your dwelling place) and bind up the hindrances of the 2nd heaven. Satan can't stop the prayers of the Just man because the prayers of the righteous availeth much. A breakthrough is more than getting your prayer answered. It has benefits such as a fresh relationship, a new anointing and healing in your body, soul and spirit. Remember that the 1st heaven is the dwelling place of man on this earth. Here we get visitation from God Himself, His Son and Spirit, angels, etc. as well as Satan, his hierarchy, demons, etc. Satan is trying to hinder the plan of God on earth. He can't fight God personally, but he will fight God's creation. Remember Satan must get permission to even fight creation. In the 1st heaven we have angels and demons coming and going. The righteous are protected by angels. These angels minister to them and for them. Satan is jealous and hates the saints. The unrighteous are controlled by Satan, their father, and demons are assigned to keep them bound. Sin is the chain that binds them to him. Jesus came to destroy sin in the flesh and set the bound captives free, (St. Luke 4:18, St. John 3:16).

Now the 2nd heaven is the dwelling place of the god of this world, the fallen one Lucifer, who is Satan, the devil and prince of the air. From his position, he is going up to the 3rd heaven to accuse the saints before God and down among men to cause havoc, disturbance and trouble. He can't be in every place at once like God, so he has ruling principalities to help rule the airways. They are also called the princes of certain kingdoms. This region operates in total deceit and darkness. They don't trust one another and they're divided. Jesus has already paraded their master Satan throughout all regions as the defeated foe. It's established in the heavenlies that the chief ruler of this world is judged and defeated. Now Satan is betting that you haven't heard or been misinformed as to his conviction.

The 3rd heaven in the center location of God's dwelling is His throne. But God is everywhere at all times. He rules totally in the 1st, 2nd and 3rd heavens. God is sovereign. God is ambient with time and eternity.

CHAPTER TWO

The <u>S</u>overeignty of a <u>T</u>riune <u>G</u>od

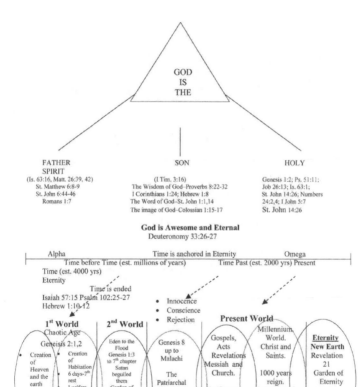

GOD IS THE

FATHER	SON	HOLY
SPIRIT		
(Is. 63:16, Matt. 26:39, 42)	(I Tim. 3:16)	Genesis 1:2; Ps. 51:11;
St. Matthew 6:8-9	The Wisdom of God–Proverbs 8:22-32	Job 26:13; Is. 63:1;
St. John 6:44-46	I Corinthians 1:24; Hebrew 1:8	St. John 14:26; Numbers
Romans 1:7	The Word of God–St. John 1:1,14	24:2,4; I John 5:7
	The image of God–Colossian 1:15-17	St. John 14:26

God is Awesome and Eternal
Deuteronomy 33:26-27

Alpha   Time is anchored in Eternity   Omega

Time before Time (est. millions of years)   Time Past (est. 2000 yrs) Present

Time (est. 4000 yrs)
Eternity
        Time is ended
Isaiah 57:15 Psalm 102:25-27
Hebrew 1:10-12

- Innocence
- Conscience
- Rejection

1st World
Chaotic Age
Genesis 2:1,2

Creation of Heaven and the earth

Earth was without

Creation of Habitation
6 days-7th rest
Lucifers created and rebel
He's cast down

2nd World
Eden to the Flood
Genesis 1:3 to 7th chapter
Satan beguiled them
Garden of Eden
Adam and Eve rule and lost because of sin.

Genesis 8 up to Malachi

The Patriarchal
Prophets
Judges
Kings
Courting Israel

Present World
Gospels, Acts
Revelations
Messiah and Church.

The Rapture

New Testament

Millennium. World.
Christ and Saints.

1000 years reign.

Satan Bound

Final Judgment. Rev 20:11
Destroyed by fire

Eternity
New Earth
Revelation 21
Garden of Eternity

No more devils
Rev 20:11

THE SOVEREIGNTY OF GOD

Webster says sovereignty is supremacy in the role of power, power to govern without external control, the supreme political power in a state. Sovereignty is excellent, of the most exalted kind, the supreme, the ruler of all, absolute and perfect. These powerful phrases give only a snapshot of God. Sovereign isn't always synonymous with God, but God is all the time sovereign. God is in every moment of time that ever was, that ever is, that ever will be, filling all space, existing and controlling with infinite awareness the affairs of the Archomai.

S : Omni – all, universally (unidirectional), he fills all points in time, every point is present and accounted for. Acts 15:18

N : Omnicompetent – able to handle any situation, having the authority or legal capacity to act in all matters. Psalm 139:2-4

A : Omnificent – unlimited in creative power. Genesis 1:1

P : Omnipotence – an agency or force of unlimited power. Proverbs15:3. Psalm147:4

S : Omnipotent – almighty, having virtually unlimited authority or influence. Genesis 18:14, Psalm 136

H : Omnipresence – Ubiquity – existing or being everywhere at the same time. Psalm 139:7-12, Matthew 18:20; Jeremiah 23:23-24

O :

T : Omniscient – having an infinite awareness, understanding, and insight possessed of universal or compete knowledge. Psalm 139:1-6; 147:5, Isaiah 40:13, Hebrews 4:13, Acts 15:18

S

There is no past or future with God, only a present. Time submits to where God's identity of Himself with His creation is only a snap shot. There is enough time to fully understand, comprehend and describe God. At best, we can offer a small photo book with a few stories. <u>God is the Father</u>; ab – He is the one who begot and protects the one we should revere and obey.

Deut 32:6 says,

In the song of Moses, it is written, to requite the Lord, is foolishness and not smart because he is thy father, the one that made thee and established thee.

<u>God the Father created man, not man is his piety created God</u>.

Have we not all one Father? hath not one God created us?
(Malachi 2:10)

Also Father is pater: a nourisher, protector, upholder. Metaphorically, of the originator or a family of company of persons animated by the same spirit as himself.

Jesus said in the prototype prayer of St. Matthew 6:9 ....*Our Father which art in heaven*.... He shows us that the Father sees (vs. 6), delivers (vs. 13), forgives (vs. 14), knoweth (vs. 32), adds to you (vs. 33). All books, chapters and verses of Scripture are a love letter and a promise backed by a God that is sovereign for those who have His **D.N.A.**–**D**ivine **N**ature **A**nimation. In His greatest hour of sorrow, Jesus Himself said, *"Abba Father, all things are possible unto thee;*...St. Mark 14:36. Abba in Aramaic means Father. It's commonly used by Jews where both parents of a real son were Jews or of a proselyte (this is a part of the covenant). It was not used when the mother was a slave. It tells the true relationship of Jesus to God. It was more than the overshadowing Mary that made Jesus the Son of God, though that was exceptionally important. But it was His obedience and faith in God from the baptism to the crucifixion on the cross and resurrection. All of this <u>s</u>ubmission, <u>o</u>bedience and <u>s</u>ervitude (S.O.S) manifested His relationship with God.

27

For as many as are led by the Spirit of God (just like Jesus was) they are the sons of God (joint heirs with Jesus). For ye have not the spirit of bondage again to fear; but ye have received the Spirit of adoption, whereby we cry Abba, Father (just like Jesus). The Spirit itself beareth witness with our Spirit, that we are the children of God.

(Romans 8:14-16)

Jesus has perfect D.N.A., because in all things He obeyed God, His Father *"and now sitteth on the right hand of God and also maketh intercession for us."* According to Romans 8:34. Remember, we also have the spirit of adoption, the Spirit helping our infirmities (physical, mental and moral weakness and flaws). It maketh intercession according to the will of God. WOW! The Father, Son and Spirit of God is presently working for us in every period of time and set of circumstances.

And we know that all things work together for good to them that love God, to them who are the called according to his purpose.

(Romans 8:28)

Let's highlight all things that work together and look at them that love God or obey God.

This doesn't work for the disobedient child because he is missing God's purpose. They must be reconciled back to God. We all used to live just like the rest of the world subject to sin, obeying Satan, the fallen prince of the power of the air. He is the spirit at work in the heart of those who refuse to obey God. What we need is to be reconciled. Strong's Concordance defines reconciled from the word kata meaning down; also meaning: to make a difference. God sent Jesus down to make a difference.

Reconciled – Katallasso properly denotes: to change, exchange; hence of persons to change from enmity to friendship. With regard to the relationship between God and man, reconciliation is what God accomplishes, exercising His grace toward sinful man on the ground of the death of Christ in propitiatory sacrifice under the judgment due sin.

28

Webster defines reconcile as meaning to cause to be friendly or harmonious again; adjust, settle, to bring to submission or acceptance.

THE ABBA PLAN

Jesus prayed *"Thy kingdom come, thy will be done on earth as it is in Heaven."* God is reconciling man.

And all things are of God, who hath reconciled us to himself by Jesus Christ, and hath given to us the ministry of reconciliation. To wit, that God was in Christ, reconciling the world unto himself, not imputing their trespasses unto them; and hath committed unto us the word of reconciliation.

(2 Corinthians 5:18-19)

Before the foundation of the world, God had a plan to reconcile us back in the Father-Son relationship. Our disobedience and sin nature would have kept us from, but God through His only begotten (not adoptive) Son God came Himself to reconcile us.

And without controversy great is the mystery of godliness: God was manifest in the flesh, justified in the Spirit, seen of angels, preached unto the Gentiles, believed on in the world, received up in to glory.

(I Timothy 3:16)

All of this sounds like Jesus is truly the Son of God and the express image of God. Allow me to break this down for you to study: the word controversy: homologoumenos: a clash of opposing views.

THE MYSTERY OF GODLINESS

1. Great – divine fullness: Ephesians 3:19; Colossians 1:19; 2:9

2. God was manifest in the flesh – the incarnation: Isaiah 7:14; 9:6-7; Matthew 1:18-25; Saint John 1:1,14; (Romans 8:3) likeness of sinful flesh, and for sin, condemned sin in the flesh: verses 4-5

3. Justified in the spirit – divine vindication: Acts 2:22-28, 36; 3:14-18; Romans 1:3-4; Ephesians 1:20-23; Philippians 2:5-11

4. Seen of angels – divine revelation: 1 Corinthians 4:9; Ephesians 3:9-10; I Peter 1:10-12

5. Preached unto the Gentiles – divine inclusion (make one the same): 1 Corinthians 12:13; Galatians 3:28; Ephesians 2:11-18; 3:1-6; Colossians 3:11

6. Believed on in the world – divine propagation (multiply): Matthew 4:23-24; 9:35; Luke 4:16-19; Ephesians 2:17

7. Received up into glory – divine ascension and exaltation: Luke 24:51; Ephesians 1:20-23; Philippians 2:9-11

God didn't make a blank trip for our reconciliation. Nor did He come to blame us for being human, but to give us his D.N.A. We must accept the Gospel and walk in the A.C.T.S. With the true revelation unfolding the mystery of godliness.

The chart on the sovereignty of God hopefully will help you to understand some of what we attempted to explain and if all fails, know that God is sovereign, Satan is already defeated and we are now the manifested sons of God by Christ Jesus. There has always been a special place God has placed His creation.

From the time Lucifer walked up and down the midst of the stones of fire upon the mountain of God, he was perfect in wisdom and beauty–even before Adam and Eve had been in the Garden of Eden. His clothing was dressed with stones of beauty, his garment was set in gold, and he was musically inclined from the inside out.

Lucifer didn't have to look for instruments. He was an orchestra of beautiful praise and worship. He was blameless in all he did from the day he was created until the day evil was found in him. That was when God, who is sovereign, banished him from the mountain of God. Satan showed up in the Garden trying to cause separation between God and His creation. We know the story. Adam and Eve missed the mark and fell from their union. But God's plan of redemption went into operation.

God said,

And I will put enmity between thee and the woman, and between thy seed and her seed. It shall bruise thy head, and thou shalt bruise his heel.

(Genesis 3:15)

Jesus came through the seed of a woman and reconciled us to God.

The History Channel has done specials on Egyptians, Pharaohs, African queens, Roman emperors and the Royal family of England. They are fascinating stories with schemes, plots, treachery and promiscuous activities. Yet, the royal bloodline has been contaminated with sin, lust and pride. The very things that God hates are what the leaders thrive on. Everyone rules according to their ability. Some did well and others were scandalous in their deeds. All of these empires and their rulers ended in their sovereignty coming to an end.

But look at the snapshot of God's Sovereignty:

Omni – all, universally (unidirectional). He fills all in time–every dimension, scope, and every point is present and accounted for. Acts 15:18 known unto God are all his works form the beginning of the world. God knows everything. He has no limits or boundaries. Kings, emperors and monarchs have their struggles and eventually die or are overthrown, but God is eternal and absolute in power. He is forever working for the believers to walk in their authority. It takes sovereignty to issue authority.

Omnipresence – Ubiquity – existing or being everywhere at the same time.

- God – (Jeremiah 23:23-24)

Am I a God at hand, saith the Lord, and not a God afar off? Can any hide himself in secret places that I shall not see him? saith the Lord. Do not I fill heaven and earth? saith the Lord.

- Christ – (Matthew 18:20)

For where two or three are gathered together in my name, there am I in the midst of them.

- Holy Ghost – (I Corinthians 2:10-13)

But God hath revealed them unto us by his Spirit: for the spirit searcheth all things, yea, the deep things of God. For what man knoweth the things of a man, save the spirit of man which is in him? Even so the things of God knoweth no man, but the Spirit of God. Now we have received, not the spirit of the world, but the spirit which is of God; that we might know the things that are freely given to us of God. Which things also we speak, not in the words which man's wisdom teacheth, but which the Holy Ghost teacheth; comparing spiritual things with spiritual.

His presence screams sovereignty; He is the God at hand. He can handle all situations. There are no secrets hidden from God, all things are naked and fully exposed to Him. He can't be blinded, shielded or forbidden by no one or anything. When believers gather together in the Name of Jesus, the omnipresence of God is there monitoring, advising and acknowledging their request– especially when we come together in Jesus' Name to praise God for His goodness. *God inhabits the praises of Israel His people* (Psalm 22:3). And is an inhabitant in our spirits when we are filled or controlled by the Holy Ghost.

Omniscient – having an infinite awareness, understanding and insight, universal or complete knowledge.

32

Psalm 139:1-6
O Lord, thou hast searched me, and known me. Thou knowest my downsitting and mine uprising, thou understandest my thought afar off. Thou compasses my path and my lying down, and are acquainted with all my ways. For there is not a word in my tongue, but, lo, O Lord, thou knowest it altogether. Thou hast beset me behind and before, and laid thine hand upon me. Such knowledge is too wonderful for me; it is high, I cannot attain unto it.

Psalm 147:5
Great is our Lord and of great power; his understanding is infinite.

Isaiah 40:28
Hast thou not known? Has thou not heard, that the everlasting God, the Lord, the creator of the ends of the earth, fainteth not, neither is weary? There is no searching of his understanding.

Acts 15:18
Known unto God are all his works from the beginning of the world.

Hebrews 4:13
Neither is there any creature that is not manifest in his sight: but all things are naked and opened unto the eyes of him with whom we have to do.

It's a powerful revelation to know God as an omniscient Savior. Satan, the enemy, has waged a powerful thought war against our minds. How many times have we heard "God doesn't know and understand what you're going through" or "You need to work that out on your own." Satan tries to get us to believe that God doesn't care, and He's too busy to assist in your time of trouble. Remember, the devil is a liar and a deceiver. David said, *"My help cometh from the Lord."*

<u>Omnicompetent</u> – able to handle any situation, having the authority or legal capacity to act in all matters.

Psalm 139:2-4
Thou knowest my downsitting and mine uprising, thou understandest my thought afar off. Thou compasses my path and my lying down, and are acquainted with all my ways. For there is not a word in my tongue, but, lo, O Lord, thou knowest it all together.

Psalm 78:17-19
And they sinned yet more against him by provoking the most high in the wilderness. And they tempted God in their heart by asking meat for their lust. Yea, they spake against God; they said, can God furnish a table in the wilderness?

Here in the Psalms we have two scenarios—one of trust and the other of mistrust in the competency of God: first the mistrust—they sinned against God by their unfaithful confidence in His ability to care and provide for them. Imagine Israel with quail in their mouths and loads of manna in their hands saying, "Can God furnish a table in the wilderness?" It was nothing short of many miracles to make it that far. Here were a group of three to five million people counting women and children, who spent forty years (fourteen thousand days) in the wilderness. If each person ate once a day, there would have been 5 million quail eaten and God fed them three meals a day with clean water, medical, clothing and education for forty years. Now read Psalm 139:1-24.

Omnipotence – an agency or force of unlimited power.

Proverbs 15:3
The eyes of the Lord are in every place, beholding the evil and the good.

The almighty God sees everything that happens. It doesn't shake God when something threatens His omnipotence because He has all power in heaven and on earth. There is no other agency or force that exists to challenge His deity. Whatever God says, that is what happens eternally, past, present and future.

Understand me, God is in control and has no reason to change. He said, "I'm Lord God and I change not," but we sometimes misunderstand Him and think in our finite minds that God has changed. Why does He allow Satan to buffet us? From a human standpoint, dealing with issues always changing and growing in grace from a limited point of view, I believe He's still omnipotent, almighty and worthy to be praised.

Psalm 24:1 tells us, *"The earth is the Lord's and the fullness thereof; the world, and they that dwell therein."* The Lord sees the heavens and the earth and the worlds to come. It all belongs to Him. David said, *"We are his people, and the sheep of his pasture"* Psalm 100:3. The shepherd watches over the sheep and leads them into green pastures and beside the still waters. And we shall not be in want because God is our provider. It's in the covenant, the will, and the contract. Read it!

<u>Omnipotent</u> – almighty, having virtually unlimited authority or influence.

Genesis 18:14
Is there any thing too hard for the Lord? At the time appointed I will return unto thee, according to the time of life, and Sarah shall have a son.

Remember the times when you didn't consult the Lord, when you were going through those harsh trials that weren't your fault? You wanted the problems to end quickly, so you tried to work it out yourself. The more you did, the worse it got and the small problem became a major mess, totally out of control.

Welcome to the club where all the participants have made the same mistake in questioning "Can I do it?" "Is there anything too hard?" My personal favorite is, "How long, Lord?" Just like Abraham and Sarah, I've questioned God many times, but I can honestly say God has done everything He promised me. Even at times when I have failed in my part of the bargain. I created Ishmaels and got second opinions on God. But God had been El-Shaddai in every situation. God is so good that there were times when He made my enemies bless me and even they today do not know why they did it. He cares for us as little children and shows us much love and patience. God wants us to increase in faith our Him so that we can manifest to the world His omnipotent power and love to whosever, believes on the Son of God. Jesus said, *"With God all things are possible"* (St. Mark 10:27B).

Omnificent – unlimited in creative power

Genesis 1:1
In the beginning God created the heavens and the earth.

God is absolute, ultimate and rules in sovereign absolutism. No one has the authority to question His omnificent creation because all that's created is a product made by God Himself. God doesn't rely upon His creation to validate His sovereignty. He's omnificent in spite of His creation. When an element of creation doesn't operate according to plan, He's still in control of everything. If you believe in creation or evolution, created evolution or evolution created, God is still omnificent.

It's good to believe His Word, the Bible, because it helps us to know and understand Him. All of creation screams loud, "There is a God" and "I credit Him for making me." Man is the only thing that has been lost in space. By space I mean occupying a realm in time and a place in creation, but not obeying His true purpose. Out of all creation we profess the greatest intelligences. We create rockets to go to the stars, ships to sail the seas, cars with telephones, navigational devices and hi-fi radios and procedures to transplant hearts, but can't cure the common cold or love our neighbor.

I read some very interesting details about God's awesome creation. I will talk about this universe only. For reference read Wilmington's Guide to the Bible page 13.

THE RELATIVE SPEED ILLUSTRATION

1. Our earth is traveling on its one axis at 1000 mph.

2. It moves around the sun at 67,000 mph.

3. It is carried by the sun across our galaxy at a speed of 64,000 mph.

4. It moves in orbit around our galaxy at 481,000 mph.

5. It travels through space at 1,350,000 mph.

6. Every twenty-four hours we cover 57,360,000 miles.

7. Each year we travel 20,936,400,000 miles across empty space.

Remember the earth is the Lord's and the fullness thereof and He created the Heavens and the Earth. All of this is a small snapshot of God in awesome sovereignty. There are many universes, galaxies, and solar systems, but only one God Who made and controls everything. God has numbered the hairs on our head.

CHAPTER THREE

The Snapshots of God's Sovereignty

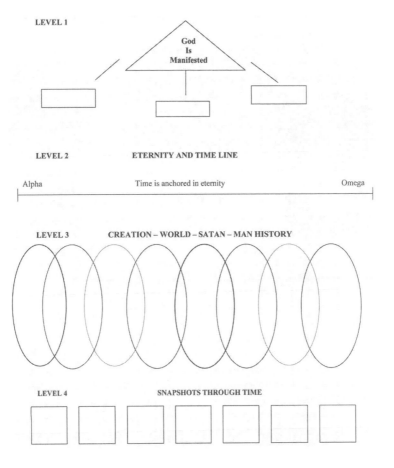

LEVEL 1

God
Is
Manifested

LEVEL 2   **ETERNITY AND TIME LINE**

Alpha   Time is anchored in eternity   Omega

LEVEL 3   **CREATION – WORLD – SATAN – MAN HISTORY**

LEVEL 4   **SNAPSHOTS THROUGH TIME**

THE FOUR LEVELS OF GOD'S SOVEREIGNTY

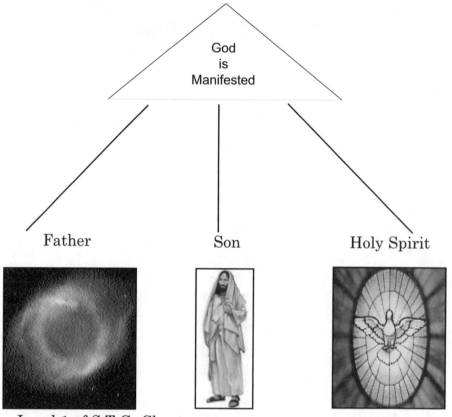

Level 1 of S.T.G. Chart

The first level of God's sovereignty is understanding that He is manifested as Father, Son and Holy Spirit to mankind. As Father, He protects with unlimited power and authority. The level that God views us from, is a complete, merciful, redemptive position. God is absolute in every way. There is nothing created, manifested or devised that is able to shatter His preeminence at any level. As the Son, He lived among us and felt our suffering and pains. He became the mediator between God and man, being God and being man Himself. There's no situation that God can't solve for man and every promise of God to man is yes. God loves us so much that He gave His life for us and His Spirit to us. As the Holy Spirit, He manifested Himself to us and revealed and searcheth all things, even the deep things of God. Scripture says: *"Now we have received, not the spirit of the world, but the spirit which is Go; that we might know the things that are freely given to us of God."* We must know the plan of God for our lives and examine each level of God's sovereignty to fulfill our destiny. On this level Satan has no authority, influence or favor.

God the Father: He is the One who begot and protects, the One we should revere and obey.

Pater: a nourisher, protector, upholder.

1. *Lord, look down from heaven and see us from your holy, glorious home. Where is the passion and the might you used to show on our behalf? Where are your mercies and compassions now? Surely you are still our Father even if Abraham and Jacob would disown us, Lord, you would still be our Father. You are the Redeemer from ages past.*

(Isaiah 63:15-16 NLT)

2. *For your Father knoweth what thing ye have need of, before ye ask him.*

Our Father which art in Heaven, Hallowed be thy name.

(St. Matthew 6:8-9 NLT)

3. *Saying O my Father, if it be possible, let this cup pass from me: never the less not as I will but as thou wilt.*

(St. Matthew 26:39)

O my Father, if this cup may not pass away from me except I drink it, thy will be done.

(St. Matthew 26:42)

God the Son: Jesus is His Name

1. *And without controversy great is the mystery of godliness. God was manifest in the flesh, justified in the Spirit, seen of angels, preached unto the Gentiles, believed on in the world, received up into glory.*

(I Timothy 3:16)

2. *The Lord formed me from the beginning, before He created anything else. I was appointed in ages past, at the very first, before the earth began. I was born before the oceans were created, before the springs bubbled forth their waters. Before the mountains and the hills were formed, I was born before he had made the earth and fields and the first handful of souls." I was there when he established the heavens, when he drew the horizon on the oceans. I was there when he set the clouds above, when he established the deep fountains of the earth. I was there when he set the limits of the seas, so they would not spread beyond their boundaries. And when he marked off the earth's foundations I was the architect at his side. I was his constant delight, rejoicing always in this presence. And how happy I was with what he created, his wide world and all the human family! And so, my children listen to me, for happy are all who follow my ways.*

(Proverbs 8:22-32 NLT)

Jesus is the wisdom of God.

3. *Christ the power of God, and the wisdom of God.*

(I Corinthians 1:24)

4. *In the beginning was the Word, and the Word was with God and the Word was God.*

(St. John 1:1)

And the Word was made flesh, and dwelt among us.

(St. John 1:14)

5. *Christ is the visible image of the invisible God. He existed before God made anything at all and is supreme over all creation. Christ is the One through whom God created everything in heaven and earth. He made the things we can see and the things we can't see, kings, kingdoms, rulers, and authorities. Everything has been created through him and for him.*

(Colossians 1:15-17 NLT)

*But unto the Son, he saith, Thy throne, O God, is for
ever and ever: a sceptre of righteousness is the sceptre of
thy kingdom.*

(Hebrews 1:8)

God the Holy Spirit: Holy Ghost, Comforter, Spirit of Truth

• *And the earth was without form, and void; and
darkness was upon the face of the deep. And the spirit of
God moved upon the face of the waters.*

(Genesis 1:2)

• *By my Spirit he hath garnished the heavens.*

(Job 26:13)

• *Cast me not away from thy presence; and take not thy
Holy Spirit from me.*

(Psalm 51:11)

• *The Spirit of the Lord God is upon me; because the
Lord hath anointed me to preach good tidings unto the
meek.*

(Isaiah 61:1)

• *And Balaam lifted up his eyes and he saw Israel
abiding in his tents according to their tribes; and the
Spirit of God came upon him. He hath said, which heard
the words of God, which saw the vision of the Almighty...*

(Numbers 24:2-4)

• *But the comforter, which the Holy Ghost, whom the
Father will send in my name, he shall teach you all things,
and bring all things to your remembrance, whatsoever I
have said unto you.*

(St. John 14:26)

• *For there are three that bear record in heaven, the
Father, the Word, and the Holy Ghost: and these three are
one.*

(I John 5:7)

Level 2 of S.T.G. Chart

ETERNITY AND TIME LINE

God is Awesome and Eternal

Time is anchored in eternity, like a ship uses an anchor to stabilize itself from drifting from its place of designation. God uses different anchors to remind us that life is temporary and short. We must not trust the carnal things in life, they're here today and gone tomorrow. Time is only used to catalog events in history. God is not controlled by time, neither is He subject to time at any level before there was a sundial, clock, or changing seasons. God was, is and always shall be. God is the author and the finisher of time. He has set the pattern for life and death. No one lives or dies without His permission. We judge life by our standards and limitations. We often ask how God could be in control with starving children in Africa, bombing in Israel and wars everywhere. God gives us a freewill and many choices. It is the will of men and the choice of individuals that affects the lives of others for evil. God is good all the time; all the time God is good. He will allow us to fail when we don't trust Him. He knows time is running out and the temporary affairs of man will not last.

> There is none like unto the God of Jeshurun, who rideth upon the heaven in thy help, and in his excellency on the sky. The eternal God is thy refuge, and underneath are the everlasting arms: and he shall thrust out the enemy from before thee; and shall say, Destroy them.
> (Deuteronomy 33:26-27)

Awesome- inspiring awe; awe; profound and reverent dread of the supernatural; respectful fear inspired by authority.

Eternity – ad; terminus, i.e. (by impl.) duration in the sense of advance or perpetuity everlasting, evermore.

Alpha   Time is anchored in Eternity   Omega

Alpha – the <u>first</u> letter of the Greek alphabet.

In the beginning God created... Genesis 1:1
The Father Alpha

1 John   In the beginning was the Word... St. John 1:1
5:7   The Word Alpha

And the Spirit of God moved ... Genesis 1:2
The Spirit Alpha

Omega – the <u>last</u> letter of the Greek alphabet

Father: *And he shewed me a pure river of water of life, clear as crystal, proceeding out of the throne of God and of the Lamb.*
(Revelation 22:1)

At the end of time   **Son**: *I am Alpha and Omega, the beginning and the end, the first and the last.*
(Revelation 22:13)

Holy Spirit: *And the Spirit and the bride say come. And let him that heareth say, come. And let him that is athirst come. And whosoever will, let him take the water of life freely.*
(Revelation 22:17)

God inhabits all eternity and linear time.

Eternity: A, time start at B through Y: Z

Time is in eternity like the Alphabet Contains A-Z.

A: The start of all;
B: Can never be first. Z the last of all and Y can never end it. (A.B. –Y.Z.). Time will always say "BYE."

Level 3 of S.T.G. Chart

For thus saith the high and lofty one that inhabiteth eternity, whose name is Holy; I dwell in the high and holy place, with him also that is of a contrite and humble spirit to revive the spirit of the humble, and to revive the heart of the contrite ones.

(Isaiah 57:15)

Of old hast thou laid the foundation of the earth: and the heavens are the work of they hands. They shall perish, but thou shalt endure: yea, all of them shall wax old like a garment; as a vesture shall thou change them, and they shall be changed. But thou are the same, and thy years shall have no end.

(Psalm 102:25-27)

And, thou, Lord, in the beginning has laid the foundation of the earth; and the heavens are the works of thine hands: they shall perish; but thou remainest; and they all shall wax old as doth a garment; and as a vesture shalt thou fold them up, and they shall be changed: but thou art the same, and thy years shall not fail.

(Hebrews 1:10-12)

Remember Time and things will always say B.Y. but God is the Alpha and Omega–He is eternal.

1ST WORLD
Genesis 1:1; Renovation Genesis 1:2

Stage 1: God Created

Genesis 1:1-2:

*In the beginning God created the heaven and the earth.
And the earth was with form and void.*

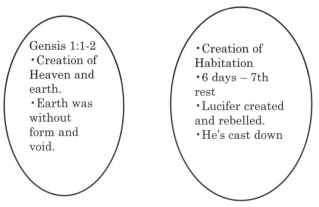

Gensis 1:1-2
• Creation of Heaven and earth.
• Earth was without form and void.

• Creation of Habitation
• 6 days – 7th rest
• Lucifer created and rebelled.
• He's cast down

Stage 2   God placed Satan as ruler and he rebelled

Ezekiel 28:11-19 – Duel Prophecy
Isaiah 14:12-15; Rev. 12:4

2ND WORLD
Genesis 1:3 to 7:24

•   **Innocences** – blamelessness
Freedom from legal guilt, simplicity
Genesis 2:1-24
Key verses – 7-8;19-20

•   **Conscience** – Consciousness of the moral
Right and wrong of one's own acts or motives.
Genesis 3:1-24
Key verses – 7,11,22

- **Ultimatum** – A final condition or demand whose rejection will bring about a resort to forceful action.
Genesis 6:1-22
Key verses – 5-7,11,17

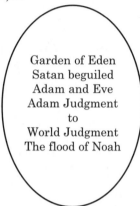

Garden of Eden
Satan beguiled
Adam and Eve
Adam Judgment
to
World Judgment
The flood of Noah

When Adam and Eve were placed in the Garden, they were innocent to iniquity, disobedience, as well as naked and not ashamed. They had fellowship, with God on a daily basis. Satan entered as a serpent and spoke to Eve. The serpent was more subtle than any other beast of the field, which the Lord God had made. Today, Satan tries hard to use what God has made and will especially succeed with cunning individuals who are crafty–prideful schemers. Adam and Eve became conscience of right and wrong when they disobeyed God. They were deceived into believing they could disobey and still have fellowship with God. But when their eyes were opened, reality set in and they hid themselves from God.

After their judgment God said, "The man has became as one of us, to know good and evil." God had to move man before he ate from the tree of life and gained eternal life without sacrifice for sin. This would have condemned mankind with the same fate as Satan with no chance of repentance.

The spirit of rejection can only breed more rejection. When Adam disobeyed it was the rejection of righteousness which turned to hatred, jealousy, murder and wickedness throughout mankind until more judgment had to be passed. First, because

48

of sin (Satan's inward nature) they lost innocence, then their home and fellowship and a son was murdered by his brother. The rebellion of his family descendants caused the Spirit of God to reject mankind. God was willing to destroy all the inhabitants of the earth with a flood. But Noah found grace in the eyes of God. Because of one man, we all had another chance to be reconciled back to God. Adam, the progenitor of mankind, missed the mark of God, but Jesus became the Savior of the world because of the mark.

3RD WORLD
From Genesis 8 to the Gospels to Revelation

Old Testament World

- Noah and Family
- Abraham, Isaac, Jacob – the Patriarchals
- The Judges
- The Prophets
- The kings
- Israel's rejections, captive, slavery
    Silent Years – God Silences (Malachi to St. Matthew)
    (Malachi to St. Matthew)

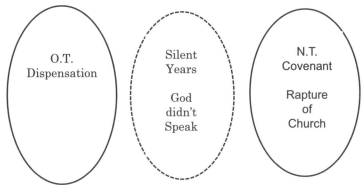

New Testament World

- John the Baptist the Ambassador
- Jesus Christ and the Gospel
- Apostle and the church
- Jews
- Gentiles
- Saints

Millennium World

Deut. 28:13–
And the Lord shall make thee the head, and not the tail; and thou shalt be above only, and thou shalt not be beneath; if that thou hearken unto the commandments of the Lord thy God.

Isaiah 35:1-10
Joel 2:1-11
Zechariah 14:1-21
Revelation 20:1-6

Messiah and Saints

Israel Head of Nations

1000-year-reign

Satan bound in chains

New Earth

Revelation 21:1–
And I saw a new heaven and a new earth: for the first heaven and the first earth were passed away; and there was no more sea.

Garden of Eternity

No more Satan, Sin, Sickness

Perfect World

Revelation 20:10–

And the devil that deceived them was cast into the lake of fire and brimstone, where the beast and the false prophet are and shall be tormented day and night for ever and ever.

Isaiah 66:22–
*For as the new heavens and the new earth, which I will
make, shall remain before me, saith the Lord, so shall you
seed and your name remain.*

The old heaven and earth is passed away. Satan has been
bound to the lake of fire. Jesus' millennium reign has ended, our
Christ has delivered the Kingdom of God and all our enemies are
under His feet. All things have been subdued unto Him. The Son
has finished His work and will step back in God with the Father
and His Holy Spirit. Then God will be again all in all according to
1 Corinthians 15:24-28.

REVELATION 23

This is the start of Revelation 23, the oneness of God. No need
for trinity of any separation. If you search the Scriptures for this
chapter, some will have trouble finding it, but it can be found in
the eternal life of the Holy Ghost in you. All who have the Holy
Ghost are living epistles and it's written in their spirits.
Understand that there is nothing that can happen to you, that will
outlast what's written in you.

Remember in St. Luke 10:17-20 when the disciples returned
with joy saying, *"Lord, even the devils are subject unto us through
thy name"* because they had been anointed with power over Satan.
They caused Satan to fall out of his territory region like lightning.
The disciples had authority to terrorize Satan and shake up his
kingdom, and nothing was able to hurt them. This alone is very
powerful. But Jesus said, *"Don't just be happy with the authority
over spirits, but rather rejoice, because your names are written in
heaven"* (paraphrase). Their names were registered in eternity,
Revelation 23.

This is the fullness of time that Paul spoke of to the church at
Ephesus (Ephesians 1:10) that in the dispensation of the fullness
of time he might gather together in one all things in Christ, both
which are in heaven and which are on earth; even in him.
Everything will go back to the original plan, all in harmony with
God, before the chaos, the insurrection of Satan, the fall of Adam
and the resurrection of Jesus.

51

Level 4 of S.T.G. Chart

The 7 Cornerstone Events and their Judgments

1. | Lucifer's Insurrection | = Isaiah 14:12-

2. | The Serpent Beguiled Adam and | = Genesis 3:13

3. | The Wickedness of Man | = Genesis 6:5

4. | The Silence Years – Malachi to | = Malachi 4 to St. Matthew 1

5. | The Rapture and Time of Jacob's Trouble– Tribulation Period |
= 1 Thessalonians 4:17
Daniel 7:1, 19-26; 12:1-4
St. Matthew 24:15-26
Revelation – 12-19

6. | The White Throne of Judgment | = Revelation 20

7. | One with God Forever– The Eternity Chapter | = Revelation 23

1. Lucifer's Insurrection	2. The Serpent Beguiled Adam and Eve	3. The Wickedness of Man	4. The Silence Years– Malachi to Matthew	5. The Rapture and Time of Jacob's Trouble. Tribulation Period	6. The White Throne judgment.	7. One with God Forever The Eternity Chapter

This album of time shows pictures in lineage time and events which are the cornerstones, (actions and reactions, cause and effects) events. Six of these events are followed by judgments of deportion, destruction, deprivation and degradation all because of sin.

Lucifer's insurrection initiated the chain of events and his final judgment and imprisonments throughout eternity and the cycle. It seems in the first six snapshots you can trace a direct line to Lucifer seeking to destroy the relationship between God and His creation. But the latter parts of the 6th and 7th snapshots show His eternal future.

As we look into this album we can see the good, the bad and the ugly. But God owns the camera, and He developes the negatives. Many times, the negatives seem useless and slow to develop. There are some angles where we can't make out what the pictures really look like to know how God will develop it. But God sees the whole picture and develops it for His purpose. Many times we see the negative page of things complete. For we know in part, understand in part but afterwhile we will see the whole picture.

GOD CREATED AND DEVELOPS THE WHOLE PICTURE

Is God in everything or is everything in God? Sometimes I don't know the answer to this question but I know that nothing happens without God's foreknowledge. Sometimes we say, "If God had only moved."

Well God doesn't have to move, because He's everywhere at all times.

Ten thousand years ago in God is the present, just as His presence is always present. God is old, but brand new. God is brand new, but ancient. He's past the present, but present in the past. He has all power. Satan's power, man's power and any and all power is subject to God. At His will He can, in His will He can, by His will He can do whatever He wants. He's invisible but is seen everywhere. People don't listen, but He never quits talking to us. Even His silence speaks louder than the sum of His creation. Some say God is distant and will not come when you call Him. But it's God that measures the distance and waits with you for Him. Study the Archomai on the chart again–the character and expression of God.

"THE ARCHOMAI THE ARCHITECT OF TOTAL EXISTENCE"

Before there was nothing, there was God. God is exnihilo meaning "from or out of nothing". But the "nothing" came from God. God has always been, therefore, when it was nothing it was God. Words can't tell you who God really is. They can only describe His character at points in eternity. Remember it's like taking snapshots and placing them in a photo album of eternity. The pictures doesn't do Him justice. God Himself must be revealed to your spirit to know Him. Only in the Word of God by the Spirit of Truth can we understand even a tiny portion of Him. God is sovereign, excellent, of the most exalted kind. He's supreme, the ruler of all, absolute, perfect free from imperfection and He's autonomous.

God is the Father, Son and the Holy Spirit.

The Character and Expression of God

God will find a way to reveal Himself to His creation. I remember the story of Helen Keller as a kid and how she couldn't see or hear. But God is so amazing in His love for us that He taught Helen to communicate with her teacher. The teacher was amazed at this miracle and began a process of educating Helen that ultimately made her an articulate individual. Ms. Keller was asked after she became a believer, "How did you get to know God?" She smiled and said, "I always knew He was there waiting, but I never knew His Name." Use this study guide to learn and understand His Name and character. We have added a little theological information to better equip you.

1. Elohim – The supreme God, the Creator. "Elohim" indicates the relation of God to man as Creator, and is in

contrast with Jehovah which indicates Him in covenant relationship with creation. (Genesis 1:1-2:3, Psalm 19:1)

2. Yehovah – self-existent or eternal one: Lord. The Jewish national Name of God. God is used with another name Adonai meaning Lord. Adonai – Jehovah, Lord God, Genesis 15:2,8; Deuteronomy 3:24; 9:26; Joshua 7:7, etc.

3. El, – Strength. El is the strong and mighty one; the Almighty; the most high God, etc. El has four expressions of His Name.

    a.   Elyon- the strongest of the strong and Mighty One. Genesis 14: 17-20.

    b.   Roi- the strong and Mighty One who sees all. Genesis 16:13

    c.   Shaddai- The Strong and Mighty One, the bosom of God. Genesis 17:1; Psalm 91:1.

    d.   Olam- The Strong and Mighty One is everlasting. Isaiah 40:28-31

4. Eloah – Deity; God, the Divine One. Deuteronomy 32:15-17; 2 Chronicles 32:15; Nehemiah 9:17; Psalm 18:31; 50:22; 114:7

5. Elah – God. Found only in Ezra 4:24; 5:1-17; 6:3-18; 7:12-27; Daniel 2:11-47; 3:12-29; 4:2-9; 5:3-26; 6:5-26

6. Tsur- Rock: Refuge Isaiah 44:8

The Main Greek Word for "God"...THEOS

Theos- The supreme Divinity; a magistrate
Theology – the study of God's relation to the world.

Theos is the New Testament word for God, origins uncertain affiliates with deity, the supreme divinity, a magistrate. Strong's says "Theos, as a noun, means (1) in polytheism of the

Greeks denoted a god or deity," Acts 14:11; 19:26; 1 Corinthians 8:5; Gal 4:8.

The word was appropriated by Jews and retained by Christians to denote "the one true God." In the O.T., "God" comes from the Hebrew words Elohim and Jehovah, the former indicating His power and preeminence, the latter His unoriginated, immutable, eternal and self-sustained existence. In the New Testament these and all the divine attributes are predicated of Him. To Him are ascribed:

His unity or monism: St. Mark 12:29; 1Timothy 2:5;
Self-existence: St. John 5:26
Immutability: James 1:17
Eternity: Romans 1:20
Universality: St. Matthew 10:29; Acts 17:26-28
Almighty Power: St. Matthew 19:26
Infinite Knowledge: Acts 2:23; 15:18; Romans 11:33
Creative Power: Romans 11:36; 1 Corinthians 8:6; Ephesians 3:9; Revelation 4:11; 10:6
Absolute Holiness: 1 Peter 1:15; 1 John1:5;
Righteousness: 1 John 17:25
Faithfulness: 1 Corinthians 1:9; 10:13; 1 Thessalonians 5:24; 2 Thessalonians 3:3; 1 John 1:9 and etc.

There is but one God and He can do all things. It's important to know Him in many ways from His unity to His faithfulness.

When I was a child my parents took the family to a toy store and allowed us to purchase some items like marbles, a checker set, a yoyo and a kaleidoscope. With the kaleidoscope you can look in one lens of the cylinder and as you turn it you see different shapes and colors, but you must hold the scope up to the light to really appreciate the view. When you study God there is only one true God and you must study Him in the light of Jesus Christ His only begotten Son. From every point of the Word, every page you turn, every chapter and verse, God is saying, "I'm here for a relationship with man. I want to reveal Myself and covenant with Him." To those who walk in the light, God keeps no secrets.

To those who refuse the light, they don't know God and can't know Him because their REJECTION has blinded their eyes. They may know the letter as the Scribes and Pharisees, but they don't know the spirit or the Word. Imagine this, men study God, write books, sing songs, and teach classes on theology, but will stand one day before God and hear God say, *" You thought you knew me, but I never knew you, depart from me you worker of iniquity."* (Matthew 25:41).

I don't care whether you're black, white, red, yellow, or brown, you must know Jesus Christ as your Lord and Savior. If you don't know Him, it doesn't matter what religion, ethnic group, your status in society, or who your mama is. If you don't accept Him as Lord and Savior, you can't and won't be saved from your sins. Because the spirit of antichrist is heavy in the land, society will say to be a responsible, moral person and when you die you're going to the big house in the sky.   WRONG! WRONG! WRONG! Life isn't based on you, but Jesus. You're saved by God's grace through faith in the Son of God. You must know Him, obey Him and be a worshipper of Him.

1. Theomacheo – to resist deity when someone fights against God; *And there arose a great cry: and the scribes that were of the Pharisees' part arose and strove saying, "We find no evil in this man: but if a spirit or angel hath spoken to him, let us not fight against God.* Acts 23:9

2. Theomachos – an opponent of deity, God-fighters, *But if it be of God, ye cannot overthrow it; lest haply ye be found even to us to not fight God.* Acts 5:39

3. Theodidaktos – divinely instructed God taught us to love one another but as touching brotherly love *Ye need not that I write unto you: for ye yourselves are taught of God to love one another.* 1 Thessalonian 4:9

4. Theopneustos – God breathed; divinely breathed in; by God's inspiration. *All Scripture is given by inspiration of God, and is profitable for doctrine, reproof, correction and instruction in righteousness.* 2 Timothy 3:16

5. <u>Theo</u>sebes – God worshipper; reverent of God, i.e. pious. *Jesus saith unto her, Woman, believe me, the hour cometh, when ye shall neither in this mountain, nor yet at Jerusalem worshipped the Father. Ye worshipped ye know not what: we know what we worship: for salvation is of the Jews. But the hour cometh and now is when the true worshippers shall worship the Father in spirit and in truth: for the Father seeketh such to worship him. God is a spirit: and they that worship must worship him in spirit and in truth.*

(St. John 4:21-24)

6. <u>Theo</u>stuges – God–hater, impious, hateful to God. They are spiteful of every Holy and righteous act committed by God, His Son and the Holy Spirit.
And even as they did not like to retain God in their knowledge, God gave them over to a reprobate mind, to do those things which are not convenient; backbiters, haters of God, despiteful, proud, boasters, inventors of evil things and disobedient to parents.

(Romans 1:28-30)

7. <u>Theo</u>sebeia – The fear or reverence of God; devoutness. *There was a certain man in Ceasarea called Corneluis, a centurion of the band called the Italian band. He was a devout man, and one that feared God with all his house, which gave much alms to the people, and prayed to God always.*

(Acts 10:1-2)

8. <u>Theosophy</u> – Webster says: belief about God and the world held to be based on mystical insight. Our authority is based upon the word of God, not New Age Meditation.

Mystical – Spiritual, symbolic: for or relating to an intimate knowledge of or direct communion with God (as though contemplation or visions). The study of God as to His relationship to the world can be summed up in St. John 3:16-17, *For God so loved the world that He gave His only begotten Son that whosoever believeth in Him should not perish, but have everlasting life. For God sent not His Son to condemn*

58

the world: but that the world through Him might be saved.
This is the true character and His expression of love to all
mankind. The haters, fighters, wicked ones, and everyone
that will believe on the Son of God and accept Him as Lord
and Savior.

Our main focus is on God and we want to reveal everything
we've learned and been taught. We aren't trying to be mystical or
profess some great revelation that only a few people understand.
But take simple Bible truths and apply spiritual and common
sense, while asking, knocking, and seeking God for answers. Most
folks don't study the Word enough to extract the meat, but settle
for much milk. But they're God's people and very precious in His
sight. I believe the deeper you get and the more you submit to
God, the more you will experience His glory. The way to get there
is through Spirit and Truth–the Holy Ghost and the Bible with a
life of humility, fasting, praying and studying the Word. Also, you
need to have proper leadership and mentorship. Find a Full
Gospel church and let God's man or woman pour into your spirit.
It's okay to go to a spirit–filled Bible College that's on the cutting
edge of God's Word. You don't have to be a minister or church
leader–just a believer.

JEHOVAH - N - THE COVENANTS

Covenant is mentioned 292 times in Scripture. In the Old
Testament (beriyth) ber-eeth'- a compact, agreement, league,
confederacy.

A covenant is the promise of certain action, provision or
protection between two individuals or parties. There are rules of
conduct, character and condition by both parties the majority of
the time.

The first covenant mentioned in Scripture in Genesis 6:18, *"But
with thee Noah will I establish my covenant God says, 'I will cause
it to stand.'"* He has the power and authority to keep his promise
in covenant. When man enters covenant he must prove or swear
by a greater force than himself. This allows him to be liable and
responsible, to give an account of himself. But God is so awesome
and omnipotent that there is no one to swear to but Himself. So

when God entered covenant He said, "Okay Father, Son and Holy Ghost, our Word has been spoken and the trinity says, "We know, We spoke it, We performed it, We've done it already from the Alpha to the Omega. Tell My covenant partners it's established in the heavens."

Now in the New Testament the word "covenant" (diatheke-dee-ath-ay-kay) means a disposition (to put together a contract, (espec, a devisory will). What is important in covenant is to meet the needs of all parties. Put together a contract spelling out the precise will and desire of both parties. If there were any questions or concerns in the old covenant, God addresses them clearly in the new covenant though Jesus Christ's coming in the form of man, through the flesh obeying God, submitted to death on the cross that we may have the right to eternal life. But the covenant also guarantees abundant life before death. Our day-to-day provision or daily bread, our health and healing etc.

The covenant is so powerful and lengthy that we couldn't do it justice in a paragraph or a chapter. This is what the authorized believers uses when warfare against the forces of Satan is waged. Our covenant is written by the Father, signed in blood by the Son and enforced by the Holy Ghost. Study the outline of Jehovah, Lord of the Covenant.

I remember a commercial a few years ago by American Express, where Karl Malden would say, "Don't leave home without your American Express Card." With AMEX you have very few spending limits. But the catch is they want you to pay all your debt at the end of the month. For some people this was great because they were able to control themselves in their business way of spending. But to others who haven't matured and have no control regarding unforeseen events that may affect their income revenue, they are constantly being taxed with penalties and late charges. Because they have the access to spend, but not the proceeds to pay on time, they are covenant breakers. AMEX set the contract terms in the application (covenant papers). You should read everything including the fine print, get to understand the terms and conditions, interest rates, grace period, etc. Know that failure could affect your credit rating and beacon score, because they will report you to the credit bureau. But our covenant (contact) with God is far better than AMEX, VISA, or Discover card. Our debt has been paid long before we ever used this credit. Life and circumstances try to collect all the time, but we are covered by the blood (life) of the sacrificial lamb. All of our sins, weights, debts, faults, shortcomings, missing the marks are paid in full. Study the outline of the One Who delivered you from bondage into prosperity.

JEHOVAH, GOD'S MOST COMMON NAME

The God of covenants, Adonai – Jehovah, the Lord our Sovereign God.

Jehovah – Jireh – The Lord will provide–Abraham–Act of Obedience(Genesis 22:13-14)–a Provision Covenant.

Jehovah – Nissi – The Lord our Banner–Israel's first victory of Amalek (Exodus 17:15)–a Victory Covenant.

Jehovah – Sabbath – the Lord of Hosts–God has charge of our protection (ects 281 times)–a Protection Covenant.

Jehovah – Shalom- The Lord is our Peace–Only God can bring peace (Judges 6:24)–a Peace in the Storm Covenant.

Jehovah – Ropha – The Lord our Healer–Obedience brings and keeps healing (Exodus 15:26)–a healing Covenant.

Jehovah – Tsidkenu - The Lord our righteousness (Jeremiah 23:6, 33:16)–a Safety Covenant.

Jehovah – Mekaddishkem – The Lord our sanctifier (Exodus 31:13; Leviticus 20:8; 21:8; 22:9, 16, 32; Ezekiel 20:12)–a Cleanliness Covenant.

Jehovah – Shammah – the Lord is present (Ezekiel 48:35)–a Covenant of His Presence.

Jehovah – Rohi – the Lord my shepherd (Psalm 23:1)–a Security Covenant.

Jehovah – Eloheka – The Lord thy God (Exodus 20:2,5,7)–a Covenant of Acknowledgement.

Jehovah – Elohay – the Lord my God (Zechariah 14:5)–a Personal Covenant.

Jehovah – Hoseenu – the Lord our maker (Psalm 95:6)–a Worship Covenant.

To illustrate, take a blank white sheet of paper and a black ink pen. Anywhere you feel like it, place one tiny dot on the paper and ask God, "Is this You in my life or is this me in Your will?"

This is the perfect conclusion:

Read   St. Matthew 7:21-23; Acts3:19-21, Romans 10:8-13; Acts 2:38; Acts 1:5-8; 2:4,42-47; Hebrew 10:25.

Follow this scriptural recipe and take the best picture of your eternal life!

CHAPTER FOUR

The Triangle of Darkness

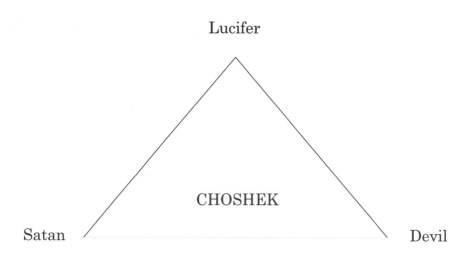

Lucifer

CHOSHEK

Satan   Devil

Lucifer –   Heylel, brightness, fallen from Heaven, son of the morning, he weakened the nations, insurrection failed, lost position with God.

Ezekiel 28 describes his looks, abilities, position and destiny.

Isaiah 14:12-15; describes his ambitiousness, self-centeredness, and final destination.

Satan – The adversary, an opponent, the arch enemy of good, the prince of this world, god of this world, to lurk for, i.e. persecute, hate, oppose, attack, accuse, resist.

I Chronicles 21:1; St. Luke 22:3,31; Revelation 20:2; 2 Corinthians 4:4; St. John 12:31; 14:30; 16:11. Revelation 20:2, 7

Devil – Diabolos accuser, slanderer, a traducer; to lower the reputation of by false accusation. To defame–

St. Matthew 4:1, 5,8,11; 9:32-33. St. John 8:44; Revelation 20:2,10.

Beelzebub – Chief of evil spirits, dung-god–

St. Matthew 10:25; 12:24-27

In the beginning God created the heavens and the earth. And the earth was without form, and void; and darkness was upon the face of the deep. And the spirit of God moved upon the face of the waters. And God said, *'Let there be light': and there was light. And God saw the light, that it was good: and God divided the light from the darkness."*

I believe God gave Lucifer a third of His angels to assist him in his assignment, and Lucifer influenced them to revolt. At this time, Lucifer decided within himself that serving God wasn't enough.

Isaiah quotes,

How art thou fallen from heaven, O Lucifer, son of the morning! How art thou cut down to the ground, which didst weaken the nations! For thou hast said in thine heart, I will ascend into heaven, I will exalt my throne above the stars of God: I will sit also upon the mount of the congregation, in the sides of the north: I will ascend above the heights of the clouds; I will be like the most High.

(Isaiah 14:12-14)

(I: ego, in Greek: Satan has a ego problem. 1. The individual is aware of himself. 2. Egotism: conceit, selfishness. Egocentric-self-centered.)

We know Lucifer's assignment was in the 2nd heaven because he's the prince of the air. Also, because he's called by Jesus as the prince of the world, Lucifer works through men, the kings of earth, like Tyrus (Ithobalas) and others. The fallen name of Lucifer is Satan, Adversary. He became the master of (darkness) choshek which has caused misery, destruction, death, ignorance and sorrow throughout our world. Satan's wickedness is everywhere and in all the things he has touched since his revolt.

> *Thou hast been in Eden the garden of God; every precious stone was thy covering... the workmanship of thy tabrets and of the pipes was prepared in thee in the day that thou wast created. Thou art the anointed cherub that covereth; and I have set thee so: thou wast upon the holy mountain of God; thou has walked up and down in the midst of the stones of fire. Thou wast perfect in thy ways from the day that thou wast created, till iniquity was found in thee.*
> (Ezekiel 28:12-15)

Found in verse 15 is the Hebrew word "matsa" meaning "to come forth, to appear or exist." In the beginning, Lucifer had it made. He was first in charge of everything as the prince of this world. He had to answer only to God. Lucifer was the master of praise and worship. But he lost his position to man. I believe before the foundation of the world God gave us the opportunity.

Scripture says,

> *...that we should be holy and without blame before him in love: having predestinated us unto the adoption of children by Jesus Christ to himself, according to the good pleasure of his will, to the praise of the glory of his grace, when he hath made us accepted in the beloved.*
> (Ephesians 1:4-6)

We were chosen before the foundation to be there at the summation of the fullness of time according to verse 10. That we should be to the praise of his glory, who first trusted in Christ (verse 12).

Don't lose your position and place in God as Satan did. He was a master at praise and worship. He was beautiful in stature and perfect in his ways, until he submitted to the sin of pride, envy and jealousy. God created him, which was good. Everything God makes is good until creation decides it doesn't need the Creator. This inner decision is birthed through pride.

God said,

Thine heart was lifted up because of thy beauty, thou hast corrupted thy wisdom by reason of thy brightness: I will cast thee to the ground. I will lay thee before kings, that they may behold thee.

(Ezekiel 28:17)

Pride will bring forth vanity, constantly looking selfishly upon ones own self–not considering the affairs and needs of others. Satan got caught up with "I". This single word or letter, "I", the way creation looks at itself to smite God's sovereign authority. God is really the only real "I" in the universe, only He controls at will.

The start of warfare began when Lucifer said "I". It was at that point his iniquity appeared or came forth. Lucifer ignited the pride that was created in himself because of his iniquity. God assigned Lucifer a job with a purpose and gave him the Garden of God as City Hall. He had access to the mountain of God to walk up and down in the midst of the stones of fire. He could come into the very presence of God at any time. With all of this honor, privilege and authority, why did he revolt against God? Because the INIQUITY- (wickedness, perversity, evil, fault, mischief, sin) in him, rose up because of pride. Some say because of the privileges and honor God stored upon him, Lucifer couldn't resist himself to be equal with God. But I say, he stopped giving the glory to God. The pride and vanity of Lucifer strengthens the iniquity within him. Also, the word iniquity is translated from the Hebrew word Avon. No offense intended by today's company, but their purpose is to sell you goods (cosmetic, superficial) to make you look and smell good, which is not a sin until thy beauty corrupts thy wisdom by reason of thy brightness or pride.

Don't let it go to your head!

God will give you beauty for ashes, the oil of joy for

mourning, the garment of praise for the Spirit of heaviness; that they might be called tress of righteousness, the planting of the Lord, that he might be glorified.

(Isaiah 61:3)

This is a promise from God to the believer of His Son Jesus. Satan can make promises, but can't keep them. The devil is a liar, deceiver and cheat. Just as there's God the Father, Son and Holy Ghost, He's sovereign. Lucifer has manifested himself as Satan, the Devil and the Dragon, he's defeated, dethroned and soon to be imprisoned and chained.

God uses man to do good and establish the Kingdom of God. The work attributes are called the proclamation of the Gospel, the Good News. Jesus is our prime example of the goodness of God. But Satan uses man as a thief, murderer and for the purpose of destruction. You might think that any man who does these things should be arrested, prosecuted and jailed. Thank God many are, but Jesus in St. John 10:10 was doing a spiritual comparison to enter the Kingdom. Now we know God is using Jesus as the door of the sheepfold. But Satan is using religious hirelings as thieves to steal (to take and carry away without right or permission) and to kill (deprive of life, defeat) and to destroy (to put an end to, ruin, kill). These men are caught up in the triangle of Lucifer. Satan is trying to build his kingdom on God's earth.

The master thief (Satan) deceives them, but for to steal, and to kill and to destroy: KJV (St. John 10:10). Because Satan is full of iniquity (Hebrew: Avon, evil, unrighteousness, wickedness) his nature is sin. All that's operating in him is to kill, steal and destroy. Remember Lucifer lost everything because of his disobedience, pride and iniquity. He wants to strike at God through creation. That's why all of creation is waiting for the manifestation of the sons of God and every time we walk in the flesh we are feeding the dragon.

God's plan was to make man in His image and after His likeness to rule this planet. Man was made a little lower than the angels. Even the angels were curious, "Why art thou mindful of man?" Satan became furious with this creation. He seeks to steal, kill and destroy it by any means possible.

67

Remember from the day that God breathed into Adam the breath of life, Satan has been trying to suck it out. It seems he is after the breath. He knows God's spirit came through his breath into man. Even though there's a difference between the spirit and breath of God, souls live by the breath of God and the Spirit lives by the spirit of God. Satan is after your soul. All of creation has His breath to live; man is the only part of creation that has God's breath in their soul. *And the Lord God formed man of the dust of the ground, and breathed into his nostrils the breath of life; and man became a living soul* (Genesis 2:7).

The soul is nephesh, a breathing creature, mind, mortally, own, pleasure, will. Satan ignited the fight in the garden battling for man's authority. After Satan was cast down to the earth and stripped of his power and authority, his plans were then to cast down and strip mankind of their power and authority by deception and manipulation; which caused man to disobey God. Satan came as a serpent in Genesis, but ate enough dust (man came from dust) and sucked enough breath to be a dragon in the book of Revelation. **Every time we fulfill the lust of the flesh we are feeding the dragon**.

God knew Satan would keep tempting mankind. Genesis 3:14 has a unique interpretation, *"...and dust shalt thou eat all the days of thy life."* We're giving him power and control over our lives. Know ye not that the unrighteous shall not inherit the kingdom of God?

> *Be not deceived: neither fornicators, nor idolaters, nor adulterers, nor effeminate, nor abusers of themselves with mankind nor thieves, nor covetous, nor drunkards, nor revilers, nor extortioners, shall inherit the kingdom of God.*
> (I Corinthians 6:9-10)

Satan has been cast out with his evil inspirations. He and his spirits control these manifestations of wickedness. Their job is to keep you ignorant, bound and out of the Kingdom of God. The Kingdom of God is the rule and reign of God; it is the will of God in the life of the believer. To live outside the Kingdom of God is to walk in the flesh (dust). Satan will be eating dust all his days.

Throughout history Satan has been after mankind. The book of Job gives insight into the spiritual activity that happens.

Look at the life of Job.

> *Now there was a day when the sons of God came to present themselves before the Lord, and Satan came also among them. And the Lord said unto Satan, Whence comest thou? Then Satan answered the Lord, and said, from going to and from in the earth, and from walking up and down in it.*
>
> (Job 1:6-7)

Satan is seeking the opportunity to use someone or something to kill, steal, and destroy, like a roaring lion seeking it's prey in the jungles of life. He's angry, disturbed and hungry for souls. The believer must be righteous and despise evil. Then the prince of this world has no advantage or control upon his life. We must submit to God and resist the devil daily. Satan is convinced that man's life is all his possession and if he loses or gains life's possessions it will affect his relationship with God. The world and its system are what the devil wants to offer in exchange for your relationship with God.

> *Love not the world, neither the things that are in the world. If any man loves the world, the love of the Father is not in him. For all that is in the world, the lust of the flesh, and the lust of the eyes, and the pride of life, is not of the Father, but is of the world. And the world passeth away, and the lust thereof: but he that doeth the will of God abideth forever.*
>
> (I John 2:15-17)

This study chart and definition will help pinpoint areas to resist the enticements that Satan offers in the worldly system:

THE ENEMY OF GOD

Lust of the eyes

The World System

Satan is the god of this world—
2 corinthians 4:4
Prince of the world – St. John 16:11

Lust of the flesh   Pride of Life

The World: the earth with its inhabitants and all things upon it.

Heb. Word trans: 1. (Eres), ground, land, earth; and it corresponds with the Greek (ge) (Psalm 22:27; Jeremiah 25:26).
2. (Cheled), a fleeting portion of time; it corresponds with the Greek. (aion), age, (Psalm 17:14; 49:1).
3. (Olam), eternity; timeout of mind; and it corresponds with the Greek.

	(aionios), (Psalm 73:12; Eccl. 3:11). **4.** (Tebel), the inhabited world; it corresponds with the Greek (oikoumene), (I Sam 2:8; II Sam. 22:16; I Chron. 16:30; Job 18:18).
Greek Word trans:	**1.** (ge), earth (Matt 5:5, 13, 18,; Rom 9:17; Eph 1:10; Rev 13:3). **2.** (aion), age (Matt 12:32; 13:22; 39-49; 24:3). **3.** (Kosmos) (Matt 4:8; 5:14; 13:35,38; 16:26). **4.** (oikoumene), inhabited earth (Matt 24:14; Luke 2:1). **5.** (aionios), eternal (Rom 16:25; II Tim 1:9, Titus 1:2).

When we submit to sin, we satisfy the flesh and glorify Satan. There is an end result:

The Results of Feeding the Dragon–Satan eats dust and spits out dirt.

The System: regular method or order

Satan sets up strongholds in the world to keep you bound, trapped and imprisoned.

THE LUST OF THE FLESH

P-power – M-money – S-Sex

God's answer–mortify and deny the flesh.

1. Adultery (moicheia): sexual unfaithfulness to wife or husband.

Thou shalt not commit adultery.
                    (Exodus 20:14; Leviticus 20:10)

Also Scripture says,
But I say unto you, that whosoever looketh on a woman to lust after her hath committed adultery with her already in his heart.

(St. Matthew 5:28)

2. Fornication (porneia): pre-marital sex and adultery, a single person with a single or married person with a single person.

Scriptures declares,
Flee fornication. Every sin that man doeth is without the body; but he that committeth fornication sinneth against his own body.

(I Corinthian 6:18)

3. Uncleanness (akatharsia): polluted lifestyle, immoral, moral impurity, soiled life.

Scripture says,
I speak after the manner of men because of infirmity of your flesh: for as ye have yielded your members servants to uncleanness and to iniquity unto iniquity; even so now yield your member's servants to righteousness unto holiness.

(Romans 6:19)

4. Lasciviousness (aslegeia): wantonness, shamelessness, outrageousness, sexual immorality, filthiness and indecency of the flesh.

Scripture says,
Who being past feeling have given themselves over unto lasciviousness to work all uncleanness with greediness.
(Ephesians 4:19)

And likewise also the men, leaving the natural use of the women, burned in their lust one toward another; men with men working that which is unseemly and receiving in themselves that recompense of their error which was meet.
(Romans 1:27)

5. Idolatry – (eidololatria): when men worship physical and mental images; times and efforts given to other things rather than the pursuit of God.

Scripture says,
Wherefore, my dearly beloved, flee from idolatry.
(I Corinthians 10:14)

For this ye know, that no whoremonger, nor unclean person, nor covetous man, who is an idolater, hath any inheritance in the kingdom of Christ and of God.
(Ephesians 5:5)

6. Witchcraft – (pharmakeia): sorcery, drug abuse, use of black or white magic, fortune telling, physics, reading, voodoo, etc.

Scripture says,
And I will cut off witchcraft out of thine hand; and thou shalt have no more soothsayers.
(Micah 5:12)

So Saul died for his transgression which he committed against the Lord, even against the word of the Lord, which he kept not and also for asking counsel of one that had a familiar spirit, to inquire of it.
(I Chronicles 10:13)

7. Hatred – (echthrai): enmity, hostility, and animosity. A feeling of disgust for another person, Satan is the master hater.

Scripture says,
If a man says I love God and hateth his brother, he is a liar: for he that loveth not his brother whom he hath seen, how can he love God whom he hath not seen?
(I John 4:20)

Hatred stirreth up strifes: but love covereth all sins.
(Proverbs 10:12)

8. Variance – (eris): strife, discord, fighting, dissension.

Scripture says,
As coals are to burning coals, and wood to fire; so is a contentious man for kindling strife.

(Proverbs 26:21)

9. Emulation – (Zelos): desiring the talents, goods, property of another person.

Scripture says,
For jealousy is the rage of man: therefore he will not spare in the day of vengeance.

(Proverb 6:34)

10. Wrath – (thumos): bad temper, bursts of rage, anger, a quick-tempered reaction to certain matters.

Scripture says,
Wherefore, my beloved brethren, let every man be swift to hear, slow to speak, slow to wrath: for the wrath of man worketh not the righteousness of God.

(James 1:19-20)

11. Strife – (erltheia): struggle, contention, conflict, a party spirit.

Scripture says,
Let nothing be done through strife or vainglory; but in lowliness of mind let each esteem other better than themselves.

(Philippians 2:3)

It is an honour for a man to cease from strife: but ever fool will be meddling.

(Proverb 20:3)

12. Sedition (dichostasia): division, rebellion, standing against others.

Scripture says,
Woe to the rebellious children, saith the Lord, that take

*counsel but not of me; and that cover with a covering, but
not of my spirit, that they may add sin to sin.*

(Isaiah 30:1)

13. Heresies (hairesis): rejection of the Holy Scriptures, God
    and the Body of Christ.

Scripture says,
*Now the Spirit speaketh expressly that in the latter times
some shall depart from the faith, giving heed to seducing
spirits, doctrines of devils.*

(I Timothy 4:1)

14. Envyings (phthonos): This is the highest form of jealousy,
    that is in your spirit, heart, soul and mind.

Scripture says,
*Be not envious against evil men neither desire to be with
them.*

(Proverbs 24:1)

15. Murders (phonos): to kill, to take a life.

Scripture says,
*But let none of you suffer as a murderer, or as a thief, or
as an evildoer, or as a busybody in other men's matters.*

(I Peter 4:15)

16. Drunkenness (methai): taking alcoholic drinks or certain
    drugs to affect or alter abilities.

Scripture says,
And be not drunk with wine, wherein is excess.

(Ephesians 5:18)

*For they that sleep sleep in the night; and they that be
drunken are drunken in the night.*

(I Thessalonians 5:7)

17. Revellings (komos): uncontrolled indulgence in pleasure,
    wild parties, orgies.

Scriptures says,

For the time past of our life may suffice us to have wrought the will of the Gentiles, when we walked in lasciviousness, lust, excess of wine, reviling, banquetings, and abominable idolatries.

(I Peter 4:3)

All that do these things shall not inherit the Kingdom of God and shall manifest the will of Satan in the world. Every time we submit our members to these works, we crucify Christ all over again. Believers must mortify the deeds of the flesh by fasting, praying and living in accordance to the Word of God. Your obedience to God is a rebuke to the spirit of disobedience.

THE LUST OF THE EYES
God's answer – keep thine eye single and treasure in heaven

The eyes can strengthen the imagination for good or evil. The heart will interpret the motive of the eyes.

The Winking Eye Story

There was a thin and short man years ago who liked to flirt with women. One day he walked through the mall and this beautiful young lady was coming his way. Chills went up and down his spine, and he started winking his eyes and hissing at her. This made the young lady upset. After being so harassed she went to the men's clothing store two doors down and told her 6'7", 300 lb husband. She described the man to her husband and directed him to the area where the incident happened.

The husband was upset because his new wife had been harassed. When he saw the man about 10 feet away, the wife pointed to him. The man turned to run, but didn't have time to get away. He began hissing and winking constantly like he had a mental problem. So when the husband laid a hand on his shoulder and spun him around to punch his lights out, he hesitated. He stepped back and said to his wife, "Honey, this man is retarded or has a medical problem. See? He wasn't winking at you. Both eyes are shutting and opening. Look at the drool around his mouth. Something is wrong with him." Then the husband let him go.

How many traps do we walk into with our eyes wide open, but our hearts closed to the Holy Spirit? Everything that shines isn't gold and everything that's gold isn't good for use. Our eyes should be used to see the glory of God.

> *All the ends of the world shall remember and turn unto the Lord: and all the kindreds of the nations shall worship before thee. For the kingdom is the Lord's and he is the governor among the nations. All they that be fat upon the earth shall eat and worship: all they that go down to the dust shall bow before him: and none can keep alive his own soul.*
>
> (Psalm 22:27-29)

No man is able to resist temptation without the help of the Lord. Satan has the recipe to trap the flesh in his snare, but when we turn to God and worship Him in spirit and truth, the lust that is appealing to the eyes cannot destroy our soul.

For many what is seen appeals to satisfy our physical and mental capacity without the direction of the Holy Spirit. It can draw away the believer from God. Scripture declares:

> *But I say unto you, that whosoever looketh on a woman to lust after her hath committed adultery with her already in his heart.*
>
> (St. Matthew 5:28)

> *Having eyes of adultery, and that cannot cease from sin; beguiling unstable souls: heart they have exercised with covetous practices; cursed children.*
>
> (II Peter 2:14)

The lust of the eyes comes from our thoughts.

> *But if thine eye be evil, thy whole body shall be full of*

darkness. If therefore the light that in thee be darkness, how great (dense) is that darkness.

(Matthew 6:23)

The eyes are the windows of the soul.

Be careful as to what you allow your eyes to gaze at. Satan has some appealing things that an empty soul may desire. Protect your eyes. They are important to your peace of mind and soul salvation.

This I say therefore, and testify in the Lord, that ye henceforth walk not as other Gentiles walk in the vanity of their minds, having the understanding darkened, being alienated from the life of God through the ignorance that is in them because of the blindness of their hearts: who being past feeling have given themselves over unto lasciviousness, to work all uncleanness with greediness.

(Ephesians 4:17-19)

The eyes reveal the intents of the heart. It seldom hides one's true nature.

THE PRIDE OF LIFE
God's Answer – submit, obey, and serve, S.O.S

The lust of the flesh and the lust of the eyes is the foundation of pride. It's about me, myself and I. I've met poor people, rich people, ugly and fair people full of pride. From Capitol Hill to Beverly Hills, it's about the almighty "I".

A self-centered person is one who focuses only on themselves, and wants people to cater to them. It causes individuals to seek the spotlight, to be lifted up in the flesh, flashy in outward appearances, to hoard up goods for oneself. Scripture says, *"Boast not thyself of tomorrow; for thou knowest not what a day may bring forth"* (Proverbs 27:1). Pride does not solely relate to shiny things, riches and expensive apparel, but to the condition of the heart.

They that trust in their wealth, and boast themselves in the multitude of their riches; none of them can by any means redeem his brother, nor give God a ransom for him.

(Psalm 49:6-7)

By the great wisdom and by the traffic hast thou increased thy riches, and your heart is lifted up because of thy riches.

(Ezekiel 28:5)

And I will break the pride of your power; and I will make your heaven as iron, and your earth as brass.

(Leviticus 26:19)

For all that is in the world, the lust of the flesh, and the lust of the eyes, and the pride of life. (I John 2:16). Satan is the prince of this world and he continually checks the souls of man in search of iniquity. If righteousness is the mark of a Godly relationship, then pride and iniquity is the mark of a sinful relationship. Every human who is born into this world, because they are born sinners, Satan believes he has the right to mark them. That's why you must be born-again of the water and spirit. Understand that when a baby is born to a born-again couple, then the child isn't born by sin and will not be shaped in iniquity. The seed of God, not the seed of sin, lives in the saved parents (read I Corinthians 7:14). By the age of accountability that child must accept Jesus as Savior. You may be born into a world of sin, but not by sin. The flesh is carnal nature, but the spirit is supernatural. Parents must train their children in the ways of God because the prince of the power of the air is Satan. He is having a field day working in the disobedience of children. Their minds can easily be blinded to the things of God and they will be caught up in the satanic vicious cycle.

The lust of the flesh, the lust of the eyes, and the pride of life are not of the Father. These are the things that caused Satan to be kicked out of heaven. His lust for power and authority, his greed for praise and honor, the iniquity to be equal with God, these are the things that caused him to lose this position, perception and power.

This is the appeal that Satan worked with Adam and Eve in the garden.

> *And the serpent said unto the woman, Ye shall not surely die: for God doth know that in the day ye eat thereof, then your eyes shall be opened, and ye shall be as gods, knowing good and evil (the lust of the flesh). And when the woman saw that the tree was good for food, and that it was pleasant to the eyes (the lust of the eyes), and a tree to be desired to make one wise (the pride of life), she took of the fruit thereof, and did eat, and gave also unto her husband with her; and he did eat (the deception of the world). And the eyes of them both were opened, and they knew that they were naked; and they sewed fig leaves together, and made themselves aprons.*
>
> (Genesis 3:4-7)

When a believer listens and obeys Satan, then they will also get more than what they bargained for. First of all, Satan is the father of lies and the master of deceit. He has been around for thousands of years. Satan doesn't play or fight fair. He will lie through his teeth and smile in your face. Never trust or rely on Satan's honor because he has none. Remember, Satan eats dust and spits out dirt (products under his control).

Judgment fell upon Adam, Eve and the serpent, which Satan used. Satan started this fight with God in the Garden of God and got kicked out of glory. Then he started a fight with man in the Garden of Eden and man got kicked out. Satan started another fight in the Garden of Gethsemane with Jesus and lost again. Every time Satan battles the Godhead he loses.

You can't win this battle walking out of the Spirit of God. For though we walk in the flesh we do not war after the flesh:

> *For the weapons of our warfare are not carnal, but mighty through God to the pulling down of strongholds: casting down imaginations and every high thing that exalteth itself against the knowledge of God and bringing into captivity every thought to the obedience of Christ.*
>
> (II Corinthians 10:3-5)

The devils will be defeated through the weapons of God. Our weapons are spiritual and designed to defeat the schemes, plots, and fiery darts of Satan. When you come to the scrimmage line and you know a fight is about to break out, use what you've got. Examples of our arsenal: some of the many methods to kick the devil's butt are fasting, praying, studying the Word, and walking in obedience.

WEAPONS FOR T.A.B.:

1. **The Word of God** – *For the Word of God is <u>quick</u>, and <u>powerful</u>, and <u>sharper</u> than any two-edged sword, <u>piercing</u> even to the <u>dividing</u> asunder of soul and spirit, and of the joints and marrow, and is a <u>discerner</u> of the thoughts and intents of the heart* (Hebrew 4:12).

2. *But ye shall receive <u>power</u>, after that the <u>Holy Ghost</u> is come upon you: and ye shall be witnesses unto me both in Jerusalem, and in all Judea, and in Samaria, and unto the uttermost part of the earth* (Act 1:8).

3. *Brethren, if a man be overtaken in a fault, ye which are spiritual, <u>restore</u> such a one in <u>the spirit of meekness</u>; considering thyself, lest thou also be tempted.* (Galatians 6:1).

4. *Moreover, it is required in <u>stewards</u> that a man is found faithful* (I Corinthians 4:2).

5. *Wherefore take unto you <u>the whole armor of God that</u> ye may be able to withstand in the evil day, and having done all, to stand* (Ephesians 6:13).

6. *Above all, taking the <u>shield of faith</u>, wherewith ye shall be able to quench all the fiery darts of the wicked* (Ephesians 6:16).

7. *And take the <u>helmet of salvation</u>, and the <u>sword of the Spirit</u>, which is the word of God* (Ephesians 6:17).

8. *<u>Praying</u>, always with all <u>prayer and supplication</u> in the Spirit, and watching thereunto with all perseverance and supplication for all saints* (Ephesians 6:18).

The Dynamics of Spiritual Warfare

9. *In whom we have <u>redemption</u> through <u>his blood</u>, the <u>forgiveness of sins</u>* (Ephesians 1:7).

10. *And now abideth <u>faith, hope, charity</u>, these three; but the greatest of these is <u>charity</u>* (I Corinthians 13:13).

11. *Wherefore <u>laying aside all malice, and all guile, and hypocrisies</u>, and <u>envies</u>, and <u>all evil speaking</u>* (I Peter 2:1).

12. *But ye are <u>a chosen generation</u>, a <u>royal priesthood</u>, a <u>holy nation</u>, a <u>peculiar people</u>; that ye should show forth the <u>praises of him</u> who hath <u>called you</u> out of <u>darkness into</u> his <u>marvelous light</u>* (I Peter 2:9).

13. *Now <u>faith</u> is the <u>substance</u> of things <u>hoped</u> for, the <u>evidence</u> of things not seen* (Hebrew 11:1).

14. *Let us <u>hold fast</u> the <u>profession</u> of our <u>faith without wavering</u>; (for he is faithful that promised)* (Hebrews 10:23).

15. *For God has not given us the <u>spirit of fear</u>; but of <u>power</u>, and of <u>love</u>, and of a <u>sound mind</u>* (II Timothy 1:7).

16. *<u>Study</u> to show thyself <u>approved</u> unto God, a workman that needeth <u>not to be ashamed</u>, <u>rightly dividing</u> the word of truth* (II Timothy 2:15).

17. *Let <u>this mind be</u> in you, which was <u>also in Christ Jesus</u>: Who being in the <u>form of God</u>, thought it not robbery to be <u>equal with God</u>* (Philippians 2:5-6).

18. *<u>Submit</u> yourselves therefore to God. <u>Resist the devil</u>, and he will <u>flee from you</u>. <u>Draw nigh to God</u>, and <u>he will draw</u> nigh to you. <u>Cleanse your hands</u>, ye sinners; and <u>purify your hearts</u>, ye double minded* (James 4:7-8).

19. *Yet Michael the archangel, when <u>contending with the devil</u> he disputed about the body of Moses, durst not bring against him a <u>railing accusation</u>, but said, <u>The Lord rebuke thee</u>* (Jude 9).

20. *There is therefore <u>now no condemnation</u> to them which are <u>in Christ Jesus</u>, who walk not after the flesh, but <u>after the Spirit</u>* (Romans 8:1).

All of these Scriptures and many more teach us the how-to's of spiritual warfare. For we fight not against flesh and blood; it's a spiritual fight that only can be won through God. The devil doesn't play by your rules and don't expect him to show remorse, regret or apologize for anything. He's already judged and condemned to the lake of fire. There's no room for repentance. Lucifer started this fight before the Garden of Eden and has spent every second, minute, hour and day trying to defeat God through creation. He's fighting a lost cause, but along the way he deceives the multitudes to join him in hell.

Therefore my people are gone into captivity, because they have no knowledge and there honourable men are famished, and their multitudes dried up with thirst. Therefore hell hath enlarged herself, and opened her mouth without measure: and their glory, and their multitude, and their pomp, and he that rejoiceth, shall descend into it.

(Isaiah 5:13-14)

All of this because man considers not the work of God, neither considers the operation of His hands. They love darkness rather then light; choshek is what lies in Satan. But the submitted believers will triumph over Lucifer, Satan and all devils.

Now thanks be unto God which always causeth us to triumph in Christ, and maketh manifest the savour of his knowledge by us in every place.

(II Corinthians 2:14)

Satan is your enemy, not God. The battle is between you and Satan, and He's no match for God! Satan is not God's equal, God has no competitor, challenger or nemesis. Don't picture in your mind God pulling the rope on one side and Satan pulling on the other side as in a tug-of-war. It hasn't been nor ever will be a tug-of-war between Satan and God. Satan must get permission to even enter into God's presence. He's subservient to God and has no choice but to obey.

Remember Job's life story? Satan was asking for permission to touch what belonged to God's servant. Many times without permission and submission, we can do nothing. Remember the demons when they met Jesus on the coast by the graveyard? They said something like this: *Cometh thou to torment us before our time? Give us permission to live in the swine.* And the swine committed suicide. The best way to defeat the devil is through submission to God.

> *Submit yourselves therefore to God. Resist the devil, and he will flee from you. Draw nigh to God, and he will draw nigh unto you. Cleanse your hands, ye sinners; and purify your hearts, ye double minded.*

(James 4:7-8)

This is the way you have complete authority and power over all the powers of Satan.

What about chapters ten of St. Matthew and St. Luke? He gave them power over satanic forces. They bruised the head of satanic forces until Jesus said, *"I beheld Satan as lightning falling from heaven."* When the believer learns that Satan's evil is not equal in power to the good in God, then Satan is in more trouble than he can handle. Let's not forget that our adversary is very deceitful and cunning. We must never underestimate our enemy.

We learned in Daniel that Satan helped to hinder the answers to prayer in a fight with good angels, but they prevailed. Satan fought for the body of Moses, but the good angels prevailed. They said to him, *"the Lord rebuke thee,"* and it was enough. In Revelation, Satan fought angels, the saints and attempted to attack the Holy City. But again, the Word defeated him, and he went to his final destination–the lake of fire. He would never fight against the saints, angels or God again.

Satan has been judged, Scripture states *Of judgment, because the prince if this world is judged* (St. John 16:11). I preached a message a few years ago about a man named Johnnie who was convicted of a crime. The jury found him guilty, and the judge passed the sentence. The man was allowed to leave jail to set his affairs in order. While released on bail, Johnnie knew he had to return at a later date to serve his sentence. During the time

Johnnie was out, he went everywhere partying all night long, gambling, drinking, using drugs and living like there was no tomorrow, for he knew that he had an appointment with destiny and had lost his freedom. Johnnie told no one that he was under judgment; he acted as though he was the king of the world. But when someone was around who knew about his conviction, he would calm down and act dignified. When he met people who were misinformed or uninformed about his impending judgement, he was a terror.

Satan is just like Johnnie. He has been judged and sentenced, but he's out on bail for a season. He's trying to deceive men into believing that he's a winner, all the while knowing that the lake of fire is his final resting place.

Because the prince of this world was judged, it has already happened at Calvary. But until then he is trying to keep believers from recognizing their authority over him. The devil believes in smoke screens, deception, lies and ignorance.

Remember, he has no room for repentance.

And the devil that deceived them was cast into the lake of fire and brimstone, where the beast and the false prophets are, and shall be tormented day and night for ever and ever.

Satan has an eternal life sentence.

And whosoever was not found written in the book of life was cast into the lake of fire.

(Revelation 20:10,15)

Will you be willing to join him?

CHAPTER FIVE

What Say You? Revival or Riot?

I remember the month I accepted the Lord as my Savior. My high school was celebrating African Culture Week. There were many planned events to educate all students... black, white and other ethnic groups. The purpose was to teach them to appreciate black achievements and respect other cultures. There was a revival started at a nearby church that my sister Olivia and her husband Woodrow D. were attending. I had a full week ahead of me, since football season was over for the Junior Varsity squad and basketball tryouts were right after school. I believed the point guard position belonged to me. Basketball tryouts were beginning, and a funny thing happened during this week.

Earlier at basketball practice, I couldn't dribble the ball without losing it. The coach and my teammates started saying "What's happening with Maxwell?" At the time, I couldn't figure it out. I didn't know why things were not working. So I stepped away for a few days, thinking I was trying too hard to do what comes naturally. I had the skills to dribble like a Globe Trotter and I could pass like Magic Johnson. The coaches and team watched with amazement how uncoordinated I had become.

While walking to class that week, I told my friends something was happening with me and I didn't know what it was. I said I felt uneasy in the pit of my stomach. I decided on the next Tuesday night I would go to the nearby revival. African Culture Week was great. Monday was fantastic and so was Tuesday, but Wednesday about 4:00 a.m., some troublemakers came out to the school and wrote on the walls "n...g...rs go home" and some other unmentionable words. The maintenance men tried to paint over it, but there wasn't enough time for the paint to dry.

Students arrived between 7:00 and 7:30 a.m. My bus was late that day, and by the time we got there, the turbulence was already in full swing. There were police cars with dogs and upset parents dropping off their children. It was a mad house. Deans and substitute teachers were patrolling inside the school and the police along with their dogs were patrolling outside. We were escorted to our classrooms.

This day felt like a repeat in history for me. At the age of six, my older brothers Vincent and Dennis and older sister, Olivia and I, plus my cousins, the Youngs, were the first black families to be bussed to an all-white elementary school in the Lake County Florida area. My father and mother hated racism and were very bold in their decision to take advantage of a choice that became available in the early 1960's. Black parents could choose to send their kids to an all-black school named Edgewood or an all-white one called Mascotte. At the time, Mascotte was closer to our home and had brand new books and better facilities, but to me the teachers were all strict.

During the first week of second grade, at the age of six, I experienced the satanic warfare of racism. I think every child in school hated our little black faces and kinky hair. They'd call us every name they could think of and they started with the "N" word and ended with the "N" word. My thoughts were, "Why in the world did my parents send us here? We must have done something wrong." I couldn't play on the monkey bars, merry-go-round, or swing set. I may have had three fights in my whole life outside family spats, but under the monkey bars was my first fight. I didn't fight the kid because he was white. I fought because I was tired of being pushed around and being denied the rights everyone else got.

It hurt so bad to be picked at, tormented and called names, that I exploded. It took about two months before some of the kids that watched for awhile started to defend us and soon walked me to class. This made me feel better and work harder to make friends. The teachers tried to smooth some things out, but I felt it was part of a mandate and didn't come from their heart. My family and I excelled in academics and that blew the principal and teachers' minds. They gave us an "S" for satisfactory and an "E" for excellent. We seldom made "B" for above average. We chose to endure the hatred, mean talking and abuse.

Remember, the fight I had under the monkey bars? The little boy and I became friends. He didn't hate me in his heart. He was just taught to hate because of his parents. So we both won the fight. I won on the playground and he won in spite of bad parenting. The way to win warfare in racism is not to be afraid to understand the other's differences.

I know now as an adult that things could have been handled differently, but then I was six years old. Thank God at Mascotte Elementary, we didn't need the police with guns, dogs and riot gear. But you better believe that the atmosphere was charged. The forces of evil and good were present, and as little children we had to make a choice. I thank God that I had a chance to make the right choice. I thank God that I made the right choice for peace and harmony. This is something that I pass on to my children. Be careful who you fight under the monkey bars of life. It might be a friend not yet properly introduced.

Now back to my story. There were assaults and insults in the bathrooms. Finally the varsity football players came together and wanted to help the teachers patrol the bathrooms and library, etc. Tension was high to say the least. I believe every teacher had to address racism as apart of his or her lesson for that day. But there was a young man in class named Emmanuel. He was a Christian and the quarterback on the football team. He decided to bring God into the conversation. It took boldness and strength and he didn't back down from the teachers or students. Everybody verbally attacked him on every side. A lesson I once learned is that, if a man will not go down easily when the odds are against him, and he is willing to defend his reputation, you can't easily defeat him. So they started calling him different names. I've always had compassion for the underdog because it reminded me of my past.

I listened to him. Yes there was a riot on the outside, but God had Emmanuel to ignite the revival on the inside. What say you? Revival or riot?

In class that day I recognized I had a choice to make; football, basketball, girls, parties or even knowing my own black history. But it wouldn't fill the void that only God could fill. I hated that someone wrote on the walls of my school, disrupted the week-long celebration and attracted national negative publicity for my high school. But in the midst of it all, God placed Emmanuel in the class to ignite the flame in me.

I went to church that week, and on Thursday night, I went to the altar, called on Jesus and received the baptism of the Holy Ghost. A few months later, I changed schools to get a fresh Christian start and that's where I started my ministry as a teenager preaching in the hallways. Emmanuel and I would fellowship from time to time. He is now a pastor and a blessed man. I changed my goals from being a high school sports star to shining for Jesus. I saw many young people saved and delivered because I chose the revival instead of the riot. You have to make the right choice.

A friend, named Bill R., and I preached up and down the hallways of my high school. We boycotted pep rallies as a protest to teachers and other students. We wanted them to know if they were fans for the world they'd have problems being fans for Jesus. Did we go overboard? Probably. Were our hearts sincere? I believe they were. Did it help us to win souls? Many souls, and lives were transformed. Today Bill is an anointed pastor in the Texas/Mexico area. It's been almost thirty years, and we are still in love with Jesus.

As I travel the nation, I meet people all the time who are sure in their minds that their own self-sacrifice is enough to please God. Their attitude is, "As long as I go with the flow everything will be all right." Well, I've got staggering news for you—God is not a game or an event that you can win or lose. God is a Spirit and they that WORSHIP HIM MUST WORSHIP HIM IN SPIRIT AND TRUTH. The truth is that God is SOVEREIGN, and He has a plan. God wants His children to have His Spirit and walk in His plan. God wants us to be in the position to take back the earth and regain our authority, by way of the Spirit and by walking in truth.

Acts 1:8 says,

> *But ye shall receive power, after that the Holy Ghost is come upon you: and ye shall be witnesses unto me both in Jerusalem, and in all Judea, and in Samaria, and unto the uttermost parts of the earth.*

Be an A.C.T.S. walker (don't worry, I'll explain this acronym later).

How many people get happy about receiving Jesus as their Lord and Savior. They join a church and are baptized in water, they put their names on the church roll and become active members. Some prophesy and may speak in a heavenly language. Some speak in an unknown language of tongues as long as the Spirit of God is the one who unctions them to speak. This is the motivation of their joy. Their rejoicing may have been a dance, flowing tears, clapping hands, stomping feet, raising their voice, or sitting in a place of mediation, but it is their expression of joy. It is all inspired by an overflow of anointing and results in a physical reaction to what is happening spiritually on the inside.

However, these expressions make up less than 10% of what is going on in the Last Day's Church. The average person stops seeking before they experience a true relationship, as if to say, "I confessed Romans 10:9 or traditional Pentecost." I tarried saying, "Jesus...Jesus...Jesus. I have enough to make heaven my home. I speak with a new tongue. I shout when the music is good. What else is there?"

Is this the ultimate purpose? What's the biblical sign of the Holy Ghost? It is a transformed lifestyle and power. Look at our example in the early Church (see the book of Acts) and compare its events with what is going on around you in the religious social clubs (oops, I mean churches) today. We've got that leftover anointing. It is already two days old (one day with the Lord is like a thousand years, so two days would put us at the year 2000). Yesterday's chosen—today's frozen.

Acts 1:8 tells us, *"But ye shall receive power!"* It does not say that you already have it. "Shall" means either will have, will be able to, or can. The promise is in the "shall". It means in all cases a hands-down guarantee. When a contractor builds a house or an apartment unit, the electrician comes to hook up the wiring. The power company sets up the telegraph pole or what "conductometric" is used. With the proper hook-up, the inspector gives the certificate of occupancy (C.O.). The house is sold or the apartment is rented. Now it is up to the new owner to pay the price to get the electricity in the house, to flip the power box and to turn on the light switch. Otherwise, he is in the house, which shall have power according to the contractor's promise, electrician's duty, Power Company's set-up, and the C.O. If the owner just sits there and is content (comfort zone), the shall is not put into effect. Nevertheless, the shall means that it can be, and that it will be able to be put into effect, but he will have to pay the price first.

Before you debate me, study this book to learn how to walk a victorious life and wage war against Satan. The believer must be properly equipped with the armor of God, and know how to use the weapons of his warfare. When living in the comfort zone, we always blame the wrong person for things that are occurring in our lives. I have information that will ignite your future. You can't help but start a revival or a riot.

> *And from the days of John the Baptist until now the kingdom of heaven suffereth violence, and the violent take it by force.*
>
> (Matthew 11:12)

John spoke revival talk to those who sought the Kingdom of God, and riot talk to those who ignored or tried to stop the flow of God's redemption plan. Let's examine the differences between revival talk and riot talk to help ignite the warfare and stop the welfare.

"Suffereth violence" in Greek is "biazo" which means "to use force; to force one's way into a thing." Before John, the Kingdom could only be viewed in the light of prophecy, but now men pressing in with an ardor resembling violence or desperation preached it. It appeared as if they would seize it by force. The word "force" in the Greek is "harpazo," which means "to snatch away, to seize." Those who are possessed of eagerness and zeal press their way into the Kingdom, instead of yielding to the opposition of religious foes such as the Scribes and Pharisees.

"The kingdom of God is preached, and every man presseth into it" (Luke 16:16). A person must storm the Kingdom to enter it. *He must have the spirit of a soldier who storms a city* (2 Timothy 2:3-4). He cannot be half-hearted, lacking spirit or energy. He cannot expect to slip into heaven. There has to be a real interest and desire, a vigorous stirring and struggle, a diligent seeking after God to enter heaven.

> *Then those men, when they had seen the miracle that Jesus did, said, 'This is of a truth that prophet that should come into the world.' When Jesus therefore perceived that they would come and* **take him by force**, *to make him a king, he departed again into a mountain himself alone.*
>
> (John 6:14-15, emphasis added)

John the Baptist preaching in the wilderness of Judea, played a very important role in igniting spiritual warfare. John was the son of Zechariah, a priest, and Elizabeth, a holy woman. We can conclude that he knew prayer holiness and most of all, dedication and sacrifice. John was ordained as the forerunner of Christ, but he was the spiritual armor bearer of the most powerful manifestation that the world would ever witness. His message was simple, yet somewhat complicated. At the same time it was simple for those with spiritual hunger and thirst, but complicated for the elite religious leaders. They thought they had it all together before John's arrival. The hungry and thirsty, on the other hand, knew that they needed more and were willing to travel into the wilderness desert to get a drink. Sometimes the things that are best for us may not be easily accessible.

93

PERCEPTIONS OF THE ELITE

The religious elite seriously questioned why their membership would go elsewhere to get what they thought was already being provided at home. So they (the elite dignitaries) went out themselves to investigate this unordained preacher who was neither mainstream, nor willing to go with the flow. They probably thought that he should have been a priest like his father. Instead, he was merely a poorly dressed, self-proclaimed prophet. Even worse, all of Jerusalem, Judea, and the region around about Jordan came confessing their sins—without a turtledove, lamb, or bullock. I'm sure they believed John was misguiding, misquoting, misinforming and misbehaving to get folks to come to the wilderness. He even neglected to get their permission from the High Priest, or a permit from City Hall. Yet, he was preaching *"Repent ye, for the kingdom of heaven is at hand,"* and making himself an ambassador to God's house. John, in their minds, was doing nothing less than starting a riot.

JOHN'S MESSAGE TO LEADERSHIP OF HIS DAY!

Riot Talk:

> *But when he saw many of the Pharisees and Sadducees come to his baptism, he said unto them, 'O generation of vipers, who hath warned you to flee from the wrath to come? Bring forth therefore fruits meet for repentance: And think not to say within yourselves, "We have Abraham to our father" for I say unto you, that God is able of these stones to raise up children unto Abraham. And now also the ax is laid unto the root of the trees: therefore, every tree which bringeth not forth good fruit is hewn down, and cast into the fire.'*

(Matthew 3:7-10)

Right from the start, John dared to make a difference in his day. He knew that he had a message and that it would have repercussions. John's message wasn't politically correct. He offended through name-calling, judging and public embarrass-

94

ment. Today, John would hear from lawyers with defamation claims, civil suits and the ACLU, NAACP, ADL, to name a few. You're talking about "igniting the warfare". In the minds of many, John crossed the line. He upset the good-ole-boys and there was a price to pay. I'm sure if it were possible, John would lose funding by the government for discrimination. He would have been blacklisted by major denominations, had interviews cancelled by major networks and wouldn't have received an invitation to the governor's mansion. And forget about the White (Right) House. Sometimes obeying the call of God on our lives makes us unpopular among our peers.

REVIVAL TALK TO THE BELIEVER:

I indeed baptize you with water unto repentance: but he that cometh after me is mightier than I, whose shoes I am not worthy to bear: he shall baptize you with the Holy Ghost, and with fire: Whose fan is in his hand, and he will thoroughly purge his floor, and gather his wheat into the garner; but he will burn up the chaff with unquenchable fire.

(Matthew 3:7-11)

John insults the religious leadership by calling them by their spiritual guilds. They were vipers (snakes) who were led in their ways by the devil. No wonder people left the synagogues and the temples in search of the reality of God. Not only did the Pharisees and Sadducees not enter the Kingdom, they blocked the doorway so others could not enter. Heaven's doors had been shut for four hundred years, and the spirit of mankind was thirsty for the presence of God. The "spiritual" religious gatekeepers of John's day were satisfied with being at ease in Zion. They had prayer, but not commitment. They sang songs, but with no expression of praise. They preached sermons—with no message. They had rituals, but no relationship. Their hearts were as hard as stones. Their spirits were cold as ice.

They had become like those mentioned in Isaiah:

His watchmen are blind: they are all ignorant, they are all dumb dogs, they cannot bark; sleeping, lying down, loving to slumber. Yea, they are greedy dogs which can never have enough, and they are shepherds that cannot understand: they all look to their own way, every one for his gain, from his quarter.

(Isaiah 56:10-11)

Today, riots sometimes start with a perception of injustice by those in authority. Often, law enforcement officers have stepped out of bounds—bringing racial tensions to a boiling point. For example, in the latter part of the twentieth century we had the Watts, McDuffie and Rodney King riots, to name a few that received national attention. The response of society to an act of perceived injustice was violence and destruction. This doesn't need to happen anymore in all societies. There are some that accept whatever dilemma is set before them and say within themselves, "That's just the way it is, and we won't complain." I believe that these individuals are far worse off in society than the rioters. Then there's a group that really can make a difference and won't, doesn't. That's the real power brokers of the world, the church, the fasting prayer warriors who speak the language of faith. They can go to heaven's court and gett a spiritual injunction against satanic plots. If people would pray, fast and seek the face of God, instead of burning cars, buildings and destroying businesses, and pray for the fire of the Holy Ghost to take control of government, then there would be an opportunity for change.

We must fast for the police force—that they fulfill their divine purpose; that they keep the law of God and order their steps by God's statutes.

We must seek God like he told Solomon,

If my people which are called by my name, shall humble themselves and pray, and seek my face, and turn from their wicked ways; then will I hear from heaven and will forgive their sin and will heal their land.

(2 Chronicles 7:14)

God told Solomon that Israel had been summoned to court because of pending judgment, but if they would be willing to change their ways, cease and desist which is to stop a practice of disobedience that he would hear from heaven, which is powerful. God is saying that He will talk to the Trinity about you. He will give them forgiveness for their sins, which is a full pardon, and heal or restore the land.

Let's continue to examine whether John had a reason to fight carnal humanism and religious leadership. In Matthew 23, Jesus describes the character and personality of the religious leadership of the day. We will study the eight woes of the Scribes and give a remedy to many of the woes.

1. **Riot Talk**: Spiritual Resistance

Jesus says the religious leaders are actors on stage—players in a part. They have a form of godliness but deny the power thereof. These men stood in the path of Heaven's entrance and refused to enter. Neither did they move to the side so that others could enter.

> *But woe unto you, scribes and Pharisees, hypocrites! For ye shut up the kingdom of heaven against men: for ye neither go in yourselves, neither suffer ye them that are entering to go in.*
>
> (Matthew 23:13 emphasis added)

Hypocrites: hupokrites; an actor under an assumed character (stage player).

John's View:
John saw that these actors wanted a part in the episode of "As the Kingdom Manifests" (As the World Turns) but they really were "At the Edge of Night" (without night vision) standing in "The Secret Storm." Riot talk is the only language they could understand.

Revival Talk: Spiritual Acceptance

Jesus spoke to those who were rejected, oppressed and cast out. They worked hard at success but always seemed to fail. These people were caught in a vicious system that was rigged for failure.

> *Come unto me, all ye that labor and are heavy laden, and I will give you rest. Take my yoke upon you, and learn of me; for I am meek and lowly in heart: and ye shall find rest unto your souls. For my yoke is easy, and my burden is light.*
>
> (Matthew 11:28-30)

John's View

John saw a change coming through repentance. The Pharisees, the common people had to change their ways and repent, the Scriptural way.

> *Therefore if any man be in Christ, he is a new creature: old things are past away; behold, all things are become new.*
>
> (II Corinthians 5:17)

Revival comes after true repentance and spiritual acceptance.

2. **Riot Talk:** Spiritual Tyrants

A tyrant of authority is a ruler who governs oppressively, brutally; one who uses authority or power harshly. The Pharisees were fascism acting spiritual tyrants who Jesus said would get extra damnation.

> *Woe unto you, scribes and Pharisees, hypocrites! for ye devour widows' houses, and for a pretence make long prayer: therefore ye shall receive the greater damnation.*
>
> (Matthew 23:14, emphasis added)

John's View

Let's get rid of the tyrants because they are not producing the right fruit. Cut them down and cast them into the fire. John knows that bad fruit can spoil and contaminate good fruit.

Revival Talk: Advocate
Even when we are tested and tried we are more than conquerors. We have an Advocate in civil matters, where normally we have to defend ourselves. Jesus is saying, "I'll meet you in court and be your Advocate or Attorney in fact.

But whoso shall offend one of these little ones which believe in me, it were better for him that a millstone were hanged about his neck, and that he were drowned in the depth of the sea. Woe unto the world because of offenses! for it must needs be that offenses come; but woe to that man by whom the offense cometh.
(Matthew 18:6-7)

Jesus is saying, "They rob the helpless in the name of religion, pray long, drawn out prayers, to be seen as well as heard; spiritual show boating. They pay the price of greater damnation."

3. **Riot Talk**: Spiritual Gehenna

Jesus tells the Scribes and Pharisees what their destiny is before they arrive as well as their converts who follow them. Be very careful as to what, where, and who you fellowship with. Everything that shines is not of gold.

Woe unto you scribes and Pharisees, hypocrites! for ye compass sea and land to make one proselyte, and when he is made, ye make him twofold more the child of hell than yourselves.
(Matthew 23:15, emphasis added)

Proselyte: *proselutos*, a newcomer, a convert from a Gentile religion to Judaism.

Gehenna - "child of *Gehenna*" means one destined to hell.

Revival Talk: Manifest Sons of God
When we become the sons of God through Christ Jesus, we die daily from ourselves and show forth the works of Christ. We don't need man's validation in all matters but the Spirit of the Spirit itself beareth witness with our spirit that we are the children of God. Roman 8:16, then revival come forth as we *"Mark the perfect*

man, and behold the upright: for the end of that man is peace" (Psalms 37:37). *"My son walk not thou in the way with them; refrain thy foot from their path"* (Proverbs 1:15).

4. **Riot Talk**: Spiritual Misguides

The Scribes spent a great amount of time spinning their wheels on subjects that appeared of great importance, but had no substance or foundation. They made a law of rituals and customs that God only gave for recommended procedure, to act as a foreshadow of the coming Christ. But they traded the outward show for the inward transformation, against divine order. They worshipped the creature and forsook the Creator.

> *Woe unto you, ye blind guides, which say, 'whosoever shall swear by the temple, it is nothing: but whosoever shall swear by the gold of the temple, he is a debtor!' Ye fools and blind: for whether is greater, the gold, or the temple that sanctifieth the gold? And, Whosoever shall swear by the altar, it is nothing; but whosoever sweareth by the gift that is upon it, he is guilty. Ye fools and blind: for whether is greater, the gift, or the altar that sanctifieth the gift? Whoso therefore shall swear by the altar, sweareth by it, and by all things thereon. And whoso shall swear by the temple, sweareth by it, and by him that dwelleth therin. And he that shall swear by heaven, sweareth by the throne of God, and by him that sitteth thereon.*
>
> (Matthew 23:16-22)

Revival Talk: Spiritual Priority
A stage and an outward show isn't what God desires of us. But inward truthfulness and repentance will bring forth a spiritual cleansing (Read Psalm 51:1-10 in your spare time). It's not lip service, but real repentance.

> *This people draweth nigh unto me with their mouth, and honoureth me with their lips; but their heart is far from me. But in vain they do worship me, teaching for doctrines the commandments of men.*
>
> (Matthew 15:8-9)

5. **Riot Talk**: Spiritual Showboats

Jesus says they were concerned with the petty parts of the law. However, they forsook and did not even touch the important issues. They scrutinized the small matters and blindly overlooked the larger and more important issues.

Woe unto you, scribes and Pharisees, hypocrites! for ye pay tithe of mint and anise and cumin and have omitted the weightier matters of the law, judgment, mercy and faith: these ought ye to have done, and not to leave the other undone. Ye blind guides, which strain at a gnat and swallow a camel.

(Matthew 23:23-24)

In a court of law the Pharisee would be cited for breach of contract (the failure to uphold their part, this violation the terms). And their character of hypocrisy would be present as circumstantial evidence for a conviction. They were contempt in judgment. They replaced mercy with duress and forfeited their faith with misfeasance. Many things they did were right but for the wrong reasons. Jesus once told His disciples, *"Do as they say, but not as they do"* to paraphrase a little.

Revival Talk: The Changing of the Guards
Before the Scribes of John and Jesus' day, God had already made provision. It was a new covenant to bless the Church. The old covenant with Israel was being replaced. This was a new and improved start. It came through Jesus, the sacrificial Lamb of God. However, the Scribes and Pharisee didn't recognize change. They enjoyed the benefits of spiritual fascism, being the religious elite.

For if that first covenant had been faultless, then should no place have been sought for the second. For finding fault with them, he saith, 'Behold, the days come, saith the Lord, when I will make a new covenant with the house of Israel and with the house of Judah: Not according to the covenant that I made with their fathers in the day when I took them by the hand to lead them out of the land of Egypt; because they continued not in my covenant, and I regarded them not, saith the Lord. For this is the covenant that I will make with the house of Israel after those days, saith the Lord; I will put my laws into their mind, and write them in their hearts: and I will be to them a God, and they shall be to me a people: and they shall not teach every man his neighbor, and every man his brother, saying, "Know the Lord:" for all shall know me, from the least to the greatest. For I will be merciful to their unrighteousness, and their sins, and their iniquities will I remember no more.' In that he saith, A new covenant, he hath made the first old. Now that which decayeth and waxeth old is ready to vanish away.

(Hebrews 8:7-13)

6. **Riot Talk**: Spiritually Filthy

Authority without ethics will bring extortion and excess. There were no limits as to what the Pharisees would do in the Name of God. They lacked moderation. Jesus said to clean up your heart and the outward man would be clean also. But the extortioner wants to look good before man even though God sees his wickedness inwardly.

Woe unto you, scribes and Pharisees, hypocrites! for ye make clean the outside of the cup and of the platter, but within they are full of extortion and excess. Thou blind Pharisee, cleanse first that which is within the cup and platter, that the outside of them may be clean also.

(Matthew 23: 25-26)

Scripture states, *"Man looks on the outward appearance, but God looks at the heart"* (1 Sam. 16:7). It is easy for man to dress the part. Remember, hypocrite means actor. Though he may not be a minister, pastor, or Christian, he can look like it from the outward appearance.

Revival Talk: Dress Could Kill

Remember, God is a Spirit and they that worship must worship Him in spirit and truth. You many not be able to dress

102

the flesh to get God's attention. *But put on the whole armor of God* (Ephesians 6) and the garments of praise and worship, trimmed in humility. It's not in the clergy collar, Bishop robes or the three-piece suits, but in your spirit.

> *Whose adorning let it not be that outward adorning of plaiting the hair, and of wearing of gold, or of putting on of apparel; But let it be the hidden man of the heart, in that which is not corruptible, even the ornament of a meek and quiet spirit, which is in the sight of God of great price.*
>
> (1 Peter 3:3-4)

7. **Riot Talk**: Spiritual Pride

The very thing that God hates the most is what the Scribes were the best at, that is, the spirit of pride, conceit, and justifiable self-respect. In today's society, it's all about me. I'm my own person, and I really don't need God. Everyone keeps telling me how great I am. I dress like a great man. I look like I'm prosperous. "I, I, I" will get you in trouble with God.

> <u>Woe</u> *unto you, scribes and Pharisees, hypocrites! for ye are like unto whited sepulchers, which indeed appear beautiful outward, but are within full of dead men's bones, and of all uncleanness. Even so ye also outwardly appear righteous unto men, but within ye are full of hypocrisy and iniquity.*
>
> (Matthew 23:27-28)

Sepulchers: A receptacle for sacred relics, tombs.
Uncleanness: Full of the works of the flesh
(Galatians 5:19-21).

Jesus says the Scribes looked the part, but the "part" was dead in them. John did not look the part at all, but was full of life and the power of God. The Scribes, according to what Paul has written to the Galatians, *"shall not inherit the kingdom of God"* (Galatians 5:21).

Revival Talk: The Chosen of God
But ye are a chosen generation, a royal priesthood, an

103

*holy nation, a peculiar people; that ye should shew forth
the praises of him who hath called you out of darkness
into his marvelous light.*

(I Peter 2:9)

The Scribes thought they were the chosen but were in all
actuality, the frozen generation. They didn't heed the warnings of
John nor the Gospel of Jesus Christ. They were praise seekers,
rather than praise givers. While the people of Jesus' day were
called out of darkness, the Pharisees in their pride refused to heed
the call of God. To move means you were standing in the wrong
place. It also means you must confess your faults and believe in
Jesus. The Scribes objected to this because of their spiritual pride.
The light will show you what's really in the house (or heart).

8. **Riot Talk**: Spiritual Self-Righteousness

*Woe unto you, scribes and Pharisees, hypocrites! because
ye build the tombs of the prophets, and garnish the
sepulchers of the righteous, and say, if we had been in the
day of our fathers, we would not have been partakers with
them in the blood of the prophets. Wherefore ye be
witnesses unto yourselves, that ye are the children of them
which killed the prophets. Fill ye up then the measure of
your fathers.*

(Matthew 23: 29-32)

In Matthew 23:1-33, Jesus described the character and
personality of the religious leadership of His day. He quoted in
verse 33, *"Ye serpents, ye generation of vipers, how can ye escape
the damnation of hell?"* The Pharisees and Sadducees made no
attempt to move into the realm of obedience or toward a fresh
move of God. They failed to perceive that there was a changing
of the guard, and that God was doing a revealed thing in the
earth.

*In with the revelation, out with the tradition. No man
putteth a piece of new cloth unto an old garment, for that
which is put in to fill it up taketh from the garment, and
the rent is made worse. Neither do men put new wine into*

*old bottles: else the bottles break, and the wine runneth
out, and the bottles perish: but they put new wine into
new bottles, and both are preserved.*

(Matthew 9:16-17)

Let us not totally disregard the old move, however. In its day,
it served a divine purpose. This, however, was the dawn of a new
day, a new era of the spiritual and supernatural. Anytime the
tradition meets the revelation, there is a conflict in the spirit.
The Pharisee represents the flesh (carnal nature) and John
represents the Spirit, the new nature. The Pharisees waited on
the restoration of Israel, but John ushered in the Kingdom of
God.

Jesus came out in the flesh and the Holy Ghost goes live into
your spirit to dwell and rule there. The old flesh came across the
bridge to submit unto the spirit, but only by faith through the
Son of God, as revealed by the Holy Ghost does this come to pass.

John came preaching,

*I indeed baptize you with water unto repentance: but he
that cometh after me is mightier than I, whose shoes I am
not worthy to bear: he shall baptize you with the Holy
Ghost, and with fire.*

(Matthew 3:11)

Here again the spirit must rule because of God's dwelling
place among mankind.

More Revival Talk

John played such an important role in the work of God that
Jesus testified:

*I say unto you, [that he's] more than a prophet. For this is
he, of whom it is written, 'Behold, I send my messenger
before thy face, which shall prepare thy way before thee.'
Verily I say unto you, Among them that are born of
women there hath not risen a greater than John the
Baptist: not withstanding he that is least in the kingdom
of heaven is greater than he.*

(Matthew 11:9-11)

What a testimony and revelation! It is a great testimony from the Son of God knowing the greatness of all the men and women of the Old Testament, from created Adam to Zecharias, John's father. You may be thinking about the Hall of Faith in Hebrews 11. Enoch's walk with God; Noah' saving the remnant of mankind; Abraham, the "Father of Faith"; Jacob (Israel), the Covenant father of the twelve tribes; Joseph, Israel's savior in famine; Moses, the greatest deliverer and meekest man whom God spoke with face-to-face; Joshua the General; the Judges; King David, a man after God's own heart; Solomon, the wisest man who ever lived; Elijah who left in a fiery chariot; Daniel, who had an excellent spirit, and many, many more.

Yet, John is identified by Jesus to be the greatest of them all. What did John do that made him so great? This question alone is worth a whole book or library. Permit me to simplify and save a little ink by saying that John's greatest service was opening the door to introduce Jesus! This was water to the thirsty, food to the hungry, hope for the hopeless, light in the darkness, salvation to a lost and dying world. The ministry of reconciliation is the most powerful spiritual activity among us, because we have all sinned and come short of the glory of God…*"notwithstanding he that is least in the kingdom of heaven is greater than he."* John represents the greatest among men of all who were under the old covenant. Jesus represents grace, truth and the Kingdom of God (heaven). John could introduce men to Him; but the least in the Kingdom are joint heirs with Christ. *"As he is, so are we in this world"* (1 John 4:17).

Remember, *"We are sons of God through Christ Jesus, we are seated in heavenly places with him. The spirit itself beareth witness with our spirit that we are the children of God."*
(Romans 8:16)

But as many as received him, to them gave he power to become the sons of God, even to them that believe on his name: Which were born, not of blood, nor of the will of the flesh, nor of the will of man, but of God.
(John 1:12-13)

106

The power he gave them was dynamite to ignite the countryside at an even greater rate or level than John the Baptist. Imagine one greater than John, here to cause an explosion through the Gospel of Jesus Christ, to change the course of history and lives of mankind, a power greater than the H-bomb. Atomic, anointed power that at the touch of grace and truth, millions upon millions of lives are transformed throughout eternity.

My God, what is the problem? Where have we faltered? Are we still on the level of the "least in the kingdom," or have we backslidden to the level of the Pharisees and Sadducees—a powerless relationship with only traces and residue of the past experiences?

God did move in the Old Testament age, but He stopped with Malachi,

> *Behold, I will send you Elijah the prophet before the coming of the great and dreadful day of the Lord: And he shall turn the heart of the fathers to the children, and the heart of the children to their fathers, lest I come and smite the earth with a curse.*
>
> (Malachi 4:5-6)

The Old Testament ends perfectly, setting up a New Testament revival and riot.

Examine yourself. Ask the questions that you fear most about the secret things and hidden agendas. Do you really have what it takes to start a riot or revival? When was the last time you called a solemn assembly of fasting and intercession? Are you pleased with "Well enough?" Remember when Rodney King said, "Can't we just all get along?" Is that your attitude? I'm reminded of a story I heard:

One Sunday in a certain town the devil himself visited a popular church. After the pastor called testimony service, the devil revealed himself. The church members, pastor included, ran out of the building screaming for fear. One lady wearing a big red hat and shoes to match stayed calmly in her seat. The

107

devil looked at her and said, "Why aren't you afraid and running like the others?" She replied, "Mr. Devil, a testimony is about something you experienced or did. Well, since I've been in this church, I've not done a thing, and I lied about my past experiences. So, I'm no threat to you, so please don't threaten me, okay?"

People oftentimes live in the basement and testify in the attic.

And they overcame him by the blood of the Lamb and by the word of their testimony; and they loved not their lives unto the death.

(Revelation 12:11)

What's in your mouth shall determine your outcome. Allow the Holy Spirit to transform your life out of darkness and trust Him every step of the way. God will give you the testimony of an overcomer. We are the real power brokers upon the earth. We have access to the Creator, angels and His will for this world. Pride will make us miss out on the promises of God. Allow your old garment of pride to be transformed to a garment of praise. Pride can only destroy, burn, and separate mankind as in racial disturbances. But praise can heal the hurting, help the less fortunate and stop prejudice. Praise can tear down the color barriers and unite the upper classes with the lower classes. Praise will start a revival that will testify of the goodness of God. I will bless the Lord at all times and His praise shall continue to be in my mouth!

I remember as a child growing up in a large family with two brothers and five sisters. I was the quiet, shy type. I was afraid to speak because my teacher told me that I had a speech impediment. Sometimes my brothers and sisters would tease me and call me tongued-tied. But as a child I had so much to say and no one who would listen. I often played alone and ate dinner and snacks in my room.

I never had many friends, but I used TV and books as an escape route. In my world I could imagine myself being open and being heard and not shying away from things that weren't under my control.

108

I remember one day the family was in the den area of the house, and I was on the floor playing with my toys. I opened my mouth and spoke, as of today I don't remember what was said, but the whole family jumped and hushed. All eyes were upon me. "Finally", someone said, "Terry spoke."

Whatever I said that day was the conversation of the hour. Maybe it wasn't what I said, but simply that I said something. How many "Terry's" are out there who have a powerful, sharp anointing to change the views of a family, city or nation by speaking out? Unfortunately he's prisoner of his or her own self-pride. Your pride is the root of your shyness. It makes you a victim of insensitivity, immaturity and ridicule. If my shyness had kept my mouth shut, the hundreds of souls I lead to salvation as a teenager in high school might not have happened, as well as the many calls of young folks wanting to commit suicide, because they thought life was at an end. By now they would have been in hell for over twenty years if I had kept my mouth shut as a youth minister.

In those days I counseled many couples not so much on my experiences, but by the Word of God and they work out their differences. The Word will show you yourself. I remember talking to other youth who were saved in times when they didn't believe that they could get a prayer through. We prayed all night long until the sun rose the following day. They received their breakthrough. Today some of them are great preachers, teachers and evangelists with effective ministries. If I had shut my mouth at the age of 17, I would have never started a radio broadcast called the Eleventh Hour of Blessing. Fresh out of high school, this radio program blessed thousands of lives in the South Florida area for years. At one point in many Christian homes they didn't watch TV until the broadcast was over. The Cosby Show had to wait. MASH was on hold. But the young preacher from Stucky Still, FL had folk's undivided attention. We were on from 8:00 until 9:00 p.m. Monday through Friday.

I didn't keep my mouth shut when a young black man, my friend, was arrested and cuffed by a policeman just for standing by his own car talking with others. The situation quickly intensified;

the officer got his gun out and radioed for back up. But the Lord spoke and said, "Talk first to the crowd and get them calm. Then talk to the officer." Just like the Lord said, it worked just fine. My friend, the young man, is a sergeant with the police department now. I thank God for placing the Word in my heart and compassion for souls.

I'm anointed to preach the Gospel, and I can't shut up. God will start a revival or a riot and sometimes both in the same service. But it's all good. I came a long way from a silent partner to a corporate spokesman. The journey between is an interesting one. Hopefully, this testimony will bless you to come out of your shyness and build your confidence in the God who desires to use your mouth. I will bless the Lord at all times and His praise shall continue to be in my mouth. God has started a revival and I've got to tell somebody.

CHAPTER SIX

Wake-up Call 911

There is some DYNAMITE lying in the churches waiting to be ignited by saints who dare to make a difference. The worldly warriors are already exploding and trying to illuminate the plans of Satan. Soon they will bring forth the Antichrist, 666. They're waging a demonically-led battle for the attention and souls of mankind. Dormant dynamite is sitting in pews, singing in the choir lofts, preaching behind the pulpit, catching every conference, and standing in every prayer line. Remember, *"The kingdom of heaven suffereth violence, and the violent take it by force"* (Matthew 11:12). If the Church doesn't take control, the world will.

> *Woe to them that are at ease in Zion and trust in the mountain of Samaria.*
>
> (Amos 6:1)

A friend of mine by the name of Gene W. called the other day, and we had a long conversation about churches on fire for the Lord. Gene and his wife Debbie are evangelists. They travel thousands of miles over this country preaching, singing, and teaching the Word of God. They are heavily anointed and you can tell that they love the people of God. In the past when Gene preached in my Fort Lauderdale Church, it blessed the congregation tremendously. His ministry seems to be one that will cause fire to fall and revival to break out. Brother Gene loves to tell me about his experiences as they traveled.

Many churches are seeking the fire presence of God and many are pleased with routine. They don't want to disturb what the founding fathers did years ago. And when a fresh new move of God comes, they totally reject it as extreme and unnecessary. I don't want to ever pastor a church that rejects the presence of God Almighty. It seems so much like the way the Pharisees acted in John's day. They were supposed to be serving God, but did only in their outward motions. When it came to obedience, submission and repentance they omitted their servitude. These churches are dormant of God's presence, but operating in His Name, surely void of His anointing.

I sure understand that everything different or new is not necessarily of God. But when something is confirmed by the Word and is a witness to your spirit, be careful not to miss your next visitation. Timing is very important in these last days. You must be on time, in tune and anointed with His spirit and power. Don't trust in the mountain of religious security and human conformity. I repeat myself again.

Woe unto them that are at ease in Zion and trusting in the mountain of Samaria.

(Amos 6:1)

Matthew Henry said, "The first words of this chapter are the contents of these verses; but they sound very strange, and contrary to the sentiments of vain words: Woe to those that are at ease!" We are ready to say, happy are those that are at ease, that neither feel any trouble, nor fear any, that lie soft and warm, and lay nothing to heart; and wise were those that do so, that battle themselves in the delights of sense and care not how the world goes. Those are looked upon as doing well for themselves that do well for their bodies and make much of them but against them this woe is denounced, and we are here told what their ease is, and what the woe is."

"I" here is a description of their pride, security and sensuality, for which God would reckon with them. (1) They were vainly conceited of their own dignities, and thought those would secure them from the judgments threatened, and be their defense against the wrath both of God and man. Those that dwelt in Zion thought that was honor and protection enough for them, and they might there be quiet from all fear evil because it was a strong city, well-fortified, but by nature and art. (2) Those that dwell in the mount of Samaria, though it was not a holy hill like that of Zion, yet they trusted in it, because it was the metropolis of a potent kingdom, and perhaps an imitation of Jerusalem; it was the headquarters of its religion; and by lapse of time the hill of Shemer became with them in as good repute as the hill of Zion ever was. They hoped for salvation from these hills and mountains. The mountains of Samaria became their comfort zone. It's easy to fall into the comfort zone when everything is going well. It's time to ignite the warfare! Get up off the seat of do nothing.

There are forces ready to destroy our lives, family, churches and nation. A few years ago, the enemies of our nation spoke loud on September 11, 2001. Wake up America: Your borders appear strong, but this attack came from within. We have defeated many outside our borders. But this attack came within our walls of security. This was a satanic attack in the name of religion. They used United and American (Airlines) to bring us to a standstill. United American is one nation under God, a good place to live and worship, but when United America trusted in Wall Street, trade towers and such, and left the principles of God's Word, we opened our borders and schools to every ungodly new age philosophy.

We're in trouble. Not only have we had the Bin Ladens, Saddams and such, but what about the sick folks who are citizens, U.S. born and raised on mom's apple pie and baseball? Some Americans have twisted views of God, country and religion. The foundation of liberty is supposed to include love, respect and character.

It has been an open house for the sick since we mourned the Oklahoma City bombing. Thank God, Timothy McVeigh has been tried and convicted and the sentence carried out for this violent act. We have also had several bombings and anthrax cases nationwide as well as in South Florida. The FBI caught the elusive and notorious Unabomber, as reported May 5, 1998 in the nation's press. Unfortunately, world society seems to be overburdened with thoughts of bombings.

Remember the snipers in the Northeast, shooting from the trunk of a car, tragedies like the one at Columbine High School in Colorado and now our youth make headlines weekly. We see them on the front pages of newspapers and on the television news programs: *60 Minutes, 20/20, Nightline, World News Tonight, Fox News, Good Morning America,* and *CNN.* You name it. We hear constant talk about how an explosion is affecting people's lives. 911 is the emergency number and, it's also the date September 11 numerically. America's wake-up call was received loud and clear, but will we doze off to sleep again?

The Refuge of the Authorized Believer

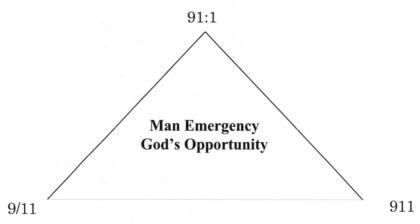

91:1

**Man Emergency
God's Opportunity**

9/11   911

Let the real 911 stand up, with no disrespect intended to the precious lives of September 11, and the professionals who served in response to our emergency calls. God knows we need these ministers of helps. As long as the Church is asleep they'll have a job. But when we wake up and call on the Lord with all of our hearts, soul and minds, that will restart a new era in the most powerful force on this planet. It's time to dwell with God, abide in His presence, remain steadfast, unmovable and always abounding. He is El-Shaddai. His is the fullness and riches of God's grace. God is the all-powerful One past impregnable. Every emergency in the making is God's opportunity to show His love and sovereignty. Every act of God's sovereignty and love is to emerge us into the presence of the El-Shaddai. When man rejects God's service and response, he will have mentally unstable religious and secular idiots to contend with–Satanic, worldly, A.C.T.S. Walkers, not Godly, but Godless. A=assiduous, C=crazy, T=Terrorists of S=Satan

> 911 = emergency number-call for assistance (Protection from harm,medical alerts, fire Protection) Quick Response Necessary.

> 9/11 = September 11th 2001; The day Americans woke up. National Response Necessary.

> 91:1 = *He that dwelleth in the secret places of the most High shall abide under the shadow of the Almighty.* Church Response Waiting.

Unfortunately, the masterminds behind these sick, unmerited acts of evil are crazy, uncontrolled maniacs. In many cases, they are merely looking for attention or have a desire to dish out vengeance; while the result is that they severely affect the lives of the innocent and unsuspecting. Often, these criminals blame the local, state and federal government for society's problems. I pray to God that this madness ceases before more law-abiding citizens are hurt. I admire the President and congress for the days following the "911" attack and how they pulled together in national prayer. But I believe its the Church, not the state that should ignite the warfare. Render to Caesar the things of Caesar and to God the things of God. Prayer and retaliation was that which followed. The problem just hid until a more opportune time arose.

The real problem behind all of this mayhem is a sleeping Church that is afraid of its God-given power. What if the Church got radical and started to tap into their explosives and anointed power from God? What if the saints in Oklahoma, New York, Washington D.C., South Florida and the rest of this country decided that enough is enough? We are tired of the lunatics stealing the press and occupying not only the news, but also the minds of many in the barbershops, washrooms, restaurants, and subways across our nation. We need to call for nationwide assemblies to fast, pray and spend quality time in fellowship with God and man.

Judgment is upon the land, especially in the United States of America. This country must go back to the old landmark of biblical training, fasting, praying, and praising God for His glory. Judgment will bring revival in this country, state, city and community. Let us look at Jehoshaphat's dilemma as an example. All at once, several nations staged war against Israel. Surrounded by the enemy on every side, no other nation came to their rescue. Did Jehoshaphat take prayer out of Judah or its schools? No. Did he abort one million babies that year? No. Did he legalize pornography, gambling, and alcohol? No. Did he call Muhammad, Buddha, or the Great Inner-Self? No. Did he sanction gay marriages? No.

Jehoshaphat, means "Jehovah has judged." Judah means "Let Him (God) be praised."

2 Chronicles - Jehoshaphat's Solemn Assembly

"And Jehoshaphat feared, and set himself to seek the Lord, and proclaimed a fast throughout all Judah" (2 Chronicles 20:3). Remember Sept. 12 when our country's leaders, including the President, Congress, Senate, Governors, Mayors and parents sought God, a Dynamic Explosion almost took place in this nation. But politics and pride rose up again. *"And Judah gathered themselves together, to ask help of the Lord: even out of all the cities of Judah they came to seek the Lord"* (2 Chronicles 20:4). National repentance always moved the heart of God, as in the case of the great city of Nineveh. To Israel it was bound up in wickedness that stunk in the nostrils of God. But after Jonah exploded in Nineveh, the city repented (Jonah 3:10). Jehoshaphat imploded in Israel and God delivered.

Then upon Jahaziel the son of Zechariah, the son of Benaiah, the son of Jeiel, the son of Mattaniah, a Levite of the sons of Asaph, came the Spirit of the Lord in the midst of the congregation... 'Thus saith the LORD unto

116

*you, Be not afraid nor dismayed by reason of this great
multitude; for the battle is not yours, but God's.'*
(2 Chronicles 20:14-15)

After Jehoshaphat prayed, God spoke through the prophet.
We ought to pray until God speaks, and we receive our answer.
The media speaks, but can't be trusted since they're biased and
carnal-minded. The politicians speak and aren't bipartisan and I
wonder who really believes them anyway. The legal system
speaks and I know justice isn't blind, not even color blind. Who's
left but the Church of Jesus Christ? I'm talking about the spirit-
filled, anointed, tongue talking, blood washed authorized
believers. You may not be a preacher, teacher or religious leader,
you might stutter like Moses, dress like John the Baptist and be
shipwrecked like Paul. But the Word of Faith is in your mouth.
Lets trust in the Lord all the way, not the system of this world.

And they rose early in the morning, and went forth into the
wilderness of Tekoa: and as they went forth, Jehoshaphat stood
and said, *Hear me, O Judah, and ye inhabitants of Jerusalem;
Believe in the Lord your God, so shall ye be established; believe
his prophets, so shall ye prosper* (2 Chronicles 20:20). In what do
we have our faith? The economy, Wall Street, corporate
America, the government, and the school system; all of these
institutions will be crushed and dissolved in the tribulation
period. Many of them are already falling. Believe in the Lord
your God, trust His prophets, be established and prosper.

*And when they began to sing and to praise, the Lord set
ambushments against the children of Ammon, Moab, and
mount Seir, which were come against Judah; and they
were smitten.*
(2 Chronicles 20:22)

Songs of Zion will bring you victory because they are directed
to God, sung about God, and intended for the children of God.
God inhabits the praises of His people. When the praise goes up,
the blessing comes down. Some people may believe that was for
the Bible days, and we can't operate the country like
Jehoshaphat did. They may say, "If our leader was to lead us

117

back to God, what religious denomination would spearhead this great revival?" Go to the only authority presented to man and recognized by God. That is the Bible, the Word of God. Joel said in the last days that God would pour out His spirit upon you. So we have the Word of God, Spirit of God, and men of God. History teaches many valuable lessons on nations that wouldn't change their evil ways. From revolutions to cold wars, a people without God that doesn't honor Jesus, that has no praise and leading of the Holy Spirit will fall from power.

And when Jehoshaphat and his people came to take away the spoil of them, they found among them in abundance both riches with the dead bodies, and precious jewels, which they stripped off for themselves, more than they could carry away: and they were three days in gathering of the spoil, it was so much.

(2 Chronicles 20:25)

Another popular Scripture states, *"The wealth of the sinner is laid up for the just"* (Proverbs 13:22). Look at the price that has to be paid in order to fulfill this Scripture: fasting, prayer, obedience to leadership, and fellowship with God. Judah may have had financial problems, but after the battle they had an abundance of precious jewels. It was God who made the enemy dress in diamonds, pearls, silver and gold, just to attack Judah (praise). However, Judah was dressed in prayer, fasting, and obedience. *"Seek ye first the kingdom of God, and his righteousness; and all these things shall be added unto you"* (Matthew 6:33). Satan wants to attack your praise—remember that God inhabits praise. The devil's plot is to fight God through the believer with any means necessary. Sometimes in battle you can't see God, because He is hidden in your praise so open your mouth and praise Him.

Look in Acts 2, the upper room experience, or read about the Azusa Street awakening. Where are the apostles and the 120 prayer warriors? Where are the William J. Seymours? Are they all dead or in their comfort zones? We need to be trained in warfare against the works of Satan. We need an attitude adjustment like John had in the wilderness. It's time for the Church to be the aggressor, to go on the offensive, and take the fight to hell's door. The believer must get a fresh anointing on his life. There's a price to pay to be anointed by God. Study the main ingredients and submit.

Dynamite will shake your city and warfare will cause changes to be made immediately. Let us shake our neighborhoods and make a difference where we live. But to do this, we must be trained to handle dynamite.

Spiritual Dynamite has four main ingredients. When mixed, they are potent.

1. <u>Fasting</u>: Heb: (tsuwm) – to cover over (the mouth) i.e. to fast; to abstain from food; to eat sparingly or to abstain from some foods. In secret – St. Matthew 6:16-18; To hear God – Zechariah 7:5-7; Chasten the soul – Psalm 69:10; The prototype fast – Isaiah 58:1-14; The 40 day fast – (Moses) Deut. 9:9, 18, 25-29; 10:10; (Joshua) Ex 24:13-18; 32:15-17; (Elijah) I King 19:7-18. (Jesus) St. Matthew 4:1-11; The 21 day fast - (Daniel) Dan 10:3-13; The 14 day fast – (Paul) Acts 27:33-34.

2. <u>Prayer</u>: Heb: (tephillah) – intercession, supplication; Greek: (proseuche) – prayer (worship); by impl. An oratory (chapel) pray earnestly, prayer; a request to God, to entreat; implore, to communicate.

Four Kinds of Prayer
a. Private (St. Matthew 6:6)
b. Open (I Corinthians 14:14-17)
c. Corporate (St. Matthew 18:20)
d. Family (Acts 10:2,30)

Seven Characters to Pray With
a. Forgiving spirit (St. Matthew 6:14)
b. Simplicity (St. Matthew 6:5-6)
c. Humility (St. Luke 18:10-14)
d. Unity of believer (St. Matthew 18:19-20)

e. Tenacity (St. Luke 18:1-8)
f. Importunity (St. Luke 11:5-8)
g. Intensity (St. Matthew 6:9-13)

The Prototype Prayer – St. Matthew 6:9-13
The Lord's Prayer – St. John 17

One of the first prayers was a blood cry prayer out of the earth. (Genesis 4:9-10).

One of the last prayers was recorded in Revelation 6:15-16. Men prayed to the rocks of the mountains, "fall on us."

3. Study the Word – Study: Greek – (spoudaios) – earnestly, promptly, diligently, instantly. Intensive intellectual effort.

Word – Hebrew – (dabar) – a word; (by impl.) A matter (as spoken of) or thing.

Greek – (logos) – something said (including the thought).

a) Scriptures – Acts 17:10-11; II Tim 3:16-17
b) Word of God – Book of the Law – Neh 8:3
c) Law of the Lord – Psalm 1:2
d) Scriptures – John 5:39
e) Holy Scriptures – Roman 1:2
f) Word of God – Heb 4:12
g) Word of Life – Phil 2:16
h) Book – Rev 22:19

Thy word have I hid in my heart, that I might not sin against thee.

(Psalm 119:11)

4. **Obedience to the Spirit** – Obedience – Greek – (hupakoe) – attentive hearkening i.e (by impl.) compliance or submission, submissive to the restraint or command of authority.

Spirit – Hebrew – (ruwach,wind) – by resemblance breath, life.

Greek – (pneuma) – a current of air, i.e. breath, a spirit. The spirit of God, the Holy Ghost, Holy Spirit.

Examples of Obedience

1. I Samuel 16:13-14, David's obedience and Saul disobedience.
2. Ezekiel 37:1-9, under submission to the spirit.
3. St. Matthew 4:1-16, The Spirit and Temptation.
4. Acts 2:1-4, being filled with the spirit.

These four ingredients will cause a spiritual wake-up and stir the anointing in the life of every believer! He can then use His authority everywhere. In the city, state and nation there will be explosions. The lives of the people will be altered drastically. These powerful explosions will not only affect the spiritual atmosphere, but the mental and physical as well. Explosions destroy the old and cause the new-and-improved to be built. Explosions cause panic, precautions and better security. Explosions are loud and get everyone's attention. In the physical, people who survive explosions are focused on life—even though death is present. God has no trouble placing them in spiritual relationships (Notice after a major tragedy how people unify and forget their petty differences.).

Jesus gave us dynamite to change millions upon millions of lives. Sadly, this Dynamic Power is seldom used. He is saying to the Body of Christ, "Explode in the towns, cities and nations. Get their attention; get them to talk about Me, and get them to focus on the Word. Let them know I can change their future. You have the Power."

USE IT OR LOSE IT

The heavenlies and all creation is waiting for the manifestation of the sons of God to set order back in the Earth. For we know that the whole creation groaneth and travaileth in pain together until now. And not only they, but ourselves also, which have the first fruits of the Spirit, even we ourselves groan within ourselves, waiting for the adoption, to wit, the redemption of our body.

(Romans 8:22-23)

The devil conned us into a spiritual set-up. But God said to Satan, "My adopted children can whip you!"

But ye shall receive power, after that the Holy Ghost is come upon you: and ye shall be witnesses unto me both in Jerusalem, and in all Judaea, and in Samaria, and unto the uttermost part of the earth.

(Acts 1:8)

The Church has access to the power and the source, just as nitroglycerin when ignited gives dynamite its explosive ability. The Word, **power** in Greek is *dunamis*, which means strength, mighty work. Dynamite is made of a porous material soaked in nitroglycerin. The saints who spend time with God can be washed and soaked in His presence. Yes, I know the Spirit is in you, but get in the Spirit also—be soaked inside and outside. Be porous, full of pores. You have a lot to get out. All creation is waiting. It's in a permeable condition.

For I am not ashamed of the gospel of Christ. For it is the power of God unto salvation to every one that believeth.

(Romans 1:16)

Nitroglycerin is <u>heavy oil</u> used chiefly in making dynamite. Like nitro, the believer must move out into the arena of power before he can be ignited with power to change his surroundings. A witness is one who bears testimony to something, attesting to a fact or event; one that gives evidence. Look at what happens when the witness becomes an anointed explosive. Better yet, look at Luke, chapter four. We can find this evidence in several Scriptures that talk about the explosive power of the Spirit on Jesus.

Full of the Holy Ghost

And Jesus being full of the Holy Ghost returned from

Jordan, and was led by the Spirit into the wilderness.

(Luke 4:1)

Power of the Spirit

And Jesus returned in the power of the Spirit into Galilee: and there went out a fame of him through all the region round about. And he taught in their synagogues, being glorified of all. And he came to Nazareth, where he had been brought up: and, as his custom was, he went into the synagogue on the Sabbath day, and stood up for to read.

(Luke 4:14-16)

Anointed to Preach
The Spirit of the Lord is upon me, because he hath anointed me to preach the gospel to the poor; he hath sent me to heal the brokenhearted, to preach deliverance to the captives, and recovering of sight to the blind, to set at liberty them that are bruised.

(Luke 4:18)

Prophetic Fulfillment
And he began to say unto them, This day is this Scripture fulfilled in your ears. And all bare him witness, and wondered at the gracious words, which proceeded out of his mouth. And they said, 'Is not this Joseph's son?'

(Luke 4:21-22)

Words of Power
And they were astonished at his doctrine: for his word was with power.

(Luke 4:32)

Luke 4:1 says, *"And Jesus being full of the Holy Ghost"* or anointed with the Holy Ghost. Many times in Scripture, when people are anointed, oil is used in the process. Heavy oil can express heavy anointing, such as when Jesus was returning in the power of the Spirit. Power and anointing cause a reaction everywhere you go from temptation in the wilderness to triumphal entrances. Church members and people you thought you knew

123

will begin to question your family tree (genealogy). You will make people angry, and cause unclean devils to cry out. What God has placed in the believer must come out. Don't try to keep this kind of dynamite (power) concealed. You must start in your own home and community.

"And he shall turn the heart of the fathers to the children, and the heart of the children to their fathers" (Malachi 4:6). The Jesus that sat and read Scriptures so many times before in the synagogue, was different from the Jesus who returned full of the Holy Ghost. Afterward, He was inspired and powerful, talking like a doer and making things happen. His followers listened to Him read the Scriptures and preach the Gospel to the poor. Worldly observers may have said, "Is that really what the poor need? Why not just toss them a few scraps here and there? Why waste time trying to revolutionize their whole way of thinking?"

But Jesus knew that God had sent him to heal the brokenhearted. These were hurting people, many with deep spiritual and emotional needs. The Pharisees could not help them, because they were carnal-minded and not sensitive to the spirit of man. These religious leaders weren't able to preach deliverance to the captive, who was not necessarily coming out of jail, slavery or physical prison. But they needed to be set free in the midst of their own life situation. Jesus came restoring sight to the blind and to those who were victims of their poverty and diseases requiring power. Looking in the natural at the Scribes of their day, listening to the hypocritical Pharisees, and learning from the Sadducees, the Israelites must have thanked God for Jesus being anointed with the Holy Ghost.

Our Mission
"Then Peter opened his mouth, and said, 'Of a truth I perceive that God is no respecter of persons' " (Acts 10:34). Listen, God will use whosoever makes himself available. John submitted, Jesus submitted, what about you and I?

But in every nation he that feareth him, and worketh righteousness is accepted with him. The word which God sent unto the children of Israel, preaching peace by Jesus Christ. (He is Lord of all:) That word, I say, ye know, which was published throughout all Judaea, and began from Galilee, after the baptism which John preached; How God anointed Jesus of Nazareth with the Holy Ghost and with power: who went about doing good, and healing all that were oppressed of the devil; for God was with him.

(Acts 10:35-38)

Is it not time for every nation, city, town, and home to be impacted as was the early Church? God is truly no respecter of persons. He can rain on the just as well as the unjust. The anointing makes the difference in the lives we touch. We must demonstrate the love of God in simplicity, and it will manifest itself in power and deliverance.

Paul says:

And I, brethen, when I came to you, came not with excellency of speech or of wisdom, declaring unto you the testimony of God. And my speech and my preaching was not with enticing words of man's wisdom, but in demonstration of the Spirit and in power: That your faith should not stand in the wisdom of men, but in the power of God.

(1 Corinthians 2:1,4-5)

Faith cometh by hearing the Word of God and is increased by demonstrating and living the Word of God.

The world does not need to hear a scribe or scholar, but a compassionate, anointed, mature child of God with a testimony. We should not spend all of our time dwelling on a rehearsal of yesterday's sermons (old manna), but on a fresh, simple, well-studied, prayerful, exhorted rhema Word of God. I may enjoy the prose of Shakespeare, the quotes of Nietzsche, the history of Rome, and the study of Black American culture, but that is not the Gospel of Jesus Christ. Nor must our speech nor sermons be built upon the King James language, interesting quotes, fallen empires or civil rights, but on the death, burial, and resurrection of Jesus Christ. He is Lord of all. John said *"All things were made by him; and without him was not any thing made that was made"* (John 1:3). *"But as many as received him, to them gave he power to become the sons of God, even to them that believe on His name"* (John 1:12).

In the power of the Spirit, we must in all things show the world Jesus Christ. When they see and recognize the love of God many will submit and obey. Jesus told His disciples, *"If I be lifted up, I will draw all men unto me."* (John 12:32) What a powerful promise to the believer and what a responsibility we have to focus all the attention toward Jesus Christ. We need to make it plain as day that everything centers on Jesus and His redemptive work. This is the testimony of God. *"For God so loved the world, that He gave His only begotten son, that whosoever believeth in Him should not perish"* (John 3:16). We must first witness this for ourselves then we can take it to the world.

Charity starts at home, then it spreads abroad. The Scripture teaches in Ephesians that Christ may dwell in your heart by faith;

> *That ye being rooted and grounded in love, may be able to comprehend with all saints what is the breadth, and length, and depth, and height; and to know the love of Christ, which passeth knowledge that ye might be filled with all the fullness of God. Now unto him that is able to do exceeding abundantly above all that we ask or think, according to the power that worketh in us. Unto him be glory in the church by Christ Jesus throughout all ages, world without end.*
>
> (Ephesians 3:17-21)

From Dormant to Dynamite. *The Merriam Webster's Dictionary* definition of dormant is: "inactive; ESP: not actively growing or functioning." The reason we aren't growing is because there's no activity in our spirits. Examine the word "dormitory," a room for sleeping. Get the message? Many of us go to Sunday morning and Tuesday night "dormitories" and get dormantised, to coin a new word. When this happens over and over, year after year, it becomes the Dormant Dynamite Syndrome.

Saints who dare to be different will crush the syndrome and ignite the warfare. It will be costly, but that's the price of power. Ask Jehoshaphat if it was worth the prayer time to enjoy the spoil. Ask the 120 prayer-warriors about the inauguration of the Holy Ghost on the day of Pentecost. I'm sure William Seymour has rejoiced because of the 120 prayer warriors that laid a foundation for his experiences. Don't look at a situation and think it only involves you. Sometimes God uses us to be the igniter of a greater plan. We are blind to the plans of God. We must act in the Spirit because this is spiritual warfare. The believer will learn how to use his weapons and stand on the principles of faith. It's going to be very explosive.

Get ready to learn that our weapons are spiritual. Learn how to use them, not abuse them and you will *Ignite the Warfare* today.

CHAPTER SEVEN

The M.O.A.B. Warrior

I felt a shaking in the ground and rumbling in the air. I looked out of the window and there wasn't a cloud in the sky. It wasn't near the fourth of July, and we hadn't celebrated Memorial Day yet. Why was the ground shaking? I turned on the T.V. and channel surfed awhile. It was CNN or one of the local news stations that had a special alert. About two hundred miles away near the Key West, the military was testing the M.O.A.B—a bomb that can penetrate deep and wide in the earth. I heard someone say, "It's the surrender bomb because after it drops on you, the only thing left for survivors to do is lift up their hands and give up." I felt its impact over a hundred miles away, and it got my attention. The military called it the mother of all bombs. They say, "In battle call for Mother." Now I love my mother but it's my Daddy that does my fighting.

In this chapter we will use the acronym M.O.A.B. but it now means Maturity of Authorized Believers. All of creation is waiting for the maturity of trained, manifested believers to grow up. It's time to learn how to use the weapons of your warfare. Everything we do must be in the Word and have a faith base. This will produce the work that Jesus did. The authorization comes from the spoken and written Word of God. The Word is quick and powerful like a missile bomb. Faith will guide you to the right place at the right time.

The weapons of our warfare must be based upon scriptural truth. We can collect from almost every book of the Bible to edify and build the last day Christian into a soldier. Jesus says that the Holy Spirit will lead the believer into all truth and teach us all things. The believer needs to know that there is a battle mounting like we have never seen before. Several years ago Americans witnessed the assault of Kuwait on their television, we stood amazed. We saw an unbelievable assault that lit the skyways. We wondered how anyone could survive such an attack with round after round of ammunition blazing through the air, tracers going up and down, sounds of bombs dropping, sirens screaming throughout the streets, and cries of woes piercing the night as forces of good and evil battled through the night both heavily armed with weapons of war.

Anytime there is a battle there will be casualties on both sides. There is still a feeling of pain and sorrow even though we accomplished our goals. In physical warfare the object of the battle is to minimize casualties. We must be trained to use the weapons of our warfare and understand their true and full purposes. In the military you are taught to know your weapon and that it is your best friend.

In this chapter you will find our weapons aren't physical but spiritual; they don't work outwardly but inwardly, to bring an outward result. One fully-armed knowledgeable saint can chase a thousand, but two can put ten thousand to flight. Imagine what a staff of ministers, a choir, an organization or the whole body of Christ could do! When you master the weapons of our warfare, which are mighty through God, you will know it's all about manifesting the will of God. Our weapons aren't given to war one against another, but to the pulling down of strongholds. In the Persian Gulf War, Saddam's strongholds had to be broken in order for Kuwait to be free. In the liberation of the Iraq people, America used bigger and more powerful weapons. The father George Bush Sr. was sparing, (but) George Bush Jr. had no mercy on Saddam. The dictator could have avoided losing his office if he had obeyed the U.N., but it took more than a U.N. mandate. Action had to speak louder than words.

Saddam was under satanic control; the prince of this world was his ruler. How else could he gas his own people and murder his enemies without guilt. If Bush had known exactly where

Saddam was during the war, one bomb was all that would have been needed. If America has used the latest weapons to strike the enemy, the war would probably have been shortened with less casualties. But the saints' weapons are far more advanced and more accurate than missiles and bombs, we have the Holy Ghost and the Word.

In the Word of God we have been equipped with supernatural weapons that can change the world, the nation, the cities and the people therein. Let us use our weapons skillfully, prayerfully and immediately. The longer it takes for the believer to learn how to use his weapon will determine the longer it is going to take for the manifestation of the sons of God to mature (Roman 8:19).

In Uncle Sam's Army it takes only 8 to 10 weeks for boot camp, and you learn how to follow orders. But in God's army it seems to take a lifetime for saints to become sons and manifest their true purpose in the earth (vs. 22). For we know that the whole creation groaneth and travaileth in pain together until now (vs. 23) and not only they but ourselves also, which have the firstfruits of the spirit. Even we ourselves groan within ourselves, waiting for the adoption, to wit, the redemption of our body.

There are some who don't rely on their training and decide after boot camp to do it their own way. Here are three of them. Look around your church or home then in the mirror and recognize the people. They are the know-it-all Christian, the Comfort Zone Christian and the Compromising Christian.

Proper training, not over-training will ignite the warfare

The Know-it-all Christian "Saint Bo": Saint Bo is just like Rambo, a one-man wrecking crew who takes things out of context, overriding the checks and balances of the Church. He's a follower but his self-righteousness keeps him too far away to hear from God. St. John 16:2 says, *"They shall put you out of the synagogues: yea, the time cometh, that whosoever killeth you will think that he doeth God service."* Saint Bo is the heavily-armed, zealous Christian that can affect everybody and everything but his own personal and spiritual problems. With his laser vision and dogmatic discerning ability he can see and zero in on everybody's problem in a flash. You can rest assured that Saint Bo will race to your call when you beckon him during trying times. He's sometimes a prophet with a word, a word from the Lord and has seen many visions of you in his so-called prayer time. You can find him misquoting Scriptures and he can pull a revelation out of anything. He has the longest drawn-out testimony and knows just what is wrong in the church. To Saint Bo the Lord doesn't only speak to the Pastor or Bishop, but to Saint Bo as well. He often wonders why the Pastor lets so many things go on in the church. If it were up to him he would stop it immediately, separating holy from unholy the first time he discerns it, not caring who he hurts.

Saint Bo is heavily-armed and dangerous, that is, dangerous to the Body of Christ and leaning to the arm of the flesh. His favorite weapons are discernment, chastisement, rebuking, after all we are soldiers fighting, against the world of sin. Saint Bo fights until he can't fight anymore. He must win at any cost. War has casualties, but Saint Bo will settle for 5 wins and 5 losses. When the Lord comes, he will reward us. Saint Bo believes he's working hard to get stars on his crown. I know by now you may recognize Saint Bo. Every church has one, well-intentioned saint who is ready to save the church from the world. Saint Bo's are like the misguided missile. Troops are killed by friendly fire, nearsighted and unskilled sharpshooters. They are armed to kill. But who or what? Sometimes I wonder if it is better to walk with the enemy than with a Saint Bo Christian. At least with the enemy you know what to expect. The lessons you will learn in this book will teach you to recognize the enemy, and the dangerous Saint Bo's. I Timothy 1:18-20 says,

This charge I commit unto thee, son Timothy according to the prophecies which went before on thee, that thou by them mightest war a good warfare; holding faith and a good conscience; which some having put away concerning faith have made shipwreck: of whom is Hymenaeus and Alexander.

The Comfort Zone "Lazy Daisy" Christian (She's not dormant but a busy body).

Nahum 2:10 *"She is empty and void, and waste: and the heart melteth..."* Lazy Daizy (or LD) grew up in the church, sang in the choir, had a calling on her life but knew she has time. With all the gifts and talents God gave her, there was no way she was going to miss the rapture.

Living in the Comfort Zone can cause you to have a form of godliness, but no power. The Bible says not to fellowship with these people, because their fellowship will leave you captive, bound in sin and lusts. The shameful part is you don't even know how or when you failed. This is what we call, being lost in the house. Looking for the part and function in position, but corrupt by religion. The religion of a god can be substituted for a relationship with God when people decide to stop seeking Jesus' presence. LD will never leave the church, and her attendance may be better than most. She starts out living for God, but will finish living for herself. In her mind God needs her. Heaven evolves around LD. When she doesn't want to sing, the Bishop, choir director or God can't make her. They'll just have to wait until she feels like it. LD wants to be the head of every board so she can designate authority and supervise. After all, she has been here the longest. "Just let some young hotshot come in here trying to get us to stretch out on God through praise and worship. I'll shut them down. Why, if we start doing those things it will take the fun out of church and membership will grow and somebody might get my job."

God has persistently allowed Lazy Daizy time to get her life in order. However, LD only wants to work with the bake sale, softball games, and fundraisers because that's where the popularity is. You see, LD wants to work around the church but not in the church. She wants to be identified with the bride, but not with the groom. When the enemy comes against her, as long as he leaves her with her pride and dignity she can get by or worse yet, her motto is "Don't stir up a hornet's nest or you might get stung." If she doesn't get too spiritual then the devil will have no need to get mad at her and attack. LD says that Act 2:38 and Roman 10:9 is enough to make it in. Lazy Daizy has the motto that is so easily adopted by many uninformed and misinformed saints and that is, "If I just can make it in, I'm going to sit down by the banks of the river and tell Jesus all about my problems. Yes, yes, yes victory will be mine if I hold my peace and let the Lord fight my battles. Then one day in the by-and-by I'll make it over. I don't need any weapons if He is going to fight for me." Well, Miss Daizy there you go again letting someone drive for you, when God has given you weapons to fight with...work out your own salvation with fear and trembling.

The Compromising Christian–Colonial Compromise

Revelation 3:16-7 *"I will spew thee out of my mouth. Because thou sayest, I am rich, and increased with goods..."* Joel said; *"Multitudes, multitudes in the valley of decision..."* Colonial Compromise (or CC as you will get to know him) sees nothing as black or white–it may not even be gray. He's not certain. CC has problems making up his mind. He has fought many battles and won some great victories, but sometimes he just doesn't feel like rebuking or resisting the devil. Though it will never be admitted, there are some things the Bible calls sin. He doesn't see any harm in it. Yes, it might be weight, but it has not developed into sin yet. If temptation isn't sin, weight isn't sin, (at least not yet) and CC has been seeking long enough to know when to get rid of it, Colonial Compromise is doing his best.

He sometimes loves the Lord and other times he has an attitude with the Father. When he tells the young men and women in church to respect each other, he means just what he says. But take protection (condoms on dates) just in case, you never know where the temptation might show up. CC has high regard for satanic plots. Didn't he come to prayer meetings in the days of Job? Solomon was a wise man and he stumbled. David and Bathsheeba still have a second son honored by the Lord. Remember Paul in Romans 7, "If it can happen to them, what about you?" Colonial Compromise is concerned but he, like many, is trying to protect others from hard times or boot camp, which is valuable learning experiences and growing in grace and truth.

CC must learn that backing and stepping down does hinder

spiritual growth. But submission and obedience to the Holy Spirit enhance growth. How many CC's out there are coasting along, feeding on how things used to be, back when? They've lost their zeal to press toward the mark of the high calling. Like a war veteran well decorated with an honorable discharge they yak, yak, all day long. They continually look back and have no vision of the future only dreams of yesterday drifting away. Colonial Compromise wouldn't be in the grandstands of glory when this last day battle will be fought if he doesn't take a solid word position and commit his life to the Holy Spirit.

Believers must be trained and balanced in the Word of God. It's time to get off the fence, the line has been drawn in the sands of time. You are either friend or foe. You can't hide behind what happened last year, last week or yesterday.

Revelation 22:11-12 reminds us,

He that is unjust, let him be unjust still: and he which is filthy, let him be filthy still: and he that is righteous , let him be righteous still: and he that is holy, let him be holy still. And, behold, I come quickly and my reward is with me, to give every man according as his work shall be.

We need a daily walk with God, a day-to-day relationship, a fresh devotion every morning, hour-to-hour with spontaneous praises in our heart. C.C. is too embarrassed to give God glory in a public place. We don't know the hour nor day that the Lord will return, but we know He is coming soon. What condition, position or compromise will He find you in. *"For the day of the Lord is near in the valley of decision"* Joel 3:14.

The maturity that we must attain as believers will come from our activity in the Word of God. Faith is the activity of God's Word in our life. The more we walk and understand the Word, the greater our faith grows and the more mature we become. Spiritual maturity comes with biblical insight.

In this Study Guide Chart the word has 3 important points; Quick, Powerful, and Sharp. This is where we get out weapons, they're quick: alert, powerful: energetic, and Sharp-decisive.

This is how the M.O.A.B. operates in day-to-day combat.

Let's Dissect A Key Scripture Explaining the Purpose of the Word.

For the word of God is quick and powerful, and sharper than any two edged sword, piercing even to the dividing asunder of soul and spirit, and of joints and marrow, and is a discerner of the thoughts and intents of the heart.

(Hebrews 4:12)

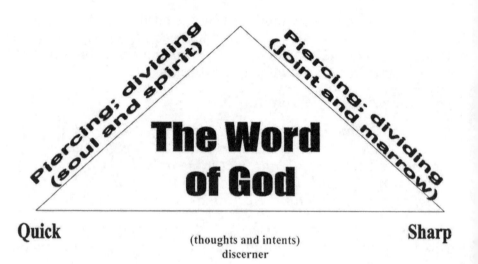

Quick   (thoughts and intents)   **Sharp**
discerner

POWERFUL

Quick – (zao); to live (lit or fig): life (-time), (a) live (-ly); living, rapid, speedy, prompt to Understand, think, or perceive, ALERT.

Powerful – (energes); active, operative: effectual (en) a fix position (in place, time or state), instrumentality (ergo) – to work; toil - as an effort or occupation, an act-deed, doing.

Sharper – (tomoteros); to cut; more comprehensive or decisive, as if by a single stroke, more keen.

Piercing – (dikneomai); to reach through i.e. penetrate; (dia)–

a channel of an act; through – after, always, among, at, to avoid. (hikanos) – to arrive, competent.

Dividing asunder – (merismos); a separation or distribution, gift; (merizo) – to part, i.e., (lit) to apportion, bestow, share, disunite.
Soul – (psuche); the thoughts, emotion, feeling, ect.; the immaterial essence of an individual life.
Spirit – (pneuma); ghost, life, a life-giving force. (pneo) - to breathe hard, i.e., breeze-blow.
Joints – (harmos); an articulation (of the body). (harma) - as a particle of union.
Marrow – (muelos); the marrow, a soft vascular tissue that fills the cavities of most bones.
Discerner – (kritikos); decisive (critical) i.e. discriminate, revealing insight and understanding.
Thoughts – (enthumesis); deliberation, device, thought. (enthumeomal) – to be inspirited i.e., ponder-think, the process of thinking, idea, notion, opinion, belief.
Intents – (ennoia); thoughtfulness i.e. moral understanding mind. The state of mind with which an act is done. (volition) – purpose, aim, meaning, significance.
Heart – (kardia); the thoughts or feeling (mind), one's innermost being, center, also the essential part.

Wake up mighty men of war, you have the most powerful weapon of them all, the written and spoken Word of God! His Word will not go out and return void. God will watch over His Word and will hasten to perform it. The real wake-up call is when the saints get up off the beds of apathy and ignite the warfare. The Word of God is the will of God. His will is His intentions, decisions and desires. What we have witnessed over the last 10 to 20 years in America is not the will of God. In the prototype prayer of St. Matthew 6, Jesus said, "Thy will be done in earth as it is in heaven."

In heaven, God's Word is established, and on earth God is operating through the life of believers. But the believer must operate in the will of God. It's like God is saying, "I can work through you, but you don't want to work in Me." The purpose of the Word is to give us liberty to flow with the plans and design that God has for us to mature and take charge. We are to walk worthy of the Lord. Everything we say and do should make God happy. In return, the joy of the Lord becomes our strength. And we the M.O.A.B. become fruitful in every good work and increase in the knowledge of God. The Word blesses and prospers us in many unseen ways. The Word pierces and divides things in us, around us and for us. It tears down strongholds of defeat that Satan establishes on our minds. Some of our thinking is stinking (it's no good), but the Word offends and destroys ungodly notions. The Word will never fail, not one joint or point. The Word is so effective that all of the Archomai stand in existence because of its use. Without the Word, nothing would be here. Nothing is nothing without the Word. Hebrews 11:3 says, "Through faith we understood that the worlds were framed by the word of God..."

The Word of God is the most powerful weapon God has given us. Out of it comes many other weapons that are and can be used effectively to wage a successful war against Satan.

Hebrews 4:12-13 says,

For the word of God is quick and powerful, and sharper than any two edged sword, piercing even to dividing asunder of soul and spirit, and of joints and marrow, and is a discerner of the thoughts and intents of the heart. Neither is there any creature that is not manifest in his sight: but all things are naked and open unto the eyes of him with whom we have to do.

None of Satan's assignments, wiles or tricks are hidden from the Word. Every demon and imp is fully exposed by the Word of God. There is no activity active outside of the control of the Word. Every instance, moment, and spark of life is subject to the Word.

Stay in the Word if you want to see clearly in the spiritual realm. All things are naked and open, seen and understood; there is no doubt in the Word, only faith. Doubt causes blindness and uncertainty. Faith brings light and confidence. Wake up and use what you have. Don't stagnate the Word of God in your life, home, church, and community.

Jesus said in Revelation 3:15-16, *I know thy works, that thou are neither cold not hot; I would thou were cold or hot. So then because thou art lukewarm, and neither cold nor hot, I will spew thee out of my mouth.* In II Timothy 3:5-7, Paul told Timothy that,

> *Having a form of godliness, but denying the power thereof: from such turn away. For of this sort are they which creep into houses, and lead captive silly women laden with sins, led away with divers lusts, ever learning, and never able to come to knowledge of the truth.*

Their learning isn't mixed with faith in God or the God of their faith that's seen in the spirit world. After walking with Jesus for awhile, your faith will began to grow and your understanding will be expanded. The Word of faith will take you to a new spiritual dimension. The Word will teach faith, and faith will reveal the Word. The Word must be mixed with faith. The Word is the vehicle and faith is the engine that moves it. Get in the driver's seat where you belong.

FAITH IS NOT KNOWING, BUT TRUSTING FAITH IS NOT BLIND, BUT SPIRITUAL. DON'T FOLLOW FAITH WITHOUT THE WORD OF GOD.

We promise in our book *The Triangle of Faith* that we will attempt to make your faith see! Faith is the activity of God's Word. Because you can't see it in the natural, it doesn't mean it's not present or working. The Word is the road map and faith is the journey. Keep going but check the map for your daily location. Faith is the result of God's work. Perhaps unseen and misunderstood by the carnal, but open and exposed to the M.O.A.B saints.

Hebrew 1:1 says,

> *Now faith is the substance of things hoped for, the evidence of things not seen.*

The "unseen" evidence of faith is visible everywhere (not seen in the natural, but visible in the spiritual and exposed by an active word-based believer). It moves around us as atoms in molecules, waiting to be discovered by Word hungry, experienced happy action-seeking children of God. Einstein discovered that the splitting of atoms would cause a hydrogen explosion of enormous magnitude which would literally change the course of the civilized world and it did. This scientific experience was so powerful that the country who processed this knowledge would be considered a world power, and share dominance throughout the 20th and 21st Centuries. This atomic power has always been here and available to whosoever paid the price to develop and process the first discovery.

The atom may not be seen; however, we know it is there, and in everything is present. The size is insignificant to the force that is behind it. Jesus said, if your faith is the size of a grain of mustard seed, you can speak to the mountain and the mountain shall move in the sea. Atoms aren't split everyday, or there would not be any earth left to stand on. Nor can anybody or anything split one. It takes something prepared and designed by purpose to do the job. There are other ingredients involved in this process, materials you don't just pick up at the corner hardware store or find casually lying around the house. It seems peculiar how God has given every man a measure of faith and faith comes by hearing and we know hearing by God's Word. Hebrew 10:38 says, *"Now the just shall live by faith: but if any man draws back, my soul shall have no pleasure in him."*

When Einstein researched and developed the correct theory of splitting atoms, this process worked out mathematically on paper, but it had to be tested beyond the ability Einstein could produce as an individual. We know God dealt every man a measure of faith. He didn't do it just because of one individual. Mankind as a whole works in unity to bring about the explosive change that is needed in the world. But as we know, this world is full of corruption and deceit. There is mistrust, greed and corruption everywhere.

The original plan of every man having faith was realized 1900 years ago. Now through the faith of the Son of God, when your faith is in Him and His faith lives through you, we have the making of the greatest spiritual atomic threat the world has ever seen. That is why the devil wants to keep us blind and carnal-minded to the things of God. When our soul draws back or acts alone, we are in no position to control or dictate the course of an insect. But Jesus, according to St. John 1:1, is the logos of God. In Hebrews, it said says He is the expressed image of the Father, the God housed in the flesh. In Revelation He said that He was the Alpha and Omega meaning He is God the Creator of the heavens and Earth. Hebrew 11:3 *"Through faith we understand that the worlds were framed by the word of God, so that things which are seen were not made of things which do appear."* What we see is the end result, not the start. Faith starts the process, works continue the patterns or motion.

The not seen evidence of Faith is through Christ Jesus; the DNA of a believer is recognized by the world when he trusts in Jesus...He moves by the unseen. Everywhere He moves, He leaves traces of His relationship. The elements are touched by Him, influenced by Him, altered by Him, bound and loosed by Him. It is His make-up or His pattern, circumstances ever-changing around Him by His faith. He must remain steadfast, unmovable and always abounding in the knowledge of Christ Jesus.

What is going to happen when the believer comes into the knowledge and understanding of the not seen evidence of Faith? When he recognizes that all of creation waiteth for the manifestation of the sons of God and not only they, but ourselves also, which have the firstfruits of the spirit, even we ourselves groan within innerman, waiting for the adoption to wit, the redemption of our body.

We already have the spirit of adoption. We cry Abba Father. By faith, Father, through Christ we are Yours, made in the Your image and likeness, living to please You by faith as a real father would be proud of his newborn son to manifest Your Name. As the Father would train him, teach him, chastise him, and love him, he can't deny him sonship because of faith (DNA) that has been patterned through his birthright.

The world may not understand our faith, but the believer must live and walk it. We understand it's not what we see with the natural eye, hear with natural ears and touch with the emotion, passion or desire of the flesh. His Word, the spirit of the Holy Ghost and our adoption papers are the promise, assurance and predestined plan of God in our lives. When you walk in the spirit, you see what your Father is doing and whatever your Father is doing is dispensing faith. In reality, faith happens in the spirit world first (this it the unseen place) and can be seen by those who are in the spirit (the rule and reign of God) and is manifested to the physical nature.

Wake up the faith of the saints. This is the training process that manifests the will of God to a dying, blinded society. The Army teaches you to trust in your training. The Navy, Marines, and Air Force do the same. In the day of battle, they say, "Have faith in your training, and don't be terrorized or dominated by your enemy, but ignite the warfare. Take it to another level. Make the enemy sorry he attacked."

In the summer of 2001, about early June, my wife and I were planning a vacation to New York City for her birthday in July. We had been to the upper part of the state but never to Manhattan. The Lord blessed us in that the whole family was able to go. We arrived in New York City around the 2nd of July and spent several wonderful days having fun, eating some great food and visiting the different sites. On the 5th of July we went to a Century 21 clothing store and my wife and daughters shopped until I got tired. I told them my feet were tired, and I was hungry. I left the store and crossed the street to find a beef hot dog and diet Coke. After a long wait on the bench, and three hot dogs later, my wife and girls came with bags of shoes and dresses. At this point I was doing just fine, my feet rested, belly full and they were spending their own money.

My wife, the prophetess, looked up and said, "Wow; what are these two tall buildings?" I told her what they were called. Then she said, "Has anyone ever tried to blow then up?" The whole family looked at her then the buildings. I told her, "I believe back in '92 or '93 some radical Muslim guys tried, but they failed." And that was the end of that conversation on the destruction of the Twin Towers.

Later we went down into Grand Central Station, but after about 20 minutes we left because the people around us were too impatient. We're from the south and we don't walk that fast. It was wall-to-wall people and no one was smiling. About two days later we left N. Y. We agreed this was the best short vacation we had had that summer, except for the Nassau Bahamas.

My wife's birthday is the 6th of July, but she has a younger sister whose birthday is on the 11th of September. What if they were born on opposite dates? My life would be totally changed. I know most of the attention is focused on New York, the Twin Towers, but also I remember the Pentagon and the third incident in Pennsylvania where mighty men and women said, "We won't stand for this. Let's roll and kick some devil's butt. They answered the wake-up call. They said "NO devil, you will not control our destiny with your twisted actions. We'd rather die for what we believe, than sit here and allow you to take our lives (it's going to be on my terms)." What can we say to the fireman, policeman, FBI and diehard citizens around the world who placed their lives on hold during the rescue efforts, the financial support and the President, the Governor, the Mayor of New York and the sacrifice of others that we will never know about? And last but not least, the thousands who perished foolishly by maniacs of religion–lunatics that don't even know God. If America is so bad then why do you live here, enjoy our freedoms, and seek our prosperity? As long as there are ten righteous individuals in the nation, the hand of the Lord will still be upon us. The attack was unprovoked and mind-blowing, but the response was quick, powerful and decisive. We know and appreciate that not all Muslims are violent people, and we are praying that they see Jesus as the true Son of God, the only begotten of our Father.

CHAPTER EIGHT

A.C.T.S. 101
The A.C.T.S. Walker in Training

When I was in college and had to select classes for my major, the first important lesson I learned was in a 101 class. A 101 class will always preview with the basics. This class will teach you foundational information that will help prepare you for the advanced materials and lessons that are sure to come before you graduate. A good understanding of the basics helps to direct and maneuver you through difficult and complex problems. In this chapter, we shall attempt to give you the training and information on what God has given to us: The How To's of Warfare, for some 101 and other 102 classes.

Jesus spent 3½ years training the apostles on the "how to's." The Holy Ghost then worked through them in the demonstration. The ACTS Walk; A=Authorized, C=Christian, T=Terrorizing, S=Satan. The book of Acts stops at 28 written chapters and today's church is in the 29th chapter. The book isn't finished. We are living and writing the last chapters of ACTS and it guarantees the continuation of the most powerful move of God in the history of mankind. Are we the ACTS walkers or the Laodicean church? The choice is ours. If we don't wake-up and answer the call, severe judgment will fall on this generation. This is the age of quick possession, little responsibility and no accountability. We won't start in this chapter with questions about who is the Boss, who has the authority and the secrets that Satan doesn't want you to know. The ACTS Walker will study his enemy's schemes, wiles and plots, yet will stay humble and submitted to God's authority. Let's learn how to take the enemy to court and declare our rights. I want all my stuff back, everything he has cheated, lied and stolen from me plus interest. This is what you must know and do: **FIRST BE AUTHORIZED.**

A–Authorized - to be given legal power. Sanctioned; rights to be placed in command; convincing force, a citation used in support of a statement or in defense of an action; also the source of such a citation.

Strong's OT - Hebrew – Authority: rabah; a prim. Root; to increase (in whatever respect): - [bring in] abundance… grow up, heap, belong, many, etc.

When the righteous are in authority, the people rejoice: but when the wicked beareth rule, the people mourn.
(Proverbs 29:2)

Strong's NT - Greek – Authority: exousia; privilege, i.e. (subj.) force, capacity, competency. Freedom, or (obj.) mastery. Delegate influence –authority jurisdiction, liberty, power, right, and strength.

All the people were amazed and said to each other, "What is this teaching? With authority and power he gives orders to evil spirits and they come out!"
(St. Luke 4:36)

Power of Attorney

Legal example: attorney – in fact – person who is authorized to act on behalf of someone else in business dealings or for other purposes. The authority to function in this way is given by a letter of attorney, or power of attorney.

The foundation of the Book of Acts has to do with the followers of Jesus using their authority as power of attorney to continue the ministry of Jesus Christ in the world system. After the Holy Ghost came upon them they shall receive power (authority; to authorize). The Holy Ghost was the attorney-in-fact to convey the authority; He stood in proxy on the day of Pentecost to oversee the transfer of power. Now understand on the day of Pentecost, Satan was watching (he had been judged and his authority taken away 50 plus days earlier). To look at it from this point of view: Jesus spent 3 days in the grave; 40 days ministering after resurrection morning. From the day of His ascension they tarried, 10 days in the upper room, and received the gift of the Holy Ghost on the day of Pentecost.

The Authorized Process:

1. Jesus died and was buried (I Corinthians 15:1-7).

2. Jesus went in the grave, Hades, Hell and whipped the devil, taking the authority that he stole from Adam and Eve (I Corinthians 15:24-28) (Colossians 2:15) (Ephesians 4:8-11).

3. Took the sting from death, which was under Satan's authority (I Corinthians 15:55-56) (Hosea 13:14).

4. Took the power from the grave and released the captive; saints of old walk the streets of Jerusalem (St. Matthew 27:52,53) (Ephesians 4:8-10).

5. And Jesus gave gifts unto men or authority unto men to carry out His will and testament. We have the power of attorney to be Apostles, Prophets, Evangelists, Pastors, and Teachers, the five-fold ministry that represent the authority of God in the earth (Ephesians 4:11).

From Genesis until the Last Supper the Will was written. At Calvary it was signed in blood. In the tomb it was sealed. Now on resurrection morning it was read throughout the spirit world. The day of Pentecost the Holy Ghost executed it. Ye shall receive power (authority) after the executor of my Will comes.

Why did the early Church walk with such authority? They understood His will. Your rights as a Christian are written in His will, not from your point of view. Satan could care less about your theology and denomination or how long you've been a believer. He also believed. But when you began to act upon the will, he knows then you have authority over him and the executor of the will of the Holy Ghost will interact to enforce every demand with a command. When a believer begins to act upon the will of God, the book of Proverbs says the people rejoice, but when Satan binds people (the wicked one), the people mourn.

Jesus said,

> *The Spirit if the Lord is upon me, because he hath anointed me to preach the Gospel to the poor; he hath sent me to heal the broken hearted, to preach deliverance to the captives, and recovering of sight to the blind, to set at liberty them that are bruised.*
>
> (St. Luke 4:18)

When the righteous are in authority, people can rejoice because the spirit of the Lord will be present. The Spirit follows the Word of God to watch over it, make sure it performs as the will has spoken. God's will is His Word. The Word tells His will. The will is the manifesting of His compassion. The Spirit witnesses His Word because it knows His will. When God anoints us, He rubs or paints us with Himself; His pleasing aroma, and fragrance. The Spirit then comes upon us also to bear witness of God's presence. We then can preach with authority the good news of the Gospel to the poor.

The first thing the poor need is the Gospel, the death, burial and resurrection of Jesus Christ and at that moment with the anointing of God and the witness of the Holy Ghost, he doesn't have to be poor anymore. When the righteous are in authority, the people rejoice. The Spirit is the executor of the will of God. It is not God's will for us to be in poverty or uninformed *"Beloved, I wish above all things that thou mayest prosper and be in health, even as thy soul prospereth."* (3 John 2). Take your authority and prosper spiritually then naturally. He has sent you, the authorized ones. God will equip you with power and authority as witnessed in St. Matthew 10, St. Luke He anointed them with power over the power of the devils. He sent you to heal the broken hearts or bound spirits/souls under satanic captivity. They've been snatched away by Satan and need to be healed and delivered. Some are church hurt people that once served God. But for whatever reason they fell prey to Satan's plots. Remember you are anointed to do this. The anointing destroys the yoke.

And it shall come to pass in that day that his burden shall be taken away from off thy shoulder, and his yoke from off thy neck, and the yoke shall be destroyed because of the anointing.

(Isaiah 10:27)

Use your authority and the people will rejoice. First, you must be under authority to be authorized with authority.

C = CHRISTIAN

Christian – Christ-like, to love Christ; of or relating to Christianity based on or conforming with Christianity, professing Jesus as Lord of your life.

Strongs 5546 NT - Greek – Christianos – a Christian follower of Christ

And when he had found him, he brought him unto Antioch. And it came to pass, that a whole year they assembled themselves with the church, and taught much people. And the disciples were called Christians first in Antioch.

(Act 11:26)

Before they were called Christians they were disciples; mathetes a learner, i.e. pupil; enrolled as a scholar: - be discipled, instruct, teach. We see here the disciples were under authority and were trained how to use and submit to authority.

Many people who are called Christians have not submitted to discipleship. Because they have little or no training, they make a mockery of the name "Christian." I believe it was Gandhi who said, "If I had not met a Christian, then I would have desired to be one." Wars have been fought and lives were lost in the name of Christianity because they tried to be Christians without submitting to discipleship and the executor of this will, the Holy Spirit.

Howbeit when he, the Spirit of truth is come, he will guide you into all truth: for he shall not speak of himself; but whatsoever he shall hear that shall he speak: and he will show you things to come.

(St. John 16:13)

The disciples first were taught and then they became Christians. There's a process to being a good Christian. It doesn't happen overnight. I can instantly accept Jesus after hearing the Gospel, but to effectively represent Him, I need to be trained spiritually and naturally on how to submit to His Word and will through the Holy Spirit.

Christians operate within their authority by the Holy Ghost that leads, guides and teaches them the will of God. In the four Gospels, Jesus teaches discipleship the "How To's" of Christianity. The Acts of the Apostles is the work of the Holy Spirit manifesting all that Jesus taught. It's here they became known as Christians by their ACTS. The Epistles are detailed testimonies, plans, training tools and procedures of Christianity. The book of Revelation is the rewards and judgments and all that was ever in the will of God. This is the book of the books, the finale where we end up the winners.

In the end Christianity will be the only religion recognized by God Almighty. Even Judaism will be submitted and conformed to Christianity. Islam will have to accept God the Father, Jesus the Son as Savior and Lord and the baptism of the Holy Ghost's submission to the Bible. Because in the end, we're still standing. Study the Word, seek His face and learn His ways.

But continue thou in the things, which thou hast learned and hast been assured of knowing of whom thou hast learned them; and that from a child thou has known the Holy Scriptures, which are able to make thee wise unto salvation through faith which is in Christ Jesus.

(II Timothy 3:14-15)

Our faith is in Christ Jesus, that's why we are Christians. We believe and trust totally that He is all Scripture says, all the preacher says, all the church says and all grandmother says. It

150

takes faith to be a Christian and the work of the Holy Spirit to stay a Christian. Faith and works produces Godly manifestations, i.e., miracles, signs and wonders. These signs shall follow them that believe. Our lives should be conforming daily to the image of the Son of God.

T = TERRORIZING

Terrorizing – to fill with terror: scare: to coerce by threat or violence; to terrify, frighten, alarm, startle, dread, trepidation

Strongs (4426) pturo – causing to fall or to fly away, to scare, frighten.

And in nothing terrified by your adversaries: which is to them and evident token of perdition, but to you of salvation, and that of God.
(Philippians 1:28)

The benefit of being an authorized Christian is the ability to terrorize Satan. We have been equipped to whip, not to be defeated by the enemy, but to conquer through Him that loves us. For the weapons of our warfare are not carnal but mighty through God to the pulling down of strongholds. We are not to be intimidated by the activity of Satan because he's the defeated foe. It terrorizes Satan when he sees an authorized Christian using the weapons of warfare, individuals who are fighting the good fight of faith, not a fleshly battle, trying to pull down other Christians and win the war of popularity.

We must warfare through God to pull down the strongholds of Satan. Let's surround the enemy's camp, his strongholds and brick-by-brick, stone-by-stone, beam-by-beam destroy it with the power of the Holy Ghost. We are appointed, anointed and assigned to terrorize the enemy. Every time a disciple becomes a Christian it terrorizes Satan. Every time a Christian is led into warfare by the Holy Spirit it terrorizes Satan. The mere presence of an anointed Christian terrorizes Satan. "Anoint" also means "Messiah the deliverer." Remember St. Luke 4:18? It was the Messiah proclamation, the anointed of God who terrorized Satan in his every move.

You are Christians, anointed ones, made in the expressed image of Jesus. Just your presence alone is intimidation and trepidation to Satan your adversary.

And when he was come to the other side into the country of the Gergesenes, there met him two possessed with devils, coming out of the tombs, exceedingly fierce, so that no man might pass by that way. And, behold, they cried out, saying what have we to do with thee, Jesus thou Son of God? Art thou come hither to torment us before the time?

(St. Matthew 8:28-29)

The devils recognized His authority and knew that when Jesus came they had to submit or be tormented before time. Sometimes we try to torment Satan before he submits, and it does not work that way. To terrorize means to cause alarm. It can be now or it will be later. Now Satan tormented these two men in the soul or spirit and they terrorized others who came that way. But when they saw Jesus, remember when the righteous is in authority the people rejoice: but when the wicked beareth rule, the people mourn. In Proverbs 29:2 only the authorized believers can ACTS Walk.

Satan hates to be told what to do by a lower creature in creation—man is a little lower than the angels. Satan was the archangel, the head of all the others including Michael and Gabriel, etc. But an authorized Christian can terrorize him because he left the will of God. (It's dangerous to be outside His will.) Outside His will you have no rights to any of the property, blessing, or favor. Regardless of where you stand or what you possess, when the will is read and executed you can and shall be moved, replaced or cast out of His territory (territory is geographical or belonging to or under the jurisdiction of a governmental authority, region district). We are His people, the sheep of His pasture and we've been brought with a price, the precious blood of Jesus. When the devil sees the will signed in His blood, the tormenting begins from Calvary to Pentecost. Fifty plus days it was signed, sealed and delivered you're permitted to ACTS Walk.

152

S = SATAN

Satan – devil, adversary, Lucifer

Strongs – 7854 OT Satan, the archenemy of good, adversary.

4567 NT satanas the accuser, the devil

Lucifer, king of Babylon, Babel means confusion king of Tyrus, prince of the air, son of the morning, slew foot, boogieman

Satan is a believer and disobedience caused him to lose his authority. When a believer loses their authority they lose their power of attorney. They look the same way–as explosive as before. But their interior substances have lost its combustion. Because they have avoided a Godly relationship, they've dried up of His anointing. The anointing is like nitroglycerin, when ignited gives dynamite its explosive ability. When the fill is gone, then the thrill is gone (no filling means less thrilling) who is the prime example that we can learn this lesson from but Satan. This is how he lost.

Hell from beneath is moved for thee to meet thee at thy coming: it stirreth up the dead for thee; even all the chief ones of the earth; it hath raised up from their thrones all the kings of the nations. All they shall speak and say unto thee, Art thou also become weak as we? Art thou become like unto us? Thy pomp is brought down to the grave, and the noise of thy violas: the worm is spread under thee, and the worms cover thee.

(Isaiah 14:9-11)

This passage of Scripture is commonly accredited to the antichrist, the satanic spirit filled servant of him. But it's Satan living through him, attempting to destroy the last day move of God. Satan when he was Lucifer the son of the morning was filled with fire from God. He even walked among the fire of God. But when he allowed pride and stopped functioning to the will of God, he began to look for what he wanted and how he saw it, instead of submitting to the will of God. When you don't submit to God, you will lose your authority. And when you loose your authority, you become complacent and dormant. Satan lost his position, power and purpose.

153

How art thou fallen from heaven, O Lucifer, son of the morning! How art thou cut down to the ground, which didst weaken the nation! For thou hast said in thine heart, I will ascend into heaven, I will exalt my throne above the stars of God: I will sit also upon the mount of the congregation, in the sides of the north: I will ascend above the heights of the clouds; I will be like the Most High. Yet thou shalt be brought down to hell, to the sides of the pit.

(Isaiah 14:12-15)

The things that make us dormant will cause our demise. At some time or somewhere Satan began to talk to himself and convince himself that walking in the fire of God and obeying God didn't matter anymore. When a believer stops submitting, serving and presenting their bodies as a living sacrifice, they lose their infilling of the fire of God's presence and become dormant. If we aren't active in obedience, then we are walking in disobedience. Have you ever wondered why Satan continued to walk in the path of destruction? Because he had no room for repentance. Satan chose not to accept or submit his will to God. Satanic pride will shut down your spirit outside the will of God. This was a part of his plan, to steal creation, which is the Glory of God, that's why he said in his heart, "I will ascend into heaven, I will exalt my throne above the stars of God. I'm really the boss, God just used me for his Glory, so I turn the tables on God, and become ruler of my own destiny." But the Bible says, *"Yet thou shalt be brought down to hell, to the sides of the pit"* (verse 15). Satan refused the fire of God so God will give him his own personal fire (hell). That's his true destiny, after its all been said and done. Satan is condemned to an eternal torment in Hell.

They that see thee shall narrowly look upon thee and consider thee, saying, Is this the man that made the earth to tremble, that did shake kingdoms; That made the world as a wilderness, and destroyed the cities thereof; that opened not the house of the prisoners.

(Isaiah 14:16-17)

Satan is a destroyer of good and when he has trapped you, he will not open the prison doors.

"IT'S ALL ABOUT ME, NOT GOD"

Satan has destroyed cities and kingdoms with his pride and rebellion.

The Word of the Lord came again unto me saying, Son of man say unto the prince of Tyrus, thus saith the Lord God; because thine heart is lifted up, and thou hast said, I am God, I sit in the seat of God, in the midst of the seas; yet thou art a man, and not God, though thou set thine heart as the heart of God: with thy wisdom and with thine understanding thou hast gotten thee riches, and hast gotten gold and silver in to thy treasures.

(Ezekiel 28:1,2,4)

The prince of Tyrus Ithobalus was convinced that he himself and I was the culprit behind his success. All the while it was satanic distribution. Now verse 3.

Behold thou art wiser than Daniel; there is no secret that they can hide from thee.

Listen to what he thought about himself, wisdom, knowledge and understanding.

Ithobalus was like the antichrist—a puppet for his master Satan. What if Ithobalus had submitted himself to God? Then he could really have the wisdom of Daniel and sit with God in heavenly places.

By the great wisdom and by thy traffic has thou increased thy riches, and thine heart is lifted up because of thy riches: therefore thus saith the Lord God; Because thou hast set thine heart as the heart of God; behold therefore I will bring strangers upon thee, the terrible of the nations: and they shall draw their swords against the beauty of thy wisdom, and they shall defile thy

155

brightness. They shall bring thee down to the pit, and thou shalt die the deaths of them that are slain in the midst of the seas.

Satan dominates the man to the degree that everything in his life was about his own glory, not God. His spirit man laid dormant to the will and obedience of God. Like his father the king, he was cast down to Hell. Like father, like son.

Moreover, the Word of the Lord came unto me, saying, Son of man take up a lamentation upon the king of Tyrus and say unto him. Thus saith the Lord God; thou sealest up the sum, full of wisdom and perfect in beauty. Thou hast been in Eden the garden of God; every precious stone was thy covering, the sardius, topaz and the diamond, the beryl, the onyx and the jasper, the sapphire, the emerald, and the carbuncle, and gold: the workmanship of thy tabrets and of thy pipes was prepared in thee in the day that thou wast created.

(Ezekiel 28:5-13)

I hope by now you understand that king Tyrus is Satan incarnated in Prince Tyrus, Ithobalus. The prince rules the natural territory but his father ruled him. The prince's kingdom would become ruins because his father's kingdom was lost from the foundation of the world. Satan used men to corrupt the creation of God. He makes them promises, then imprisons them. He also destroys their will. These men don't seek God anymore, but their own satisfaction. Satan was covered in ten stones, representing kingdoms of men. He lost his covering in heaven and is trying to cover himself with stonyhearted men.

This is Lucifer's Nature

S.I.N.

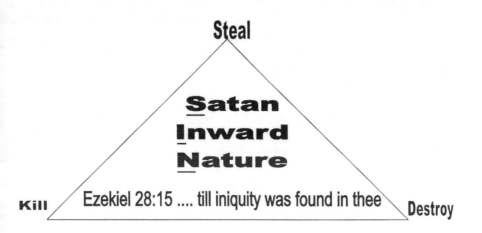

Steal

Satan
Inward
Nature

Kill   Ezekiel 28:15 .... till iniquity was found in thee   Destroy

Hierarchy is a ruling body of clergy organized into ranks; persons or things arranged in a graded series.

For such are false apostles, deceitful workers, transforming themselves into the apostles of Christ. And no marvel, for satan himself is transformed into an angel of light. Therefore, it is no great thing if his ministers also be transformed as the ministers of righteousness; whose end shall be according to their work.

(II Corinthians 11:13-15)

To defeat the devil and pull down his hierarchy, the ACTS Walker must put on the whole armour of God, daily through fasting, praying, studying the Word, and submitting to the Holy Spirit. Submit to God, resist the devil and he will flee from you. The ACTS Walker must know his enemy.

Satan has many wiles (methods, plans, and schemes to deceive and entrap the believer).

These are the main areas:

1. Satan's Hierarchy

<u>Principalities</u> – Gr: Arche; Chief rulers or beings of the highest rank and order in Satan's kingdom (Ephesians v.1:21; 2:2; Col. 2:10). This is Satan's seat of authority. He is the prince of darkness, prince of this world and all wickedness and evilness comes by his authority. "Prince" means a ruler (St. John 14:30; 16:11).

<u>Powers</u> – Gr: Exousia, authorities, those who derive the power from an executive, the will of the Chief rulers (Ephesians 1:21; Col. 2:10). This is the demons who work side-by-side with Satan to carry out orders to control nations, state, and cities. They personally cause disruption in governments heads of states with greed, lust, abortion, wars, etc.

<u>Ruler of Darkness</u> – Gr: Kosmokratopas, work-rulers of the darkness of this age, the spirit rulers (Daniel 10:13-21; Ephesians 1:21; 6:12; Col. 1:16-18). These demons and imps keep races and people divided by veils of darkness. They stop the harmony of peace, understanding and trust among mankind. They plant hate, envy and strife among men.

<u>Spiritual Wickedness</u> – Gr: pneumatikos ponerias- that of the wicked spirits of Satan in the heavenlies (Ephesians 1:21, Col. 1:16-18). These foul spirits seek to control the worship of God. They don't want pure and true worship coming from mankind. They seek to control preachers, mayors, the legal system, compromising Christians, presidents and many others. New age, physics, and cults are all under the control of spiritual wickedness in high places. The high place is a place where orders come from. It is a place of information: TV, newspapers, radio, pulpits...the demon's desire to control these places.

THE DEVIL WANTS TO BE KEPT SECRET!

1. Satan's Kingdom cannot hold us

Colossians 1:13
Who hath delivered us from the power of darkness, and hath translated us into the kingdom of his dear son.

FACT - We have been delivered from the power of darkness into a marvelous light and into the Kingdom of God. The body will still suffer from the results of being born into a world ruled by Satan, but the spirit-man or eternal man can sit in the heavenly places with Christ Jesus.

2. Satan does not own anything legally

Colossians 1:16
For by Him (Jesus) were all things created that are in heaven, and that are in earth, visible and invisible, whether they be thrones, or dominions, or principalities, or powers: all things were created by Him, and for Him.

3. Satan can be controlled by you

St. Luke 10:17-19
And the seventy returned again with joy, saying Lord, even the devils are subject unto us through thy name. And he said unto them, I beheld Satan as lightning fall from heaven. Behold, I give unto you power to tread on serpents and scorpions, and over all the power of the enemy: and nothing shall by any means hurt you.

FACT - Not only does Jesus possess the authority but He gave it to His disciples. They went forth with such authority that Jesus saw Satan flee from heaven (heavenlies) with lightning speed to see what was happening in his kingdom, the authorized believers were causing shock waves in the spirit world. Demons were screaming, imps were running and the oppressed, depressed and suppressed were set free. Real anointed ministry superseded all of Satan's stolen authority.

159

4. Satan's Limited Power

Job 1:12
And the Lord said unto Satan, Behold all that he hath is in thy power; only upon himself put not forth thine hand. So Satan went forth from the presence of the Lord.

FACT – Satan cannot do anything he desires to the believer, he cannot attack without permission. We may by disobedient to God and open the door for unnecessary suffering, but even in our disobedience we are still covered by grace. God sometimes allows Satan to buffet us.

5. Satan's Limited in Temptations

I Corinthians 10:13
There hath no temptation taken you but such as is common to man: but God is faithful, who will not suffer you to be tempted above that ye are able; but will with the temptation also make a way to escape, that ye may be able to bear it.

FACT – This is, of course, as long as you follow the leading of the Lord and don't be drawn away. Jesus said, "My yoke is easy and my burden is light." If you resist the devil, and stay submitted to God, Satan is limited to the level of temptation he can present to the believer. But if you're drawn away and yoked with sin, temptation has no escape route. Read and study Israel's wilderness journey. They rejected God and were rejected by God because they yielded to Satan.

6. Satan Wants to Keep the World in Darkness

2 Corinthians 4:3-4
But if our gospel be hid, it is hid to them that are lost: In whom the God of this world hath blinded the minds of them which believe not, lest the light of the glorious gospel of Christ, who is the image of God, should shine unto them.

FACT – Satan does not want the truth to come out and that is why he fights the great commission (St. Matthew 28:19-20).

Satan has already been defeated (past-tense). Jesus is the light of the world. Satan is the Chosek of the world. In the light we have life, joy, peace and abundant living. But in the darkness, there's fear, pain, hatred and death. Satan wants to keep the world misinformed about salvation. Many times he acts in the name of God to deceive the people. As long as they never hear the true Gospel and experience the full Gospel, they will follow a lie. He is the father of all lies. Satan will offer you religion with no relationship. Satan will tell you what you want to hear, to satisfy your flesh. Satan will make you feel good about yourself.

Remember Apostle Peter's revelation of Satan's method and procedures in I Peter 5:8-9:

> *Be sober, be vigilant: because your adversary the devil, as a roaring lion, walketh about, seeking whom he may devour: Whom resist steadfast in the faith.*

In warfare against Satan, the believer must cast all cares, concerns, and situations before the Lord. The Lord will inspect and examine our motives, plans and desires because what we care for will affect our heart and relationship.

WE ALL MUST HAVE OUR TRAINING IN WARFARE (BOOT CAMP)

What's recorded in St. Matthew 6:32-33 is the next best thing to waging a successful battle of warfare against Satan. *Seek ye first the Kingdom of God.* "Seek" means "to restore to, go to, to go in search of, look for, to make a search of iniquity" as earlier stated. God's Kingdom will always supersede the world's offers. Jesus said in the 32nd verse *"For after all these things do the Gentiles (world) seek: for your heavenly Father knoweth that ye have need of all these things."* Spiritual warfare should not be fought just for things. The plan of God is made manifest in the lives of mankind. In the Kingdom of God, we have everything that we need. Satan will try to use the worldly resources to tempt us into disobeying God's plan as He did with Adam and Eve in the garden. The Garden was a Comfort Zone for Adam.

God had not originally planned to put Adam out. However, because of sin, Adam had to go through what we call Boot camp—a time of testing and learning to submit to God. By the sweat of his face toiling in hardship and by the third pain of death—sorrow in child bearing. Adam and Eve's wills had to be broken. We all would have paid an equal price had Jesus failed in the wilderness (boot camp).

WILDERNESS WARFARE (TIME TO MATURE)

Led by the Spirit, Jesus went into the wilderness. Heaven proved that without the necessity of life, we can survive without yielding to Satan's most promising worldly offers. Adam lost his warfare in the garden. Jesus won our warfare in the wilderness. Adam was a living soul and Jesus was a quickening spirit. Adam blamed, Jesus claimed (I Corinthians 15:45-50).

After looking at the example of Adam, the first natural man and Jesus, the first perfect spiritual man, let us look at Adam's environment it was a garden with all the supplies Adam ever needed including companionship. He had a good job with great hours and retirement benefits which were eternal life. Jesus' wilderness environment was full of wild animals, cliffs, and valleys with no companionship, but Satan tempting him. His job would last only 3½ years with a shameful death on the cross. Jesus did not have had food or drink but stood in obedience. Adam had food and drink, but yielded to Satan's offers. Romans 14:17 says, *"For the kingdom of God is not meat and drink; but righteousness, and peace, and joy in the Holy Ghost."* What Jesus brings from His wilderness (boot camp) experience, righteousness, peace, and joy to the believers' life, Adam left us a curse (Genesis 3:17).

TEMPTATION OF CHRIST

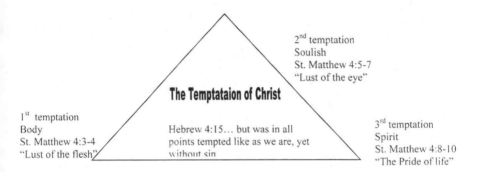

2nd temptation
Soulish
St. Matthew 4:5-7
"Lust of the eye"

The Temptataion of Christ

1st temptation
Body
St. Matthew 4:3-4
"Lust of the flesh"

Hebrew 4:15... but was in all
points tempted like as we are, yet
without sin

3rd temptation
Spirit
St. Matthew 4:8-10
"The Pride of life"

<u>Temptation #1</u> The Body - Matthew 4:3

And when the tempter came to him, he said, if thou be the Son of God, command that these stones be made bread. But he answered and said it is written, Man shall not live by bread alone, but by every word that proceedeth out of the mouth of God.

Note: Satan twisted and tried to misuse Scripture. His assumption was that Jesus was hungry enough to misuse His authority. This is the temptation of the flesh. Don't let the process of worldly cares cause you to stumble in the wilderness.

<u>Temptation #2</u> The Soul - Matthew 4:5-7

Then the devil taketh him up in the holy city and setteth him on a pinnacle of the temple, and saith unto him, if thou be the Son of God, cast thyself down: for it is written He shall give his angels charge concerning thee: and in their hands they shall bear thee up, lest at anytime thou dash thy foot against a stone. Jesus said unto him, It is written again, Thou shalt not tempt the Lord thy God. (this temptation is mental/mind)

Note: Satan's misuse of the definition of Scripture. God will send His angels to save the suicidal (one who purposely tries to harm himself). God is faithful and doesn't respond to man's temptation (tempting is used to draw man because of a desire or need). God is sovereign.

Temptation #3 The Spirit- Matthew 4:8-9

Again the devil taketh him up into an exceeding high mountain, and showeth him all the kingdoms of the world, and the glory of them; And saith unto him, all these things will I give thee, if thou wilt fall down and worship me.

Note: Satan showed Jesus his own property but now under Satanic influence. Jesus wouldn't in any way accept the Kingdom in their present state. (10) *Then saith Jesus unto him, get thee hence, Satan: for it is written, Thou shalt worship the Lord thy God, and him only shalt thou serve.* Note that the earth is the Lord's and the fullness thereof, the world and them that dwell therein. Observe what Jesus told Satan during His temptation, when the trials of His faith were in session.

We must keep the faith and stop failing the test. Yes, Satan has persuaded many to bow and heed to temptation, but Jesus, through this wilderness experience, mortified the flesh so that Satan could tempt Him in nothing. What a testimony. All children of Israel's except for a few died in wilderness experience. In order to go into the Promised Land, God has to kill our carnal, complaining ways. We must die before we can enter into the manifestation of the promise. After that, the Holy Ghost shall come, and we shall receive power. We have to die from the carnal to manifest the power of God. Moses viewed the Promised Land but did not get to walk in it. We have the ability, but not the maturity in Christ's power to fulfill our God appointed destiny.

After the test is over or boot camp is finished, you are ready to have power and maturity in the spirit.

WILDERNESS EXPERIENCE (THE BEST TEACHER)

Jesus had to be baptized with the Holy Ghost and God was His witness and testified of His obedience. God gave His Son confirmation of His purposes.

Matthew 4: *"Now Jesus is prepared to go through the wilderness experience."* This is the time of refining and testing. God will perfect you wholly according to I Thessalonians 5:23: *"And the very God of peace sanctify you wholly and I pray God your whole spirit and soul and body be preserved blameless unto the coming of our Lord Jesus Christ."*

The body, soul and spirit of the trinity of men must work as one in obedience to God.

The Body of Flesh–must be mortified. Flesh and blood cannot enter the Kingdom of God. The natural man (Gr. Psuchikos, sensual) is a man living under the control of the fleshly passions and physical desires.

The Spiritual Man–is spiritual. This is a man under the control of the Holy Spirit and the things of God.

The Soul Man–is the emotional one who lives according to his feelings and imagination. He thinks he knows God but only in forms of religion. He can quote Scripture and cry "holy," but can't live right, always blaming someone or something else for his troubles.

There are at least two processes by which God can perfect man wholly. One way is the Word, and the other is the wilderness. Anytime you want to move on in God, you will take one of these routes.

Hebrew 4:12
For the word of God is quick and powerful, and sharper

than any two edged sword, piercing even to the dividing asunder of soul and spirit, and the joints and marrow, and is the discerned of the thoughts and intents of the heart.

Since Jesus is the Word, God had no need to test Himself (the Word). But Satan did tempt Him in the wilderness. Matthew 4:1-11 tells the story, but for the record, we will attempt to show how he was tested body, soul and spirit.

Satan's aim in warfare is to destroy your relationship with God, mankind and yourself by any means necessary. But Jesus stayed in the power of the Holy Ghost. St. Luke 4:14 says that Jesus returned in the power of the spirit into Galilee. Warfare doesn't weaken but strengthens the saints. Warfare mortifies the flesh, submits the soul and ignites the purposes of the Spirit.

THE TRIANGLE OF MAN (I THESSALONIANS 5:23)

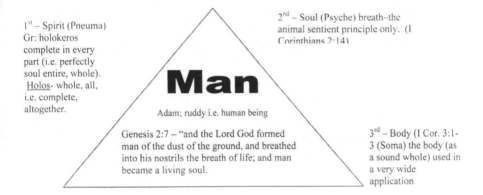

1ˢᵗ – Spirit (Pneuma) Gr: holokeros complete in every part (i.e. perfectly soul entire, whole). Holos- whole, all, i.e. complete, altogether.

2ⁿᵈ – Soul (Psyche) breath–the animal sentient principle only. (I Corinthians 2:14)

Man

Adam; ruddy i.e. human being

Genesis 2:7 – "and the Lord God formed man of the dust of the ground, and breathed into his nostrils the breath of life; and man became a living soul.

3ʳᵈ – Body (I Cor. 3:1-3 (Soma) the body (as a sound whole) used in a very wide application

BODY, SOUL, SPIRIT (TOTAL MAN)

I Thessalonians 5:23
And the very God of Peace sanctify you wholly; and I pray God your whole spirit and soul and body be preserved blameless unto the coming of our Lord Jesus Christ.

First, the battle was fought in the body. Satan requested Jesus to turn stones into loaves of bread. Jesus countered with "Man shall live by the true bread" (Himself), and the Word of God. Satan tried to affect the body of man, (see John 1:1). Secondly, they fought in the soul area dealing with temptation or tempting the Lord our God (Satan affecting the souls of man). Then saith Jesus unto him, *"Get thee hence Satan; for it is written, Thou shall worship the Lord thy God and him only shalt thou serve."* Last, but not least, his final quest to live in the Spirit of man, the place of worship!

POWER IN THE SPIRIT

Matthew 4:23
And Jesus went about all Galilee, teaching in their synagogues, and preaching the gospel of the kingdom, and healing all manners of sickness and all manner of disease among the people.

Note: Jesus first taught them that He preached the Gospel of the Kingdom of God, followed by signs, wonders and miracles. Whatever He taught or preached was what the Father was telling Him. Jesus said the works that I do is what I see the Father doing. My meat is to do the will of God and finish His works. The believer must not get sidetracked with the worldly or political systems. It is good to know what is going on in the world. However, it's better to know the Kingdom activities. The world has Watergate, Whitewater and corruption in its government. But the Kingdom has righteousness, peace and joy in the Holy Ghost. Isaiah said, "The government shall be upon his shoulder that he is the government of God." Revelation teaches that Jesus will crush the world government.

If a believer follows our example of power in the Holy Ghost, he will catch on fire and walk in power (dynamite) and he will manifest the power of God to a dying world. Just like the explosion caused people's curiosity to arouse, people will begin to watch and follow the Church again; our pews will be filled with hungry lives seeking to be transformed. The drunks will start drinking a new wine. The drug addict will get re-hooked to a new high that is the rock of ages, instead of Cocaine Rock. The prostitute will become a fisher of men instead of a solicitor of man. The homosexual will find true love instead of deception. The whites and blacks will walk in true fellowship like in the days of early Azusa 1906 when the blood of Jesus wiped away mistrust and color barriers. Jews and Gentiles will fellowship in harmony. Muslims, Hindus and Catholics will be spirit-filled and praising Jesus as Lord of all.

Roman 8:14-19:

For as many as are led by the Spirit of God, they are the sons of God for ye have not received the spirit of Bondage again to fear; but ye have received the Spirit of adoption, whereby we cry Abba Father. The Spirit itself beareth witness with our spirit that we are the children of God: And if children, then heirs of God and joint-heirs with Christ, if so be that we suffer with him, that we may be also glorified together. For I reckon that the sufferings of this present time are not worthy to be compared with the glory, which shall be revealed in us. For the earnest expectation of the creature waiteth for the manifestation of the sons of God.

CHAPTER NINE

*The Acts of the Five Fold Ministry
The Body builders*

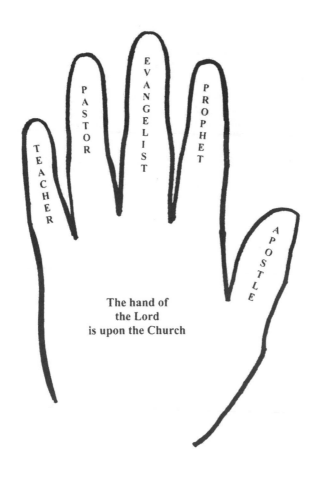

The hand of
the Lord
is upon the Church

The older I get the more difficult it is to workout. I have more equipment lying useless in the garage, a membership at the Lord's Gym (a free one for Pastors), dresser drawers full of sweat pants and closets full of jogging shoes. I'm just like you. I get more exercise going to buy these things than I do using them. What a shame, shame, shame. In the past I haven't had the luxuries in my life that I have now.

When I was young, I used to lift weights under my neighbor's big oak tree 5 days a week, run two miles a day and play full court basketball for 2-3 hours a day. I wonder sometimes what happened and then I remember that I got married, had children and started pastoring. We have a mortgage and two color TVs. Now I struggle to walk 30 minutes 3 to 4 days a week. Today the heaviest weight I lift is all the books I carry when I'm preparing to write or preach. Don't even mention full court basketball. These days at 5'11, I'm not tall enough to play a center and will play only one end of the court and wait for them to return and pass me the ball, though I still know how to shoot. I guess, as life would have it, we change as our responsibilities come and go. There are some things that shouldn't change too much like getting rest, exercise, and a good diet. These things help build the physical body and keep it at peak performance. I confess, I could have done a better job on God's temple, and believe me I've paid for my shortcomings. But in spite of my failures, God has spared me and helped in time of trouble.

In this chapter we're going to deal with the body builders, the Authorized Christians Terrorizing Satan ministries. Study the Scriptures yourself and read other writings to help understand how to be a body builder. We use the hand to represent the Hand of the Lord upon the Church. Each finger will be used to illustrate the Gift of God given to build them in the body. Each finger plays and supports a different part but holds the same print (finger prints). They can all be used to identify the owner of the hand.

This hand will help the Church fulfill its function, and we can know when the Hand of the Lord is upon us. We can also say, "the Spirit of the Lord is upon us."

Read Ezekiel 37:1
*The hand of the Lord was upon me, and carried me out in
the spirit of the Lord, and set me down in the midst of the
valley which was full of bones.*

So the Hand of the Lord is the Spirit of the Lord working in
the life of the believer.

St. Luke 4:17-18 says,
*When the book was delivered to Jesus and he stood to
read, The Spirit of the lord is upon me, because he hath
anointed me to preach the gospel to the poor; he hath sent
me to heal the broken hearted to preach deliverance to the
captives, and recovering of sight to the blind, to set at
liberty them that are bruised, to preach the acceptable
year of the Lord.*

The Hand of the Lord was upon Jesus, even standing and
reading the messianic Scripture.

The Prophet's Vision–The hand of the Lord will work through
you.

We were in a revival service in Miami Beach, Florida, and God
was manifesting Himself. At the end of the service we started a
prayer line for those who were sick and under attack. From the
time we laid hands upon the first person, the Holy Spirit began to
slay folks all over the church. I reached a particular individual
who had a problem in his stomach area. I didn't know at the time
precisely what to do, but the Lord said not to touch him and to
point toward his belly. So I obeyed the Lord, and the moment I
pointed, the person bent over and fell forward. This wasn't new to
me, it happened many times and in most services. The amazing
thing was that God opened the eyes of a prophet, and he saw
another hand coming out of my hand going into the individual's
body and healing him. God said, "Don't touch just point, and I'll
do the rest." Understand this, when the Word of God has been
preached, miracles, signs, and wonders will come from the spoken
Word. The Hand of the Lord will work through you as well as
upon you.

God has not taken His hand off the Church or lost a finger since the day of Pentecost. Every finger is just as important as the other. But each finger has the same fingerprint outside and the same DNA inside. They all operate different functions, but every finger has a unique purpose and it is to fulfill. Ephesians 4:11-16.

And he gave some apostles and some prophets; and some evangelists; and some pastors and teachers.

In this chapter, we will learn the purpose, plans, and positions of the five-fold ministry and also the 10 functions and purposes of His fingers operating in the Church and the Body of Christ.

Function – the normal or characteristic action of anything; the special duty or performance required in the course of work or activity.

Purpose – to plan, intend or resolve. What one plans to get or do intention; aim.

We will use Strong's and Webster's to help define the function and purposes of the five-fold ministry. We will use the Holy Spirit and our experiences where permitted to define the spiritual role of the five-fold ministry.

Ephesians 4:12 (A)–*For the perfecting of the saints.*

Perfect – Webster's definition – being without fault or defect; exact, precise complete.
Perfecting – Strong's 2677 katartismos, from 2675 (katartizo-to complete thoroughly i.e., repair (lit. or fig.) or adjust; complete furnishing.
Function and Purpose: *That ye may stand perfect and complete in all the will of God* (Colossians 4:12). *Having therefore these promises, dearly beloved, let us cleanse ourselves from all filthiness of the flesh and spirit, perfecting holiness in the fear of God* (II Corinthians 7:1).

Ephesians 4:12 (B) *For the work of the ministry.*

174

<u>Work</u> – Webster's definition – toil, labor task job (have-to do) the energy used when a force is applied over a given distance.

<u>Work</u> – strong's 2041 ergo (to work); toil (as an effort or occupation) doing labour.

Function and Purpose: *And meet for the master's use, and prepared unto every good work* (II Timothy 2:21).

Ephesians 4:12 (C) *For the edifying of the body of Christ.*

<u>Edifying</u> – Webster definition – instruction and improvement esp. in morality. Edify.

<u>Edifying</u> – Strong 3619 – oikodome is from oikos 3624 and doma 1430
doma 1430 – to build edifice, roof housetop
oikodome – architecture, a structure, confirmation building
Function and Purpose: **But we do all things, dearly beloved, for your edifying** (II Corinthians 12:19).

Ephesians 4:13 (D) *Till we all come in the unity of the faith.*

<u>Unity</u> – Webster's definition – the quality or state of being or being made one. Oneness.

<u>Unity</u> – Strong's 1775 henotes oneness, i.e. (fig) unanimity heis 1520 one, abundantly, man, one, only.

Function and Purpose: *And all that believed were together, and had all things common* (Act 2:44).

Ephesians 4:13 (E) *And the knowledge of the Son of God.*

<u>Knowledge</u> – Webster's definition – understanding gained by actual experience, range of information, clear perception of truth.

<u>Knowledge</u> – Strongs 1922 epignosis recognition full discernment.

Function and Purpose: *And to know the love of Christ, which passeth knowledge, that ye might be filled with the fullness of God* (Ephesians 3:19).

Ephesians 4:13 (F) *Unto a perfect man.*

<u>Perfect</u> – Webster's definition – being without fault or defect exact, precise, complete.

Perfect – Strong's 5046 teleios complete (in various applications of labor, growth, mental and moral character, etc.).

Function and Purpose: *That the man of God may be perfect, thoroughly furnished unto all good works* (II Timothy 3:17).

Ephesians 4:13 (G) *Unto the measure of the stature of the fullness of Christ.*

Measure – Webster's definition – an adequate or moderate portion a suitable limit.

Function and Purpose: *According as God hath dealth to every man the measure of faith* (Roman 12:3).

Stature – Webster's definition – quality or status gained (as by achievement) natural height.

Function and Purpose: *And Jesus increased in wisdom and stature, and in favor with God and man.* (St. Luke 2:52).

Fullness – Webster's definition – filled, complete esp. in detail. Having volume or depth of sound, completely occupied with a thought or plan.

Function and Purpose: *For it pleased the father that in him should all fullness dwell* (Colossians 1:19).

Measure – Strong's 3358 metron; limited portion (degree)
Stature – Strong's 2244 helikia; maturity
Fullness – Strong's 4138 pleroma; completion

THE FUNCTIONAL CHURCH

Ephesians 4:14 (H)
That we henceforth be no more children, tossed to and from, and carried about with every wind of doctrine, by the sleight of men, and cunning craftiness, whereby they lie in wait to deceive.

Ephesians 4:15 (I)
But speaking the truth in love, may grow up into him in all things, which is the head even Christ.

Ephesians 4:16 (J)
From whom the whole body fitly joined together and

compacted by that which every joint supplieth, according to the effectual working in the measure of every part, maketh increase of the body unto the edifying of itself in love.

God loves us so much that not only did He send His Son to die for our sin, He also gave Him gifts to leave as a reminder of His love. The five-fold ministry is precious to the body and must be received with thanksgiving, appreciation and respect.

The last day Church must have the unction to function. They're ACTS Walkers who've heard the wake-up call. They're ready to go in the trenches to kick some devil butt. Allow me to introduce you to the winning team.

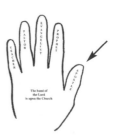

And He gave some apostles:

The thumb that can touch every finger. Gr apostolos, a delegate, one sent with full power of attorney to act in the place of another, the sender remaining behind but backs the one sent. In the case of Christians, it means God sends them to do what He would do if He went Himself. What authority God has given this office of believers!

It is very important for the apostle to walk in total subjection and obedience. This believer must listen, understand and carry instruction to the letter. A lot is dependent upon his willingness to act in the place of God. He is a representative for God before men and both will examine his motives. Titus, an apostle, was sent to Corinth for the financial business. Paul said,

Providing for honest things not only in the sight of the Lord, but also in the sight of men. And we have sent with them our brother, whom we have often time proved

diligent in many things, but now much more diligent upon the great confidence which I have in you. Whether any do enquire of Titus, he is my partner and fellow helper concerning you: or our brethren be inquired of, they are the messengers of the churches, and the glory of Christ.

(II Corinthians 8:21-23)

There are over twenty apostles recognized in New Testament Scriptures.

Here are a few of those listed:

1   Jesus Christ (Hebrews 3:1)

2.   Epaphroditus (Philippians 2:25)

3.   Paul (Galatians 1:1)

4.   The Twelve (Matthew 10:2-4;
          Mark 3:16-19)

5.   Junia (Romans 16:7)

6.   Apollos (I Corinthians 4:6-9)

7.   Timothy (I Thessalonians 1:1)

8.   Matthias (Acts 1:26)

9.   Barnabas (I Corinthians 9:5-6)

10.   Andronicus (Romans 16:7)

11.   James, the Lord's brother

12.   Titus (II Corinthians 8:23)
          (Galatians 1:19; 2:9)

WE KNOW THAT THERE WERE FALLEN APOSTLES—

Judas, false Apostle, *"For such are false apostles, deceitful workers, transforming themselves into the apostles of Christ."* II Corinthians 11:13

The Greek word Apostlos translated apostle again means one sent forth, a messenger.

Hebrews 3:1
Wherefore Holy brethren, partakers of the heavenly calling, consider the Apostle and High Priest of our profession, Christ Jesus.

The first group in Scripture is the twelve who followed Him, Mathias replacing Judas. The book of Revelation called them the apostles of the Lamb, as mentioned in Revelation 21:14 *"and the wall of the city had twelve foundations and in them the names of the twelve apostles of the Lamb."* In the gospel they are called "apostles" in Matthew the 10th chapter. The second group basically was headed by apostle Paul and other anointed early church leaders, some called missionaries, bishops, etc. Not all of them received Scriptural recognition by name or title, but their works will speak for them in the day of judgment and rewards. Some were possible women and non-Jews.

My personal journey to understand my call as an apostle started as a teenager. It was during a night vision and out of body experiences. I was only fourteen years old, I was fasting and praying alot in these days. Being a high school student and battling the forces that control our public schools, I needed help. Some of my friends lived compromising lifestyles, professing to be Christians, but living like heathens. I told the Lord that before I started playing the church game, to please take me home to heaven. I didn't want to hurt or crucify Him again. God told me to live in spite of my failures.

I had some close calls as a teenager; some days I felt like just giving up. Many days it was hard and lonely, but the Holy Spirit would come upon me in my weakest moments and encourage me to move forward. I thought I was missing out on fun and excitement being a church boy. I would hear at the lunch table about the events of last night and the weekends. I remember nobody would call me because all I had to talk about was Jesus, the church and sometimes sports. They all respected me, but were really afraid to socialize with me, because they didn't want to stop doing what they liked. Teachers and students would ask for prayer and opinions, but not how to permanently change the problem.

It was during this period of time that one night I laid down to rest and the second my head hit the pillow, I felt electric shocks all over my body and an awesome presence in my room. I sat up in my bed and then began to walk around the room, but my body was still laying there. I looked at myself, and I was at peace. I felt this tugging, and when I looked up, I began to rise at will. It was fun and exciting. Then I felt a greater tugging and could hear a voice saying, "You can come up higher." So I looked through the ceiling, the clouds and earth's atmosphere and like a rocket I took off and as I rose I saw my house, neighborhood and eventually the earth decrease until they were no longer visible. Where I was I don't know (1st, 2nd, or 3rd heaven). I knew the Lord would take care of me body, soul, and spirit as I moved to the next dimension. While I was there, the Lord began to show me visions of present and future events. It was revealed then that I had the gift of being an apostle upon my life, but it would be awhile before I walked in the manifestation of that gift. In my next book I will share several more experiences and what I saw in that vision.

From the age of fourteen until nineteen I had about twenty of these visions and experiences. The Lord knows the who's and what's to help us be encouraged and direct us to the appointments in life He has set up. The hand of the Lord was upon me heavily because the foundation of my ministry was being established. The Holy Spirit has manifested the works of each office in me when the Lord required it to be so. But over the last fifteen years the gift of apostle has been manifested through the Holy Ghost more frequently. To me, the work is more important than someone believing that I'm called. Many are called, but few are chosen because of their obedience to the call.

180

We know that the ACTS of the apostles didn't cease with the 28th chapter of Acts (the only other book that has not finished being fulfilled or written is Revelation). Lastly, as I've studied Church history and examined the move of God in these last days, the gift of the apostle comes out of the Holy Ghost. I know there are apostles today, who have the qualifications that are necessary for the last day ministry and that can be found in Scripture. The present day apostle must be upon the foundation of the apostles of the Lamb, where Jesus is the chief cornerstone, their doctrine must be the godly anointed Word of the Holy Scripture and a personal relationship with the chief Apostle Jesus Christ.

We must take the attitude and position of the Apostle Paul. Paul's authority and commendation were from God, not man.

For we dare not compare ourselves with some that commend themselves, but them measuring themselves among themselves are not wise. But we will not boast of things without our measure, but according to the measure of the rule, which God hath distributed to us, a measure to reach even unto you.

For we stretch not ourselves beyond our measure, as though we reached not onto you: for we are come as far as to you also in preaching the gospel of Christ: not boasting of things with out our measure that is, of other men's labors; but having hope, when your faith is increased, that we shall be enlarged by you according to our rule abundantly. To preach the gospel in the regions beyond you, and not to boast in another man's line of things made ready to our hand. But he that glorieth, let him glory in the Lord. For not he that commendeth himself is approved, but whom the Lord commendeth.

(II Corinthians 10:12-18)

If you're called and anointed by God, He has given you the measure and authority, not to brag, boast or try to outpreach or prophesy one another, but to build up the body to the high measure of Christ. The apostles' day isn't over in the Church.

Christ is the head of the body, but throughout New Testament Scripture they were used in authority even stirring up other gifts. And in this final hour why would God take away the position that best represent His authority in the earth; to build a house properly you don't destroy the foundation.

> *For I think that God hath set forth us the apostles last, as it were appointed to death; for we were made a spectacle unto the world, and to angels, and to man.*
>
> (I Corinthians 4:9)

The Apostle must be humble, obedient and prepared to suffer for the gospel. At no time are we to be in competition with ourselves or any other office. Paul said in 1 Corinthians 4:6,7,9 NLT,

> *Dear brothers and sister, I have used Apollos and myself to illustrate what I've been saying." If you pay attention to the Scriptures, you won't brag about one of your leaders at the expense of another. What makes you better than anyone else? What do you have that God hasn't given you? And if all you have is from God, why boast as though you have accomplished something on your own?" Then he adds, "But sometimes I think God has put us apostles on display, like prisoners of war at the end of a victor's parade, condemned to die."*

We have become a spectacle to the entire world, to people and angels alike. Our dedication to Christ makes us look like fools, but You are so wise! We are weak, but You are so powerful! You are well thought of but we are laughed at. To this very hour we go hungry and thirsty, without enough clothes to keep us warm. We have endured many beatings, and we have no homes of our own. We have worked wearily with our own hands to earn our living. We bless those who curse us. We are patient with those who abuse us. We respond gently when evil things are said about us. Yet we are treated like the world's garbage, like everybody's trash, right up to the present moment (9-13). This may look like a glamorous office, but trust me. If you don't know and have some doubt about your calling, apostle, prophet, etc...

then keep your mouth shut and serve the Lord with humility. Know this, whatever your call, there are demons and devils assigned by Satan to destroy, discourage, and deceive you. But God has anointed you for that office when He called you—anointed with power and the Holy Ghost to walk in your calling.

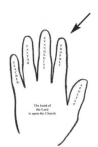

The authority of the Prophet –

The Pointer, Set Direction,
Points and Directs

Then the word of the Lord came unto me saying, Before I formed thee in the belly I knew thee; and before thou camest forth out of the womb I sanctified thee, and I ordained thee a prophet unto the nations. Then said I, ah, Lord God! Behold, I cannot speak: for I am a child. But the Lord said unto me, say not, I am a child: for thou shalt go to all that I shall send thee, and whatsoever I command thee, thou shalt speak. Be not afraid of their faces: for I am with thee to deliver thee saith the Lord. Then the Lord put forth his hand, and touched my mouth. And the Lord said unto me, Behold, I have put my words in thy mouth. See, I have this day set thee over the nations and over the kingdoms, to root out and to pull down, and to destroy, and throw down to build up and to plant.

(Jeremiah 1:4-10)

It appears that Jeremiah's ministry was predestined for the purpose of God. The Scriptures also state that *"for whom he did foreknow he also predestinated to be conformed to the image of his Son"* (Romans 8:29). God has foreknowledge. He knows ahead of time what the outcome will be. God sets circumstances into motion. He orders the courses of life to bring glory to His Name. Before the foundations of the world, God was at work. He has solved the problems we encounter before they are ever introduced to us. The catch is you must walk in the authority to experience and witness the success of your destiny.

Many people allow life challenge to be the champion, they neglect the powerful potential that God has placed in them. What if Jeremiah had not heard the prophetic voice of God about his future? Israel's status was already in dire straits. Their backsliding would lead again to more captivity. Israel might have said that God wouldn't deliver us from our captors. Being so rebellious has led them again away in chains and shackles. But their problem wasn't the slave master. For their captors were only one of the sources that God was using to rid them of their backsliding. God wanted Israel to conform to His image and stop being so hardheaded and rebellious. God spoke to Jeremiah, *"Be not afraid of their faces for I am with thee to deliver thee."* The deliverer needed deliverance because he had not matured into his prophetic call. "God's hand touched his mouth. And the Lord said unto me, Behold, I have put my words in thy mouth." When dealing with hardheaded people you need all the help you can get.

God's Word is law. It's backed up with authority. Jeremiah needed to know his authority when dealing with Israel. God would back him in every area of his ministry. Jeremiah had authority over kingdoms and principalities. Looking at their faces doesn't determine where they stand in the matter. It can't affect where you stand. If you are given authority over them, you have no reason to be afraid of their principalities, powers, the rulers of the darkness of this world, spiritual wickedness in high places according to Eph. 6:12.

Jeremiah was ordained, formed and brought forth as a prophet to root out, to pull down, and to destroy and throw down that which exalts itself against the purposes and place of God.

He also had as much authority to build and to plant that which brings glory to God and establish God's Kingdom in the midst of Israel's trial period. When walking in obedience, the same prophet who pronounced destruction can also declare jubilee and blessings. Israel obeying God was the position that he wanted to establish through Jeremiah's ministry. The prophet must be ready to

184

revenge all disobedience, when their obedience is fulfilled. When God is delivering the deliverer, they are given authority to cast down satanic and demonic strongholds and deliver the captive for their oppressors.

Sometimes deliverance is a process. Spiritual deliverance deals with things in the spirit of man, physical deliverance deals with the flesh of man and natural deliverance deals with the soul or mind of man. All of these areas must be subject to God before the building process can be completed. God has a plan and purpose. We must get in the position to establish His authority first in us as believers, then in our surroundings and abroad. The prophet Jeremiah is just one of the prime examples of a prophet in Scripture that God is using as a model for today's prophets.

THE GIFT OF THE PROPHET

This is the most common office in Scripture, from the days of the flood. Noah preached and prophesied coming events. Prophet is the gift of speaking under the inspiration of God's Spirit. It includes both prediction and proclamation, and neither one should be minimized despite the abuse of the gift today. The role of a prophet and the gift of prophecy are not necessarily one in the same. There are prophets who prophesy and preach because of their anointing, yet there are times when the gift of prophecy is upon the individual and they do not hold the office of a prophet but are being used. Some prophecies can come by the Holy Spirit moving in a setting. It doesn't matter who holds what office or how mature or deep they are in Christ. Most people think that prophets are strange and mystical. But Jesus is the best example of a prophet, and if the prophet or prophetess doesn't walk in love and harmony with the Holy Spirit, he or she needs deliverance and a spiritual check-up. By the way, this goes for any office. Your gift will make room for you, not give you an excuse to be rude or arrogant. Christ the Head of the body gave gifts to the body to help, not hurt the body. Listen, apostle and prophet, you act as though the body belongs to you and sometimes you think you have unrestricted control over God's property. Humble yourselves and learn how to serve the local Church. If God has called you then He will give sufficient ability to carry out the task in love and kindness. I've met people who were afraid of the apostles and prophets. When they met them there was no love and because of intimidation you abused the gift. That's not the purpose of the gift.

This reminds me of a story I heard. A father bought his sons a cute little puppy, and the boys fell in love with it. They took care of it; they groomed and washed it every day. They fed it four times a day and played in the yard with their pet. But now the summer had passed and school was starting back again; the children were enrolled in a distant boarding school. It was time to leave their home and travel to school. During the year, the family would visit them. This was easier to do rather than have the kids fly home on a plane with strangers.

Time had arrived again for the kids to come home for the summer and after their arrival, the first thing they wanted to see and enjoy was their gift. But time has made a change in their pet. They went to the backyard and asked their father who stole the cute little puppy and replaced it with this furious rottweiler. The gift had grown out of their control. The father had control, but the children were afraid! Remember the father is there to protect the children, because they are his seed. A good father knows how to give good gifts to his children even if he has to replace them from time-to-time. Don't let time cause you to abuse the gift of prophecy.

The gift of prophecy is so important for the body to walk in their authority. Prophecy sets you up on the present and next move of God. It reveals God's action in every situation. Remember, there's no authority outside the will and move of God. The prophet also manifests the word of wisdom. This is revelation concerning the divine purpose in the will of God. He will speak of the things to come. A prophet is a discerner of spirits, has sharp insight into the life of a believer, understands motives and intentions, hears and sees in the spiritual realm. Also the Word of knowledge is knowing facts about people, places, or situations past, present and future. The prophet must have night vision.

This is the ability to see in the dark matters, closed matters and reveal the hidden things.

One of the first prophecies in Scripture is,

And the Lord God said unto the serpent, because thou hast done this, thou art cursed above all cattle, and above every beast of the field, upon thy belly shalt thou go, and dust shalt thou eat all the days of thy life: and I will put enmity between thee and the woman and between they seed and her seed: it shall bruise thy heal and thou shalt bruise his heel.

(Genesis 3:14-15)

God takes prophecy seriously. It expresses part of the authority He gave to the body through the life, death, and resurrection of His Son.

But unto every one of us is given grace according to the measure of the gift of Christ. Wherefore he saith when he ascended up on high, he led captivity captive and gave gifts unto men

(Ephesians 4:7-8)

Just as God prophesied upon Satan concerning his demise, defeat and loss of authority, He also spoke of our victory, triumphant and spoils of victory (now that He ascended, what is it but that He also descended first into the lower part of the earth? He that descended is the same also that ascended up far above all heavens, that He might fill all things.), and He gave some apostles, and some prophets. Satan had some authority and some gifts. But the power of the resurrection revealed the relationship that Adam lost. Jesus took it all back, gifts included.

Just as there are false apostles there are false prophets; I think there are more prophets in this day (at least more people calling themselves prophets). So the chance of more false prophets is expected. On a positive note, God spoke to Joel saying,

And it shall come to pass, afterward, that I will pour our my spirit upon all flesh; and your sons and your daughters

shall prophesy, your old men shall dream dreams, your young men shall see vision.

(Joel 2:28)

It's important to remember that gifts come before repentance. At best, we prophesy in part. But after awhile we will know it all. Prophecy is a powerful gift that is recognized by God's divine authority. And the Spirit of the prophets are subject to the prophets. Yes man or woman of God, you can hold your peace.

For God is not the author of confusion but of peace as in all churches of the saints.

(I Corinthians 14:32-33)

The Evangelist – the Preacher is a reacher–It goes a little further than others.

Euaggelistes from euaggelizo – to announce good news, the gospel. (er, yoo; neut of a prim (food); adv well: - good, well (done).

There are several stages of evangelism in the New Testament.

1. Pre-Christ – John the Baptist   St.   Matthew   3:1-12
2. Present Christ period – Christ and the disciples St. Matthew 4:17; 10-1, ect.
3. Post-Christ period – Apostles Day of Pentecost St. Matthew 28:18-20; Act 2. ect

Yes, John the Baptist did the work of an evangelist. When we take a closer look at his ministry, John was very productive in compelling people to hear the Good News. He spoke with authority and power. John's services were not in the synagogues or temples, but outside open-air services, preaching, teaching, and baptizing them immediately. In these days came John the Baptist, preaching in the wilderness of Judaea, and saying:

Repent ye: for the kingdom of heaven is at hand. Then went out to him Jerusalem, and all Judea, and all region round about Jordan; and were baptized of him in Jordan; confessing their sins.

(St. Matthew 3:1-2;5-7)

John was such a great evangelist that all the countryside came to hear this explosive message. Jesus said, *"of those born of woman, there had not risen one greater than John the Baptist."* John preached an evangelistic message that stormed the Kingdom of heaven like a Macy's Day Half-Off Sale. John started the New Testament off with evangelism. Preach an uncompromising message: John preached revival and started a riot.

Jesus continues the evangelism by manifesting Christ and the Kingdom of God after the temptation in the wilderness:

"Now when Jesus had heard that John was cast into prison he departed into Galilee." (St. Matthew 4:12)

Jesus became the evangelist of the hour. From that time, Jesus began to preach, and to say, *"Repent: for the kingdom of heaven is at hand."* Notice John preached the same message in the wilderness.

Jesus preached in the towns and cities. And Jesus went about all Galilee teaching in the synagogues and preaching the gospel of the kingdom, and healing all manner of sickness and all manner of disease among the people. And his fame went throughout all Syria and they brought unto him all sick people that were taken with divers diseases and torments and those which were possessed with devils and those, which were lunatic, and

189

those that had the palsy and he healed them. And there followed him great multitudes of people from Galilee, and from Decapolis and from Jerusalem and from Judaea, and from beyond Jordan.

(St. Matthew 4:23-25)

The work of a true evangelist is authority over devils, changing lives, destroying yokes and preaching the good news of the Kingdom of God.

And Jesus came and spake unto them saying, all power is given unto me in heaven and in earth. Go ye there fore and teach all nations, baptizing them in the name of the Father and of the Son and of the Holy Ghost: Teaching them to observe all things whatsoever I have commanded you: and lo, I am with you always, even unto the end of the world. Amen.

(St. Matthew 28:18-20)

This is the gift of carrying the gospel throughout the world. It is the gift that specializes in preaching the Good News to the world. Missionaries are also called evangelists. All believers must do the work of an evangelist, but all believers aren't called to be evangelists. Every church needs the ministry of evangelism operating. Jesus went from town to town preaching the Kingdom of heaven is at hand, and God backed His ministry. God anointed Him with the Holy Ghost and Jesus went about doing good, healing all that was oppressed by the devil.

In St. Matthew the 10th chapter, Jesus sent His apostles out on evangelist crusades and many signs, miracles, and wonders took place. The gift of the evangelist extends the borders of the New Testament Church. That's when the work and the anointing will show strong when one performs the work of an evangelist. Philip is also an example of his ministry in action (Acts the 8th chapter). Also, study the work in Samaria, how the deacon/evangelist turns the city upside down and preaches Jesus.

The authority of the believer was strong in the life of Philip. When he finished the role that the Holy Spirit had him to perform in Samaria, Philip called for the apostle to be established during the work in Samaria. He didn't try to set up a ministry headquarters or create a five-year revival for financial security. Philip was led by the Lord and kept personal interests out of spiritual work and God blessed him to go to the next job in Azotes and preach all the way to Caesarea.

The Pastor – the ring finger. It connects the groom to the bride.

The word "pastor" means "shepherd"—Greek. Poi: men, a supervisor, feed rule. There's only one true shepherd, Jesus Christ of Nazareth, but there are many under shepherds, supervisors, feeders and rulers. Jesus said, *"I am the Good Shepherd, the Good shepherd giveth his life for the sheep."* (St. John 10:11) The gifts of the pastor is in full operation when a shepherd give his life for his sheep. He must have a life of prayer; every sheep in the fold needs a prayer covering, someone praying in the spirit for them, with them and about them.

By nature sheep need guidance. There's a time in all of our lives when we don't make the right decisions, or the best choices. Many times we stray away from the fold and protection, but a praying shepherd will ask God to lead us and protect us even when we don't deserve it. Moses was a good under-shepherd who had a congregation of approximately four million. I wonder how many times Moses had to stand in the gap for a hard-headed, stiff-necked, unappreciating group of complainers. Israel kept Moses praying. Standing in the gap was a daily activity for Moses. Yes, this pastor gave his life and opportunity for the Promised Land because of the people. After awhile of ministering to His disciples,

Jesus asked the question, *"Who do men say that I the Son of man am?"* We know the story, how some said John the Baptist and others said one of the prophets, but they were only at first saying what others said about him. But when He asked them, they really had no answer of their own, until the spirit of God revealed it unto Peter. I wonder what would have happened if Jesus had not asked them this question or Peter was absent that day.

Do you know your pastor by the spirit or have you come to know the fleshly man? This is a gift with authority and power. He's a doorway to revelation and enlightenment. God has given him a charge to keep. His time is valuable and his efforts must not be taken for granted. A pastor must lead with joy, but when the congregation is not willing to submit and walk in total obedience, then his work becomes grievously irritating. Please don't grieve your pastor. Souls can be lost and lives will continue in bondage, if your pastor does his job without support.

His Own Dreams and Visions

I wonder how many pastors have said, "If I wasn't a pastor, I'd be rich, successful and happy." Surprise! I know! I've said it, my pastor friends have said it and many others, if they would be honest and confess. We have the most powerful position on the planet second to none. But people make us want to quit and find employment immediately somewhere else. Our congregation thinks that we are rich so that's why they don't give tithes and offerings. Then they complain about where the money is going. After they give that whole dollar, they wonder why we have programs to send the pastor on a three-day vacation, from Wednesday after Tuesday night Bible study to Saturday evening, so he can prepare for Sunday morning.

Now I know that this is not the scenario in every church, but there are hundreds of pastors leaving the ministry every month. There are thousands suffering from "burnout". Did you know that 65% of pastors make less than minimum wage? Eighty-five percent of pastors don't have medical insurance. Ninety percent don't have a retirement plan worth discussing. I believe that 80% of the souls who are saved are directly led by a pastor, but his salary matches 20% of his own congregation. It is a shame how we have treated the core gift of the five-fold ministry. The pastor's gift is the one gift that the church can't do without. But they take more abuse than any other office. The average pastor's daily activities range from taxi driver to dishwasher. I once read that a housewife's duties are so many that if she were paid a fair salary in today's market, it would be $80,000 a year, with a month's vacation. And we know how valuable a housewife is. She's super-mom.

The average pastor, not the televangelist or those boys who are blessed to pastor thousands, but I'm talking about the pastor of 25, 100 and maybe 500 people, the small churches, storefronts, school cafeterias, etc., these pastors work hard. Many times, 8-12 hours on a secular job, then free for the church. They take their own family time and money to keep the church from closing and/or splitting. Many times is the mortgage on their homes diverted, the car payment, made late, or family vacation funds disappear to the church because someone in the church got angry and didn't tithe that month. Sometimes the pastor has another lady stealing his attention, his wife gets jealous, but can't say anything because the other women are the church and ministry. His children are hurt because the people mistreat their parents and they are caught in the crossfire of a leader trying to please two families. Most pastors don't complain because they try to practice what they preach. When one pastor fails, in the mindset of some people all of them are failures, they blame the closest pastor to them. Sometimes folks leave the church because of what a pastor across town did. I wonder why we don't stop to call 911 when a policeman is dirty, or defend ourselves when a lawyer is crooked, or operate on ourselves when a doctor makes a mistake. Please appreciate and respect the gift of the pastor because Jesus Himself is our great shepherd, the pastor of our souls.

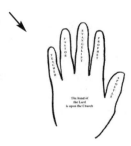

The teacher – small enough for every office to accommodate, every office must teach.

The teacher – didaskalos – an instructor (gen. Or spec.): doctor, master, teacher; to guide the studies of; to impart the knowledge of doctrine.

To receive the gift of authority you must have a teachable spirit. To teach, you must be taught. Teaching is the daily substance of life that is needed from day-to-day to fulfill and enjoy your purpose, plans and position in life. Teaching is the glue that makes preaching, prophesying, psalms, hymns and any other act of God's Word applicable.

And it came to pass, when Jesus had ended these sayings,
the people were astonished at his doctrine: for he taught
them as one having authority, and not as the scribes.

The Savior, our Apostle, Prophet, Good Shepherd taught people the ways of God while He was evangelizing. To receive your healing, you must be taught on how to trust God. To receive the financial blessing, you must be taught to give tithes and offering. To have a successful marriage, you must be taught the principles of finding a wife, intimacy, communications and patience. To raise children in this perplexed society, you must be taught on how to train up a child, because if the Holy Ghost hasn't taught you, how can you be a good leader exercising the gift itself? The gift will teach you to handle your experiences. A good leader will teach by his experiences in God and the Word of God. God sends His authority by the Holy Ghost. His job is to teach them to observe all things, whatsoever Jesus has commanded us... this is the great commission.

This nation must be taught the ways of God. The reason we have so many complex problems in this society is because we aren't teaching the Word of God. We teach the M.E.S.S. Math, English, Science, Social Study and a foreign language, but nothing in our public schools teaches about the values, principles and commandments of God. This is offensive, disturbing to some and a spiritual mistake to others. Especially in these troubled times. We already have secular humanism. Our school system has become a training ground for more suicide bombers. The school system already has kids with guns, knives, and drugs. Let's pray for teachers and students to get good Christian teaching, great home teaching on morals and a personal relationship with the Holy Spirit.

Jesus is the real teacher we need in our lives. Yes, I know that we allowed prayer to be taken out of the school. As long as there are tests and tough teachers our children will pray. As long as they're lunatics bringing guns and knives, children and teachers will be praying. I know this sounds awkward, but at the end of the day, trust me, it's true. Yes, I hope we get at least a quiet time in every school morning, midday or at last period for corporate prayer led by a Holy Ghost filled, Bible-believing teachers, students and principles.

When we learn to be taught then we can realize the authority that's already ours. We don't have to wait too long to fulfill the Great Commission.

But ye shall receive power after that the Holy Ghost is come upon you. And ye shall be witnesses unto me both in Jerusalem, and in all Judaea, and in Samaria, and unto the uttermost part of the earth.

(Acts 1:8)

All of these people must be taught the Word of God. God will, through the Holy Ghost, back the teaching with demonstrations of signs, wonders, and miracles. In order to get them to believe, you must do like Philip with the Ethiopian in Acts the 8th chapter.

And Philip ran thither to him and heard him read the prophet Esaias, and said understandest thou what thou readest? And he said, How can I, except some man should guide me? And he desired Philip that he would come up and sit with him.

(Acts 8:30-31)

The man was hungry for revelation and had the Scripture in his hands; but he needed a teacher, a preacher to explain the Word of God. Philip was filled with the Holy Ghost (the great teacher and guide for all believers) and the Ethiopian was searching for truth. How many people do you know who have a Bible, can read but never get revelation or proper interpretation because they don't have the Holy Ghost, Bible training, or some anointed leader teaching them with authority? They can't understand. When was the last time you stopped a chariot and got on board to bring life to a dying soul? So many church folks have a form of godliness, but no power or revelation. *"Go ye into the entire world teaching them what I taught you,"* said the Lord. Become an A.C.T.S. walker and start where you are, allowing the Holy Ghost to teach through you.

THE POSITION

Jesus' manifested the five-fold ministry with unlimited authority, from the baptism by John to the cross. And after the resurrection, He shared His gifts. Throughout His ministry, angels, demons, devils, kings, governors, Scribes, Pharisees and centurions recognized that Jesus had authority from God.

And when Jesus was entered into Capernaum, there came unto him a centurion, beseeching him, and saying Lord, my servant lieth at home sick of the palsy, grievously tormented. And Jesus saith unto him, I will come and heal him. The centurion answered and said, Lord, I am not worthy that thou shouldest come under my roof: but speak the word only, and my servant shall be healed. For I am a man under authority, having soldiers under me; and I say to this man go and he goeth; and to another come and he cometh; and to my servant, do this and he doeth it. When

Jesus heard it, he marveled and said to them that followed,
verily, I say unto you, I have not found so great faith, no not
in Israel.

(St. Matthew 8:5-10)

The centurion had no doubt that Jesus held a position of authority. He understood protocol. Please learn protocol and soveriegnity. Then not only will your gift work, but all of heaven's host will assist you in ministry.

Are they not all ministering spirits, sent forth to minister
for them whoso shall be heirs of salvation?

(Hebrew 1:14)

We have angels that travaileth over our next decision, they are ascending soldiers of God here to assist the believers and they go where God assigns them. Also Paul said in Romans:

We have the Spirit of God that leads us and maketh
intercession for us with groaning which cannot be uttered.
And he that searcheth the hearts knoweth what is the mind
of the Spirit because he maketh intercession for the saints
according to the will God.

(Romans 8:26-27)

The gifts that Jesus has given us will release the power and authority in our lives.

Wherefore I put thee in remembrance that thou stir up the
gift of God, which is in thee by the putting on of my
hands.

(2 Timothy 1:6)

Paul tells us that if your gift is stagnated find an anointed leader and let him lay hands on you to release authority in your life. So we have others so they can help us fulfill our purpose. Most of all, we have Jesus the Author and Finisher of our faith; *who for the joy that was set before him endured the cross, despising the shame, and is set down at the right hand of the throne of God.* The author is the writer, the founder. He knows all about it. He's the finisher. He has completed the job before you start. In His perfect will there's no embarrassing moments, no uncertainties, no doubts about the victory.

Jesus has laid the foundation and opened up the way. He led captivity captive, He has all power in His hands, He has conquered the grave and took the sting from death and gave gifts unto men. Let it be known throughout the heavenlies that Jesus is the Christ, the Son of God, proven by His own testimony. *"No man taketh away my life, I will lay it down and take it up in three days."* Jesus, the Father and the Holy Spirit are working as one in the resurrection. The Father said *"This is my beloved Son in whom I'm well pleased."* The Son said, *"Into thine hands I command My spirit and after the third day the Holy Spirit said, it's time to get up!"* But while His physical body was in the grave (Jesus) the Christ-man went to hell and delivered the captive, He also chained the devil and took the keys, declared victory over the grave, took the sting from death, all of this was just before breakfast. From death to resurrection:

And behold, the veil of the temple was rent in twain from the top to the bottom and the earth did quake and the rocks rent, and the grave were opened and many bodies of the saints which slept arose and came out of the graves after his resurrection and went into the holy city, and appeared unto many.

(St. Matthew 27:51-53)

What did the resurrected saints say to the people of the Holy City? I believe that they testified that Jesus came down and set us free. We're on our way to heaven and He was so kind as to allow us a few hours to stop by and testify the truth. He has all power and authority and some spoils (gifts) for the Church. You witness His triumphant entrance in Jerusalem several days ago and then you crucified Him. But we witnessed His triumphal departure, and we glorify and honor Him.

Jesus is presently seated on the right hand of God, a place of honor and authority, and according to the prayer of Jesus in St John 17:9-10,

198

I pray for them: I pray not for the world, but for them which thou hast given me for they are mine. And all mine are thine, and thine are mine; and I am glorified in them.

The gifts are given to mature the Church to the position that we can glorify Jesus Christ. The Church must know the place of God. He gives us gifts and talents and called us out of darkness to spread the gospel to as many that will receive it and be living epistles, prime examples of apostles, prophets, evangelists, pastors and teachers to the Body of Christ and the light of the world. Our position is that we are truly the light in a dark world, the city that is seated upon the hills.

*As he is so are we to this world. There is no **fear** in love; but perfect love casteth out fear: because **fear** hath torment. He that feareth is not made perfect in love.*
(I John 4:17B, 18)

*For God hath not given us the spirit of **fear**; but of power and of love and of a sound mind. Be not thou therefore ashamed of the testimony of our Lord, nor of me his prisoner: But be thou partaker of the afflictions of the gospel according to the power of God.*
(II Timothy 1:7-8)

We have all of this plus more, working for us. How can we live defeated lives? I believe it takes a great effort on our behalf to fail. It's certainly not in the plan of God.

CHAPTER TEN

The Authorized Believer

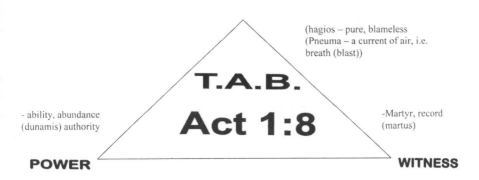

HOLY GHOST

(hagios – pure, blameless
(Pneuma – a current of air, i.e.
breath (blast))

T.A.B.

Act 1:8

- ability, abundance
(dunamis) authority

-Martyr, record
(martus)

POWER   WITNESS

Have you ever heard the expression," Keep a tab on it?" This sometimes means, watch or keep track of the expenditures, because we don't want the final cost to go over a particular amount. A TAB is also a projection or a short strip attached to an object to facilitate opening, handling or identification. Sometimes when discussing a tab, we're talking about a bill or a check, as far as a meal in a restaurant. But most of the time, when we hear or use TABS, we're dealing with some cost to account for.

As we begin this chapter on The Authorized Believer (TAB), we're still counting up the cost to walk in our position of authority.

But ye shall receive power, after that the Holy Ghost is come upon you and ye shall be witness unto me both in Jerusalem, and in all Judaea and in Samaria, and unto the uttermost parts of the earth.

(Acts 1:8)

Now please keep a T.A.B. on this. There is cost involved to receive power to be a witness perhaps at great expense if you're a young rich ruler. Maybe you might be asked to give up everything. If you're a widow woman with your last morsel of bread, you might be required to feed the prophet. If you live in the palace, you might go to prison for righteous living. You might have to love not your life until death. So keep accurate your T.A.B. on this walk with God. You're a witness of His Holy Ghost power; you're a record keeper with power and authority.

I remember watching the Olympic basketball games when I was a child. I believe the Americans were playing the Russians; the game was close and the Americans had never lost to anyone. They had their job cut out for them that day. The Russians were a very good team and were playing their best game. It all came down to the final seconds on the clock. I don't actually remember all that happened, but I do remember this, the buzzer sounded and the Americans thought they had won the game. Then someone came out of the audience acting like he had the authority to put seconds back on the clock. This gentlemen went to the officials and referees and persuaded them to change the time on the clock. By doing so they changed the outcome of the game. Well as fate would have it, the Russians scored and the buzzer sounded.

The American players stood in disbelief! I imagine they felt powerless. Who was this person, where did he come from, and who gave him the authority to add seconds to an already determined outcome? What was supposed to be a golden moment turned tarnish. The American team boycotted the award ceremonies and refused to this day to accept the second place silver metal. Now there may be some difference in how the story unfolded, but that's the way I remember it. By the way, who was that guy anyway? Surely he was not authorized to make such a call!

Remember:

When the righteous are in the authority, the people rejoice: but when the wicked beareth rule, the people mourn.

(Proverbs 29:2)

I walked into a place of business one day to get an approval on some paperwork. It had to be signed and approved by this particular agency. I thought that this would be easy, because everyone there was dressed professionally and looking like they were important. I was as usual, very professional and polite. I walked up to the counter and asked for direction. The young lady on the other side of the desk was having a bad day, she was mean and nasty. I wondered if I had come at a bad time. I admit my voice is heavy and melodious, because I am a minister. Maybe she thought I was going to preach or complain. I knew then this wasn't going to be easy. For the sake of peace, I smiled and cheered up my voice tone, but Ms. Thing was determined to be difficult. So I backed away from the counter to take inventory of the situation. I didn't want tension to escalate.

I decided that greater is He that is in me than him that's in the world. So, I decided to come back to the counter and use some Holy Ghost anointed authority. I refused to allow the devil to make me miss my blessing. The paperwork I had was to get the approval on the ministry's daycare. To this date the school has blessed thousands of disadvantaged children and improved the lives of low-income families. But the devil knew if he could stop it or hinder it, his kingdom of darkness would have a stronger grip on the community. After I finally broke through this barrier, I spoke to a supervisor who was worst than her receptionist. She said to me, "I wouldn't help you if I could." Wow! I just stared at her in amazement. I was in shock; you see, I was at the zoning department in the city of Fort Lauderdale office where my tax dollars pay their salaries. Now I know this wasn't a black thing, even though they were white. But this was a church thing. The devil hates real ministries, more than separation of black, brown, yellow and white. If we come together as races it isn't as threatening as when we gather as a mighty church of all colors. You want to see real authority? Go to the church where the Lord is leading you, rather than where the faces reside that you are familiar with. Everytime there is a major move of God, race has to take a backseat. There's only one race that matters, and the Holy Spirit has ordained it as the Christian race. Don't misread the essence of my message. At the end of the day, I still have to defend and make people aware that I am here. I'm one of God's creations and because of obedience, Jesus died and left me boss. Not only me, but also all who believe and trust His Word. We are the authorized believers.

Question: Who has the Power to control situations on the earth as it is in heaven?

Verily I say unto you, whatsoever ye shall bind on earth, shall be bound in heaven: and whatsoever ye shall loose on earth shall be loosed in heaven. Again I say unto you, that if two of you shall agree on earth as touching any thing that they shall ask, it shall be done for them of my Father, which is in heaven. For where two or three are gathered together in my name, there am I in the midst of them.

(St. Matthew 18:18-20). Answer: T.A.B.

Question: Who has the Power to control the Atmosphere, no matter what the circumstances?

And when he had called unto him his twelve disciples he gave them power against unclean spirits, to cast them out and to heal all manner of sickness and all manner of disease. And as ye go, preach, saying the kingdom of heaven is at hand. Heal the sick, cleanse the lepers, raise the dead, cast out devils: freely ye have received, freely give.

(St. Matthew 10:1,7-8). Answer T.A.B.

Question: Who has the Power over the flesh and things that hinder our Spirit?

For though we walk in the flesh, we do not war after the flesh for the weapons of our warfare are not carnal but mighty through God to the pulling down of strong holds, casting down imaginations and every high thing that exalteth itself against the knowledge of God and bringing into captivity every thought to the obedience of Christ; and having in a readiness to revenge all disobedience, when your obedience is fulfilled. Do ye look on things after the outward appearance? If any man trust to himself that he is Christ's let him of himself think this again, that as he is Christ even so are we Christ's. For though I should boast somewhat more of our authority, which the Lord hath given us for edification; and not for your destruction. I should not be ashamed.

(II Corinthians 10:3-8). Answer: T.A.B.

Question: Who has the Power of angels, the blood and testimonies of Victory?

And there was war in heaven: Michael and his angels fought against the dragon; and the dragon fought and his angels, and prevailed not; neither was there place found any more in heaven. And the great dragon was cast out; that old serpent, called the Devil and Satan, which deceiveth the whole world: he was cast out into the earth, and his angels were cast out with him, and I heard a loud voice saying in heaven, Now is come salvation, and strength, and the kingdom of our God, and the power of his Christ: for the accuser of our brethren is cast down, which accused them before our God day and night. And they overcame him by the blood of the Lamb and by the word of their testimony: and they loved not their lives unto death.

(Revelation 12:7-11). Answer T.A.B.

Question: Who has the Power of revelation knowledge?

Thou hast put all things in subjection under his feet. For in that he put all in subjection under him: he left nothing that is not put under him. But now we see not yet all things put under him.

(Hebrews 2:8). Answer T.A.B.

Question: Who has the Power over devils and demons but also their name is written in heaven?

And the seventy returned again with joy saying, Lord, even the devils are subject unto us through thy name. And he said unto them, I beheld Satan as lightning fall from heaven. Behold, I give unto you power to tread on the serpents and scorpions, and over all the power of the enemy: and nothing shall by any means hurt you. Not withstanding in this rejoices not, that the spirits are subject unto you, but rather rejoice, because your names are written in heaven.

(St. Luke 10:17-20). Answer T.A.B.

Question: Who has Power to work at every level, irregardless of whom is present?

And he withdrew himself into the wilderness, and prayed. And it came to pass on a certain day, as he was teaching, that there where Pharisees and doctors of the law sitting by, which were come out of every town of Galilee, and Judaea and Jerusalem: and the power of the Lord was present to heal them.

(St. Luke 5:16-17). Answer T.A.B.

Question: Who has the Power of seeking the Kingdom first, then possession of all things?

(For after all these things do the Gentiles seek:)

For your heavenly Father knoweth that ye have need of all these things, But seek ye, first the kingdom of God, and his righteousness; and all these things shall be added unto you.

(Matthew 6:32-33) Answer T.A.B.

The purpose of the believer's authority started long before the Church age. We can trace events from when Satan was kicked out of heaven into the earth.

How art thou fallen from heaven O Lucifer, son of the morning! How art thou cut down to the ground, which didst weaken the nations! For thou has said in thine heart, I will ascend into heaven; I will exalt my throne above the stars of God: I will sit also upon the mount of the congregation in the sides of the north: I will ascend above the heights of the clouds: I will be like the most High. Yet thou shalt be brought down to hell, to the sides of the pit.

(Isaiah 14:12-15)

Satan has a lot to do with the believer's authority because after his rebellion in heaven, he was cast down to earth. Satan decided that he could rule the heavens and earth through God's own creation. I guess Satan figured that would cause creation to rebel also against the Creator. Maybe he figured that all of God's hope was in what He saw. And if he could destroy it God would pay for cutting him out of the eternal ruleship plan. So Satan said within himself, I'll gain entrance into mankind and destroy God and man from within. It seems that God had placed so much trust in mankind. I'll deceive and destroy them, I'll make them curse God to His face and surely God will have to destroy them because of their rebellious ways.

So Satan enters as a snake in the Garden of Genesis and became a dragon by the time he reached Revelation. But along the way, things didn't work according to his plans and purposes.

They that see thee shall narrowly look upon thee, and consider thee saying, Is this man that made the earth to tremble, that did shake kingdoms: that made the world as a wilderness, and destroyed the cities thereof. That opened not the house of his prisoner? All the kings of the nations even all of them, lie in glory, every one in his own house. But thou art cast out of their grave like an abominable branch and as the raiment of those that are

slain, thrust through with a sword, that go down to the
stones of the pit; as a carcass, trodden under feet.
(Isaiah 14:16-19)

The big bad devil is defeated and shall be disposed of. He is and shall be cast out, cut down like road kill laying aside the Highway of Eternity. Who will expose him? The answer is the T.A.B. Doing the A.C.T.S. walk. They've been informed about their authority. They know their purpose, God's plan and their position. We have the keys of authority, the keys of the Kingdom, and we know the difference between warfare and welfare. Every believer that has a teachable spirit can be trained to defeat Satan from the first fight to the final battle. Now these are the things that the devil doesn't want you to know. He will try to stop the flow of God into your life, stagnate the anointing and keep you in the dark about your destiny. But we will teach you about night vision, the ability to see the unseen, hear the unheard and touch the untouchable, to dispose and expose with a overwhelming suppose!

The devil started his plot in the Mountain of God, and Jesus defeated him in the Garden of Gethsemane. In Eden Adam lost his authority to Satan. In Gethsemane, Jesus defeated Satan and restored authority. Sometimes the battle between Jesus and Satan is fought in mankind's submission to one or the other. The world is subject to Satan and the Church must be subject to Jesus, our Messiah and Deliverer. David recorded in Psalms,

Why do the heathen rage, and the people imagine a vain
thing? The kings of the earth set themselves and the
rulers take counsel together, against the Lord, and
against His anointed saying, "Let us break their bands
asunder, and cast away their cords from us. He that
sitteth in the heavens shall laugh: the Lord shall have
them in derision." Then shall he speak unto them in his
wrath, and vex them in his sore displeasure. Yet have I set
my king up on my holy hill of Zion. I will declare the
decree: the Lord hath said unto me, Thou art my son; this
day have I begotten thee. Ask of me, and I shall give thee

the heathen for thine inheritance, and the uttermost parts
of the earth for thy possession.

(Psalm 2:1-8)

I know that this is a Messianic Psalm, dealing with how the Lord is to be rejected, but Jesus said, *"If they reject me then they will reject God and you the believer. If they persecute me than they will persecute you also."* The rejecters and persecutors are from the seed of Satan. Satan has planted his seed in them and they are fulfilling their father's will in the earth. The Lord will laugh at them and cause them to experience derision or ridicule, God will mock them because of their stupidity. The Lord shall deal harshly with them. The place and position Satan has been trying to achieve that is to set upon the Holy Hill, because of his rebellion he lost it. And God shall set us up as kings and priests because of our obedience and submission to the Word of God. In the earth God has given us all we need to defeat Satan.

Psalm 2: 8 said,
Ask of me and I shall give thee the heathen for thine inheritance, and the uttermost part of the earth for my possession.

Ask for the things that Satan has stolen and God said I would give them back to the believer. Remember, God is reconciling the world back to Himself and He will not force it, but love it with kindness. The heathen rage because Satan has deceived them. But when faced with the authority of a true believer they have no might to resist.

"The earth is the Lord's and the fullness thereof, the world and they that dwell within." All belong to God even the uttermost parts of the earth belong to God. So the devil has no rights to anything. Jesus told His disciples, *"But ye shall receive power, after that the Holy Ghost is come upon you"* and *"Ye **shall** be witnesses unto me in both Jerusalem, and all Judaea, and in Samaria, and unto the uttermost part of the earth."* (Acts1:8)

This of course is after the resurrection. Satan was defeated, and lost power and authority, this fulfilled a promised. Remember, the Word (shall) guarantees a promise. Next let's find the plan of action to make all of this work according to God's purpose.

THE PLAN FOR AUTHORITY

And he gave some, apostles; and some prophets; and some, evangelists; and some, pastors and teachers; for the perfecting of the saints, for the work of the ministry, for the edifying of the body of Christ. Till we all come in the unity of the faith and of the knowledge of the Son of God unto a perfect man, unto the measure of the stature of the fullness of Christ: that we henceforth be no more children tossed to and fro, and carried about with every wind of doctrine, by the sleight of men, and cunning craftiness, whereby they lie in wait to deceive. By speaking the truth in love, may grow up into him in all things, which is the head, even Christ: from whom the whole body fitly joined together and compact by that which every joint supplieth, according to the effectual working in the measure of every part, maketh increase of the body unto the edifying of itself in love.

(Ephesians 4:11-16)

God has given grace according to the measure—what is the measure that has been given? Whatever the needs are at any given time, God has given grace for it. Grace is given to make us sufficient in all things that we may abound to every good work. God will release more authority when we learn and mature in our calling. The Church must be perfected (mature) to work in the ministry and the authority is released as the Father's will and work is performed. Let us look further at the gifts that Christ gave to the Church.

The Authority of the Believers (Acts 2:42-3:13)

And they continued steadfastly in the apostle's doctrine and fellowship, and in breaking of bread, and in prayers. And fear came upon every soul: and many wonders and signs were done by the apostles. And all that believed were together, and had all things common and sold their possessions and good and parted them to all men, as every man had need. And they continuing daily with one accord in the temple and breaking bread from house to house, did eat their meat with gladness and singleness of heart, praising God and having favour with all the people. And the Lord added to the church daily such as should be saved.

(Acts 2:42-47)

The fear that came upon every soul was the result of the T.A.B.. Everyone acknowledged that God supernaturally used these men. The normal routine has been eclipsed by the power of God. Remember, wherever the power of God is enacted or active, His authority is present. These men walked with Jesus and presently received the Holy Ghost and power according to Acts 1:8—"POWER IS AUTHORITY." As a result of this power, the people submitted to their authority. People gave what was necessary to help those with genuine needs. This is not a form of communism with a dictatorship by natural force, but the work of the Holy Spirit through submitted men and women of God. They were focusing on the spiritual blessing and the fellowship and well-being of their brethren. When men seek the Kingdom of God, the real king appears and supernatural blessings follow. God began to demonstrate how His Kingdom system supercedes the worldly system.

Remember the studies in the previous chapter on how God used the five-fold ministries as representatives? They have the power of attorney to execute matters. They will go from glory to glory and established Kingdom principles. People will find that it is more blessed to submit to them and receive this same authority. The revelation of the corporate anointing was upon them. They knew that one could chase a thousand and two could put ten thousand to flight.

The believers were given power over the power of Satan, and they had the authority to cancel all of Satan's contracts. Because of sin, Satan has a right to attack many people's lives and without reservation he is doing his best to fulfill his purpose. Peter and John went up together in the temple at the hour of prayer, being the ninth hour. One of Satan's victims who was attacked before his birth (Satan is cruel to attack an unborn fetus) was a certain man lame from his mother's womb. He was carried and they laid him daily at the gate of the temple which is called Beautiful to ask alms of them who entered in the temple. This man was still suffering from birth unto now. He's about to be introduced to the apostles, the T.A.B. messengers of the Kingdom.

When he saw Peter and John about to go into the temple, he asked alms of them. The physical cry for help is only temporary. It lasts from day-to-day, pain-to-pain, sorrow-to-sorrow, never ending till death sets in. But a spiritual cry will move the hand of God. This cry speaks the language of faith. You will learn this language in the Dynamics of Spiritual Warfare Series (Triangle of Faith).

Peter, fastening his eyes upon him with John, said "Look on us." Peter was discerning who was asking for help. It's important not to cast your pearls before swine. Peter said to the man, "Look on us. We have the authorization by the manufacturer to replace the broken parts. We are authorized to do more than deal with the physical man." Then Peter said, "Silver and gold have I none; but such as I have give I thee: in the Name of Jesus Christ of Nazareth rise up and walk."

I don't think for a moment that Peter was broke or poor. After all, they had all things in common and usage of the treasury to distribute as the needs were. What I believe took this conversation to the next level was when he said in essence, "You're asking the wrong person (man) for the wrong thing (money). You don't know what you need so let me help you. Rise up and walk. Now you can help yourself and stop depending on others for what you have the ability to do." And as an extra incentive, Peter took him by the right hand (fellowship) and lifted him up: and immediately his feet and anklebones received strength. What if Peter had given him money and went on to prayer? That man would have spent the money and been placed in the same position the next day. Nothing would have been changed. The poor, hurting, etc...needs the gospel, warfare, not man's welfare. His physical challenge still would have been the champion or ruler of his life.

Peter showed him physically by lifting him, what was happening spiritually.

Faith with works reveals the intent of God. God already knows. He's waiting for the believer to ignite the warfare as an A.C.T.S. walker. The man lept, stood up, walked and entered with them into the temple, walking, and leaping and praising God. Because Peter allowed God to flow in him the man received a miracle and gave God the glory. You see why fear came upon every soul? These things weren't happening everyday. This was a public act that could be verified.

> *And all the people saw him walking and praising God: and they knew that it was he which sat for alms at the Beautiful gate of the temple: and they were filled with wonder and amazement at that which had happened unto him.*
>
> (Acts 3:9-10)

Amazement is expected when the T.A.B. walk in their authority while seeking the Kingdom of God in every matter. In every situation, we must see what God is doing or hear what God is saying, then follow through. Watch for the hand of the Lord moving. And as the lame man who was healed held Peter and John, all the people ran together wondering. We as believers will not leave them in a state of wonder and amazement. But plainly let them know that Jesus in the answer. And when Peter saw it, he answered unto the people,

> *Ye men of Israel why marvel ye at this? Or why look ye so earnestly on us, as though by our own power or holiness we had made this man walk. The God of Abraham and of Isaac, and of Jacob, the God of our fathers hath glorified his Son Jesus; whom ye delivered up, and denied him in the presence of Pilate, when he was determined to let him go.*
>
> (Act 3:12-13)

God is so good that even in the expo facto crucifixion of His Son, He still blessed His people.

Now the last question is, "What are you planning to do about your TAB? Are you going to submit to the fresh move of God or make excuses on why you can't pay the price for the power of God in your life?" How many crippled, hurting, or dying people are waiting for you to pay for the TAB?

STOP BEING A CHEAPSKATE.

CHAPTER ELEVEN

The Acts Walk
The Leading to Chapter 29!

When I was a young evangelist, one of the things that I enjoyed doing the most was breaking the powers of darkness upon people's lives. I had spent days, weeks, and months fasting and praying for a deliverance ministry. I wasn't married and had my own business, so time was under my control. There were services that I was a part of, when the move of God was so powerful that everyone in the building was slain by the Holy Ghost. I refused to pray for the last one or two people, because I didn't want to be the only one left standing. Sometimes the people would be slain for a half hour or more. So the two or three of us who were left standing would just talk and praise God. There were many salvations and miracles that took place. From time to time I visit some of those churches to see if the power of God is still flowing.

We experienced the days of Pentecost and dynamic street revivals. We didn't have TV cameras and the national media recording our every move. God has ordained the ACTS walk chapter 29 style for us in this last day. Most of the churches and ministries that opened their doors were small to medium congregations. Many had women pastors and high percentages were minorities. I don't today and didn't in the past, care about the size of the church, denomination, or the color of the people. All God wants is for people to be hungry for a move of God (an ACTS walk). I watch today's major ministries and appreciate

215

how far the church has come. Thank God for the pioneers of the past (Billy Graham, Rex Humbard, Oral Roberts, and T. L. Osbourn). You can see miracles, signs, and wonders on the big screen and Black, Asian and Latino pastors with national ministries. TBN and the 700 Club have a Pentecost anointing and are two of the most popular television ministries in the world. The Sky Angel Cable Network, B.E.T. Gospel and the Word Network allows us to see ministries that would have never had the exposure in times past. They don't seem to shy away from the move of God. But I've been in the trenches and nothing for me has come easy.

Presently, I pastor pastors and mentor leaders. I believe one day we will lead thousands of pastors. This vision is growing into a revelation worldwide ministry. Every step of the way, God has provided. Now that I'm older (not old), I know that the righteous will not be forsaken and His seed begging bread. We have the seed of God in us, which is the Word of God. The authority of the Word keeps us from becoming beggars and panhandlers.

The key to the ACTS Walk is obedience, submission, and availability. As a young man, obedience was something my father taught me. He told me to do it right the first time, tell the truth all the time because truth can stand alone, but a lie needs help. Obedience to me is a direct form of truth and trust. The ACTS walker must trust the leading of the spirit of the Lord, (spirit of truth). When we trust the truth, it is easy to obey or submit. Jesus Himself had to submit to the move of God. Jesus said, "The works that I do is what I see My father doing. I make myself available so that the Father can use Me." The Father doesn't use us and not provide for us. As we seek the rule and reign of God (Kingdom of God), obey Him, submit to His will, all things that the Father has become available to us as heirs of God. Remember Psalm 24:1, "The earth is the Lord's, and the fullness thereof; the world, and they that dwell therein." He knows how to lead us, protect us, and provide for us. He's Jehovah Jireh. As a young man, I learned how to fight the devil and as a mature Christian, I am learning to terrorize Satan. Yes, I'm fasting, praying, and studying the Word of God (doing homework). But now I have more authority and stability. I've been there and done that and I know it works.

God said in Joel 2:28,
And it shall come to pass afterward, that I will pour out my spirit upon all flesh; and your sons and your daughters shall prophesy, your old men shall dream dreams, your young men shall see visions.

This is to happen during and after Israel's restoration, what I call ACTS Chapter 29, the authorization of the last day church, "We shall be a force to be reckon with, a mighty army of one. That is led by one spirit, with one mind and no color, race, or denomination"

In Joel 3:9-10 God says,
Proclaim ye this among the Gentiles; prepare war, wake up the mighty men, let all the men of war draw near; let them come up: Beat your plowshares into swords and your pruning hooks into spears: let the weak say I am strong.

The Church must stop being a wimp and playing patty cake. We have a job to do. This isn't Mission Impossible; we are the winners, not the whiners. A winner is led by the spirit of God; a whiner isn't led by anything but complaints. Paul says in Philippians 4:13, *"I can do all things through Christ which strengtheneth me."* It's time to walk the walk and talk the talk. You are in Acts 29.

Romans 8:14-19,
For as many as are led by the Spirit of God, they are the sons of God. For as ye have not received the spirit of bondage again to fear; but ye have received the Spirit of adoption, whereby we cry Abba, Father. The Spirit itself beareth witness with our spirit that we are the children of God: And if children, then heirs, heirs of God and joint-heirs with Christ; if so be that we suffer with him, that we may also be glorified together. For I reckon that the sufferings of this present time are not worthy to be

compared with the glory, which shall be revealed in us. For the earnest expectation of the creature waiteth for the manifestation of the sons of God.

Look at what happens to the believer after the Holy Ghost comes—he receives power. The Holy Ghost possesses the Kingdom of God, and in the Kingdom there is power. When power or dynamite is used, it gets someone's attention. Kingdom living is explosive and the best place to set off your first explosion is home, casting out every devil and demon, because you have the authority to terrorize Satan's kingdom. So, where is it we need to go? And how do we apply this to today?

But ye shall receive power, after that the Holy Ghost is come upon you: and you shall be witnesses unto me both in Jerusalem, and in all Judaea and in Samaria, and unto the uttermost part of the earth.

(Act 1:8)

Let us Follow the Steps of the Early church

Jerusalem means "possession of peace." In the above context it means "home", starting with your immediate family and loved ones. Jerusalem is a place of peace and worship. This is where all beginners should get their experience and training in warfare and on how to use the weapons of warfare. Make all your mistakes in a place of peace and forgiveness. This is the place where the Church started and then spread out. There is a danger in staying in Jerusalem too long. It can become a comfort zone for the unproductive. The best way to stay in Jerusalem is to be a worshipper, intercessor, or a praiser. But DON'T SIT IN ZION TWIDDLING YOUR FINGERS. If you're assigned to Jerusalem, then keep active in the will of God.

David said, *"There is a river, the streams whereof shall make glad the city of God, the holy place of the tabernacles of the most High"* (Psalm 46:4). As believers, we are led by the Holy Spirit and witnesses to the goodness of God. That testimony is like a river flowing streams of salvation to whomever will hear it. Inside every believer is the riverbed that carries the flow of the

218

Holy Spirit. Be prepared. God may choose your river to overflow and flood all around you with the salvation message.

ACTS Walk

And when the day of Pentecost was fully come, they were all with one accord in one place. And suddenly there came a sound from heaven as of a rushing mighty wind, and it filled all the house where they were sitting. And there appeared unto them cloven tongues like as of fire, and it sat upon each of them. And they were filled with the Holy Ghost, and began to speak with other tongues, as the Spirit gave them utterance. And there were dwelling at Jerusalem Jews, devout men, out of every nation under heaven.

(Acts 2:1-5)

Pentecost. What a grand occasion to introduce the person of the Holy Spirit to the families of the earth. The Holy Spirit only testifies of Jesus Christ. The Life of Christ is the best witness of how much God loves mankind. We can see how powerful the home-based ministries of witnessing and testimonies are as we read Acts 2, verses 41 through 47 (see also verses 6-39).

Then they that gladly received his word were baptized: and the same day there were added unto them about three thousand souls. And they continued steadfastly in the apostles' doctrine and fellowship, and in breaking of bread, and in prayers. And fear came upon every soul: and many wonders and signs were done by the apostles. And all that believed were together, and had all things common; and sold their possessions and goods, and parted them to all men, as every man had need. And they, continuing daily with one accord in the temple, and breaking bread from house to house, did eat their meat with gladness and singleness of heart, praising God, and having favour with all the people. And the Lord added to the church daily such as should be saved.

(Acts 2:41-47)

The Trials of Your Faith

Judea, a Roman province, represents rural people outside of Jerusalem. This could symbolize your country, traveling from town to town a long distance away. To witness in Judea is more of a challenge than at home. Your testimony is tested; your faith is tried, your authority is scrutinized; but there is more warfare than there is welfare going on in Judaea. In Jerusalem things are easily attainable, but in Judaea you must take it by force. There are more territorial demons to battle, false teachers, pagan worshippers and hard places. "In those days came John the Baptist preaching in the wilderness of Judaea." Like life in the wilderness, it takes commitment and sacrifice to endure the dry spells that come in your Judaea experience. There are caves and dens in the sides of the mountains and cliffs. But, along with the hardship Judaea offers a great move of God. *"Then went out to him Jerusalem, and all Judaea, and all the region round about Jordan"* (Matthew 3:5).

In the Judean wilderness there is even religious opposition.

But when he saw many of the Pharisees and Sadducees come to his baptism, he said unto them, O generation of vipers, who hath warned you to flee from the wrath to come? Bring forth therefore fruits meet for repentance.
(Matthew 3:7-8)

It is a place of testing and temptation.

Then was Jesus led up of the spirit into the wilderness to be tempted of the devil... (Matthew 4:1) *Then the devil leaveth him and, behold, angels came and ministered unto him* (Matthew 4:11). *But, just as the Father was with Jesus, the Lord is with you even in the wilderness or dry places. Peter gives us an example of other types of testing we might face as he stood before the religious leaders.*

And it came to pass on the morrow, that their rulers, and elders, and scribes, and Annas the high priest, and

Caiaphas, and John, and Alexander, and as many as were of the kindred of the high priest, were gathered together at Jerusalem. And when they had set them in the midst, they asked, 'By what power, or by what name, have ye done this?' Then Peter, filled with the Holy Ghost, said unto them, 'Ye rulers of the people, and elders of Israel, If we this day be examined of the good deed done to the impotent man, by what means he is made whole; be it known unto you all, and to all the people of Israel, that by the name of Jesus Christ of Nazareth, whom ye crucified, whom God raised from the dead, even by him doth this man stand here before you whole. This is the stone which was set at nought of you builders, which is become the head of the corner. Neither is there salvation in any other: for there is none other name under heaven given among men, whereby we must be saved.' Now when they saw the boldness of Peter and John, and perceived that they were unlearned and ignorant men, they marvelled; and they took knowledge of them, that they had been with Jesus.

(Acts 4:5-13).

The Uttermost Parts of the Earth

If you are not called, appointed and anointed for a worldwide ministry, then please, do not go. Yes, yes, yes, I know,

Go ye therefore, and teach all nations, baptizing them in the name of the Father, and of the Son, and of the Holy Ghost: teaching them to observe all things whatsoever I have commanded you: and, lo, I am with you always, even unto the end of the world.

(Matthew 28:19-20)

But we must remember the point Paul made when he told the church at Rome:

For as we have many members in one body, and all members have not the same office: ...having then gifts differing according to the grace that is given to us, whether prophecy, let us prophesy according to the proportion of faith; or ministry, let us wait on our ministering: or he that

*teacheth, on teaching; or he that exhorteth, on exhortation;
he that giveth, let him do it with simplicity; he that ruleth,
with diligence; he that sheweth mercy, with cheerfulness.*
(Romans 12:4, 6-8)

Ministry as a missionary is the deep water, highest mountain, "stripes above measure," "in prison more frequently, "in deaths often."

Paul says in 2 Corinthians 11:24-25,
*Of the Jews five times received I forty stripes save one.
Thrice was I beaten with rods, once was I stoned, thrice I
suffered shipwreck, a night and a day I have been in the
deep.*

Read verses 26 and 27 of 2 Corinthians 11, and then study Paul's history. Realize that his last stop was at the gallows of Nero's chopping block. Paul concludes in 2 Timothy 4 that it is worth it all. "But watch thou in all things, endure afflictions, do the work of an evangelist, make full proof of thy ministry (v. 5).

To go into the uttermost parts of the world, you must be very watchful and prepared to suffer for the gospel's sake. This is not the job for novices and babies, but for the steadfast, immovable, meat-eating, mature saints. Your life and character will be seduced, enticed and threatened daily. *"For I am now ready to be offered, and the time of my departure is at hand"* (2 Timothy 4:6). I would guess that this was the apostle's last stop before eternity, and if there is a time and a place to prepare, the outward, upward evangelistic field would definitely be it.

I have fought a good fight, I have finished my course, I have kept the faith. (2 Timothy 4:7). If you are called to "the uttermost parts," know that there are devils and demons waiting in line just to get you off course, and make you give up the faith. The believer must look at himself through God's eyes of Faith, Hope, and Love to bear the cross of this calling. Remember, "No cross, no crown."

Henceforth there is laid up for me a crown of

righteousness, which the Lord, the righteous judge, shall give me at that day: and not to me only, but unto all them also that love his appearing.

(2 Timothy 4:8)

I am so glad that God is a righteous judge, and also a merciful one. We are taught, *"Let us not to be weary in well doing; for in due season we shall reap, if we faint not"* (Galatians 6:9). Similarly, Paul said, *"For I reckon that the sufferings of this present time are not worthy to be compared with the glory which shall be revealed in us"* (Romans 8:18).

Now about that time Herod the King stretched forth his hands to vex certain members of the Church. And he killed James the brother of John with the sword. Why didn't Herod attack all of the Church? Because some were dormant (in their comfort zone, CZ), and not a threat.

If you are called as a missionary, please go. If you are not called, then financially and prayerfully support others who are. This is a place for the chosen, not the frozen. Few ministries have the anointing to make a worldwide change. This is neither a denominational ministry, nor a TV or radio ministry. These things are secondary, but necessary. The uttermost parts of earthly ministry have the greatest sacrifice for those who are called. And the returns may not include your name in lights as a speaker on TBN sponsored programs, conferences with Billy Graham or your name in the Who's Who of religion. You may be hated and despised.

ACTS Walk

But the Jews stirred up the devout and honourable women, and the chief men of the city, and raised persecution against Paul and Barnabas, and expelled them out of their coasts. But they shook off the dust of their feet against them, and came unto Iconium. And the disciples were filled with joy, and with the Holy Ghost.

(Acts 13:50-52)

This evangelistic team experienced persecution from the men

and women of Antioch, but they pressed on anyway.

The Scripture is saying here that dynamic power comes after the Holy Ghost arrives. Power is the ability to act or pursue. Effective power goes beyond the scope of normal acts—beyond the comfort zone. As we need to mention again, the Comfort Zone is a popular place; it is where most Christians reside. There is little opposition or conflict in the Comfort Zone. It is a place full of complacent Christians. Webster says "complacence" means, "self-satisfied, unconcerned calm or secure, satisfaction with one's self."

"Woe to them that are at ease in Zion, and trust in the mountain of Samaria" (Amos 6:1). Zion is the centerpiece of Jerusalem, which is the city of David, the site of the Messiah's reign and God's dwelling place. However, Zion in Amos' day was a place for the complacent. The leaders here acted like the leaders in Samaria—and God sent them a strong warning or rebuke.

ACTS Walk

Now while Paul waited for them at Athens, his spirit was stirred in him, when he saw the city wholly given to idolatry. Therefore disputed he in the synagogue with the Jews, and with the devout persons, and in the market daily with them that met with him. Then certain philosophers of the Epicureans, and of the Stoics, encountered him. And some said, 'What will this babbler say?' others said, 'He seemeth to be a setter forth of strange gods:' because he preached unto them Jesus, and the resurrection. And they took him, and brought him unto Areopagus, saying, 'May we know what his new doctrine, whereof thou speakest, is? For thou bringest certain strange things to our ears: we would know therefore what these things mean.' (For all the Athenians and strangers which were there spent their time in nothing else, but either to tell, or to hear some new thing.)

(Acts 17:16-21)

The Athenians are an example of what happens when we stay in the Comfort Zone of Zion. We will not utilize the power that is promised in Acts 1:8. How many believers hear Romans 10:9-10 about confessing and believing and stop yielding, seeking and growing? Because they still shout, speak in King James tongues and dance a little, they are content. But they become stagnant, not flowing in the current of anointing, not advancing or developing into sonship. The experience of God is bubbling up in their soul, but nothing is flowing out of their spirit. The Comfort Zone tempts you to say, "I am doing fine; and it doesn't take all that." The problem is when you cut off the out-flowing waters, the spring becomes stagnate, calm, and eventually polluted with its environment. I beg you, keep the waters flowing, so the rivers can flow freely from your spirit. The fact is, we must revive our spirits—before we can transform their lives. *"They which do hunger and thirst after righteousness... shall be filled"*(Matthew 5:6).

As a further part of the ACTS walk, we need to look at some of the settings we find ourselves in as we attempt to witness to them.

PLACES OF WITNESSING

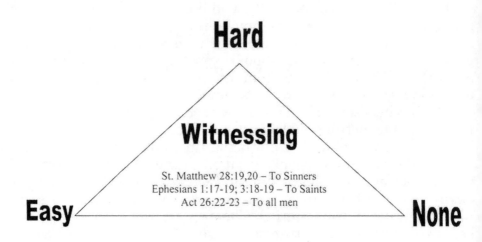

Witness – Greek: martureo from (martus – a martyr, record, witness) charge, give evidence, bear record, have (obtain, of) good report, testify give testimonies

Witnessing – bearing testimony to something

But sanctify the Lord God in your hearts: and be ready always to give an answer to every man that asketh you a reason of the hope that is in you with meekness and fear.
(I Peter 3:15)

Every believer has a commission to witness to the lost and encourage the saints. We have the commission to communicate with all mankind. Jesus said *"Go ye therefore and teach, all nations."* Teach them what I taught you is a command, not an option. But the believer must be ready to give an answer to the questions and inquiries of the world. Also, we must have the proper attitude. Remember we must win the lost, not whip the lost. Keep your witnessing biblical and wholesome, no tricks, gimmicks or puzzles. The Apostle Paul said, *" I had God's help, witnessing both to small and great, saying none other things than those which the prophet and Moses did say should come."* Witnessing is telling the truth about what you know, saw or heard, it's the truth the whole truth and nothing but the truth, so help me Lord!

Sinners need witnessing to hear the gospel (the death, burial and resurrection of Jesus Christ). But saints also need witnessing, especially to hear testimonies. This encourages us to keep seeking the Kingdom of God and to abstain from the very appearance of evil. Living in the world can blind your eyes to the move of God. We must be able to comprehend with all saints what is the fullness of God. Then are we really able to give an answer to all men. And they will see operating in our hope, the exceeding greatness of God's authority in the body, the ACTS walkers. It's all leading to chapter 29.

EASY
In Religious Gathering!
Church, gospel concerts, funerals, weddings, baptism.

Social Events!
Job picnics, graduations, and family dinners at restaurants, festivals.

Home Entertainment!
Cookouts, teatime, family prayer hour, new neighbor, old neighbors.

Service Places!
Doctors office, car repair shop, bookstore, barber shop, mailman.

HARD
Anti-Religious Setting!

1. This is where witnessing can lead to arguments, fights, and unnecessary interaction.

2. This is also where they are laws, rules, and warnings about religious conversation.

Social Statues!
1. To dress like a bomb, smell like a garbage can and expect people to take you serious.
2. To women, some men will only listen for a chance to flirt.
3. To men, some women don't want Jesus just give them a man.
4. To all, make sure it's the Lord leading you, not your flesh to socialize.

Character or Color Barriers!
1. It's hard to witness to someone who has seen hypocrites.
2. It's hard to witness to people you've hurt.
3. It's hard to witness to people who are prejudice.
4. Dress so that there's no sexual enticement.

No Witness!
Ten Greatest Reasons

1. I'm shy! I'm scared! I'm afraid!
2. What if I make a mistake?
3. I'm not sure what to say!
4. They won't believe that I'm real!
5. Nobody wants to hear about God!
6. I'll let my pastor come and talk to them!
7. I don't know enough Scripture!
8. They're not of my religion!
9. They don't need to be preached to by me!
10. I got time to do it later!

Acts Walk

And it came to pass, that, while Apollos was at Corinth, Paul having passed through the upper coasts came to Ephesus: and finding certain disciples, he said unto them, 'Have ye received the Holy Ghost since ye believed? 'And they said unto him, 'We have not so much as heard whether there be any Holy Ghost.' And he said unto them, 'Unto what then were ye baptized?' And they said, 'Unto John's baptism.' Then said Paul, 'John verily baptized with the baptism of repentance, saying unto the people, that they should believe on him which should come after him, that is, on Christ Jesus. When they heard this, they were baptized in the name of the Lord Jesus. And when Paul had laid his hands upon them, the Holy Ghost came on them; and they spake with tongues, and prophesied. And all the men were about twelve.

(Acts 19:1-7)

Hard Witness

Hard Witness is when you can't get your message across plainly due to circumstances beyond your control. Sometimes this would involve language barriers, color barriers, or economic factors. People are more apt to listen to someone they can identify with and trust. Jesus dined with sinners, but the Pharisees shunned them. Whom do you think they trusted more, and whom do you think won more converts? Don't try to change someone's language, customs, or habits until you show her love, respect, and a better way of life. This may not be your lifestyle applied to their day-to-day circumstances. Show them how Jesus would live their life, not how you would live it. And try not to remind people continually about their mistakes. Promote the love of Jesus and His death, burial, and resurrection (the Gospel). For this is the *"power of God unto salvation to everyone that believes"* (Rom. 1:16).

Acts Walk

And from Miletus he sent to Ephesus, and called the elders of the church. And when they were come to him, he said unto them, 'Ye know, from the first day that I came into Asia, after what manner I have been with you at all seasons, serving the Lord with all humility of mind, and with many tears, and temptations, which befell me by the lying in wait of the Jews: and how I kept back nothing that was profitable unto you, but have shewed you, and have taught you publicly, and from house to house, testifying both to the Jews, and also to the Greeks, repentance toward God, and faith toward our Lord Jesus Christ. And now, behold, I go bound in the spirit unto Jerusalem, not knowing the things that shall befall me there: save that the Holy Ghost witnesseth in every city, saying that bonds and afflictions abide me. But none of these things move me, neither count I my life dear unto myself, so that I might finish my course with joy, and the ministry, which I have received of the Lord Jesus, to testify the gospel of the grace of God. And now, behold, I know that ye all, among whom I have gone preaching the kingdom of God, shall see my face no more. Wherefore I take you to record this day that I am pure from the blood of all men. For I have not shunned to declare unto you all the counsel of God'.

(Acts 20:17-27)

To put it mildly, Paul had some hard times. Why did he endure them? *"Therefore I endure all things for the elect's sakes, that they may also obtain the salvation which is in Christ Jesus with eternal glory"* (2 Timothy 2:10). So others could be saved.

No Witness

No witness is what most of the Church is producing now! Some are ashamed, fearful, and bound by forces of evil. To them Paul would say:

Wherefore I put thee in remembrance that thou stir up the gift of God, which is in thee by the putting on of my hands. For God hath not given us the spirit of fear; but of power, and of love, and of a sound mind. Be not thou therefore ashamed of the testimony of our Lord, nor of me his prisoner: but be thou partaker of the afflictions of the gospel according to the power of God. Who hath saved us, and called us with an holy calling, not according to our works, but according to his own purpose and grace, which was given us in Christ Jesus before the world began.

(2 Timothy 1:6-9)

Authorized Christians Terrorizing Satan is the Acts Walk. All believers are armed—but few are dangerous. I say armed because there is power in believing and confessing. But one becomes dangerous when he adds possession to his believing and confessing. Look at this example: a man says, "I've got a bomb wired to me and I'm going to destroy this building." He'll certainly get my attention. But if it's revealed that he doesn't have what he confesses, then believe me, I'll not only call the police, but also the mental hospital. This man is a danger to society and himself.

Satan will challenge you about belief, confession and especially possession. An undercover policeman is treated just like any other person until he reveals his badge and gun. Then he earns special respect. Believers must have Jesus as their prized possession to defeat the wiles of Satan.

Just your authority in Christ will remind Satan how Jesus whipped him silly after the crucifixion. And Jesus rose with all power in heaven and in earth in His possession. He confessed it on resurrection morning. I believed it over 25 years ago and I believe it today. The devil is a liar; I know he's scared. He's afraid that somebody will read this book and become un-dormatized and re-authorized and break the syndrome.

We will look now at some of the syndromes that hinder our ability to wage spiritual warfare. These will include the "Laodicean Syndrome," the "Ichabod Syndrome," and the "Saul Syndrome," and will comprise the next three chapters. All three lead to complacency.

CHAPTER TWELVE

The Laodicea Syndrome
The Thrill is Gone

Have you ever gotten tired and not cared about your relationship with God, the Church family or marriage, etc.? Remember when you first received the Lord in your life, the excitement, and the fire burning in your spirit? You didn't want to think no evil, hear no evil, or kill a fly. When it was time for church you were ready an hour ahead of time. Saturday night you would prepare and press your clothes for Sunday morning. Remember that? As you drove to church and someone would pull out and cut you off in traffic, it was alright because you were ready to make a joyful noise unto the Lord and not curse the idiot out.

When you got to church on time, you sat as close to the front as possible because you didn't want to be sitting in the back with the gum chewers, note passers and church dating club. It didn't matter how long the service was because you wanted to be there. The pastor has his first closing, second closing and sometimes a third, but you didn't mind. Some of the church family had more problems than you could number. You discovered that everybody didn't come to church to praise the Lord, but you had patience and prayed for them.

You didn't gossip, but you prayed and kept your mind on the Lord. Remember that?

What was that that went through you when you saw your spouse for the first time? Was it love at first sight? What about the fragrance that caught your attention, the first time you touched? Your blood pressure went up and your pulse raced when he/she entered the room. Cupid couldn't have done a better job firing his arrows. As you gazed into your mates eyes and said, " I do", you did it till death do you part. Remember that? I've got one question for you. Now think before you answer. What happened? You can't tell me that somewhere along the way something didn't happen. You start out hot and on fire and now I don't know what to think. Some days I hear "hosanna" and other days I hear "Crucify him."

I'm reminded of a story I heard on the radio about an old couple. The husband and wife were riding in the family pick-up to the movies and along came another truck in their direction. It looked like there was only one person in it, but the closer they got, they were able to make out it was two. It was a young couple just married and so in love that they were sitting close to one another. The wife of the old couple looked at her husband and said, "I remember when we used to sit close like that." Well, the husband being a wise man still in love with his wife, said, "Honey, I haven't moved." When your relationship is getting lukewarm or cold, check your position.

THE 7 CHURCHES OF ASIA SPIRITUAL GAGE

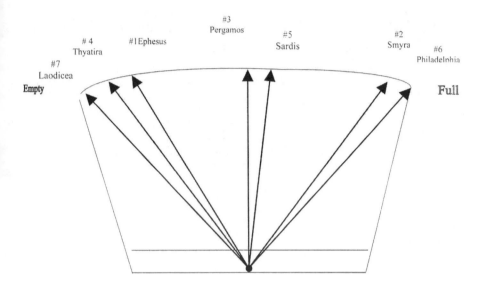

These churches have a personal characteristic as well as national, historical and dispensational representation. It's sometimes difficult to pen any one trait on a specific time or dispensation, but there's overwhelming evidence through history. Our studies would lead us to believe that we are living in the days of a lukewarm Church, some of these ministries almost empty of the presence of God. We have more material possessions and millionaires than ever before in the history of mankind. "We are rich and increased with goods, and have need of nothing." We are so blessed that we think we don't even need God, just a strong economy. Because of the blessing he stored upon Philadelphia, because of their love and trust in God, we are reaping the prosperity of righteous living from our forefathers, but remember blessing without dedication and commitment only leads to compromise. Check your position on the chart by studying the Church's character. Are you lukewarm or hot, full or empty?

Background of Laodicea

Loadicea was called by Ramsey (op. cit., p 413) *"the city of compromise"*.

They were lukewarm in works. *"I know thy works, that thou art neither cold nor hot. So then because thou art lukewarm... I will spew* (Greek is emeo. To vomit) *thee out of my mouth* (Revelation 3:15-16) Charlie Ryrie writes, "Near Laodicea were hot mineral springs whose water could be drunk only if very hot. When lukewarm, it became nauseating (Revelation, p.31). According to His words here Christ apparently has more respect for fiery hot fanaticism or for icy cold formalism than for lifeless and lame lukewarmness, according to *Wilmington's Guide to the Bible*, page 547. When the waters are hot it has medicinal uses to cure disease or relieve pain. When believers are hot and on target they can cause healing in the Body of Christ and relief. The minerals are the substances that fight sickness and disease. The minerals are activated when the water is hot. But when the waters are lukewarm, it has a bitter affect that causes the acids in the stomach to be nauseated. The lukewarm waters are like the church of Laodicea. They have the minerals but there's a compromise in the midst. So what's in the midst of them? It isn't healing the body, but hurting the body.

When we go through moments of lukewarm stages, we can't trust in the flesh. Find a hot ministry or church and get the fire of the Holy Spirit burning again in your life. We all have heard stories about individuals who went from rags to riches. But what about Laodicea? They had rags in their riches.

> *Because thou sayest, I am rich, and increased with goods, and have need of nothing; and knowest not that thou art wretched and miserable, and poor, and blind, and naked.*
> (Revelation 3:17)

Rags are waste pieces of material, no longer used as a part of the main stream apparel, torn or separate. Many believers are torn and separated from the last day move of God. The Church must not glory in things. Prayer shouldn't stop when the needs are supplied. Many believers stop pursuing God when they achieve levels of worldly success. Then the process of deteriation begins. When we stop or become stagnate, normally we fall apart. We are then rich with the world, but ragged with God.

Lay not up for yourselves treasures in heaven where moth and rust doth corrupt and where thieves break through and steal. But lay up for yourselves treasures in heaven where neither moth nor rust doth corrupt and where thieves do not break through nor steal. For where you treasure is, their will your heart be also.

(St. Matthew 6:19-21)

Eastern treasures were of fine clothes, polished armour, weapons of war; gold and jewels. Moth and rust were as destructive to most of them as thieves. Compromise will steal the real treasures and cause spiritual corruption.

The young rich ruler of St. Luke 18, was rich in worldly goods like Laodicea. But something was in his waters. It kept him from the stage that God desired to promote him to.

Now when Jesus heard these things, he said unto him, Yet lackest thou one thing, sell all that thou hast, and distribute unto the poor, and thou shalt have treasure in heaven: and come, follow me. And when he heard this he was very sorrowful: for he was very rich.

(St Luke 18:22-23)

God never had a problem with treasure or riches because heaven has streets of gold, not compromise and spiritual ignorance. God has real treasures that will last throughout eternity. In the Garden, Adam was blessed and rich. In the beginning God intended for His creation to be wealthy and blessed.

And a river went out of Eden to water the Garden and from thence it was parted, and became into four heads. The name of the first is Pison: that is it which compasseth the whole land of Havilah, where there is gold; and the gold of that land is good: there is bdellium and the onyx stone.

(Genesis 2:10-12)

(Bdellum-Hebrew. Bedolach, something in pieces, a fragrant of ambegum, or pearl) (Number 11:7).

(Onyx Stone – Hebrew. Shaham, to blanch; a gem of a pale green color) All of this was at Adam's fingertips, but compromise caused him to lose it all. We are living in the most blessed times of human history. We have more garbage in this day than kings had wealth yesterday. I see the making of young rich rulers daily, instant millionaires with the stroke of the pen. But in spite of all of this, we're not appreciative of our daily bread. Million dollar entertainers, computer wiz kids, and athletes are still attaining more wealth than ever before in the history of mankind without Jesus. They are rags in the midst of their riches. The word "compromise" isn't the exception, but the rule! Remember when we used to say if that was me, I'll do such and such? I've never compromised or sold God short. Remember before we had a TV in every room and three car garages with an expense account how we fasted and prayed to be the representation of God's blessings in the last days? We preached prosperity and didn't have bus fare. But look how far the Lord has brought us, and in such a short period of time. Remember when we said, "Lord if You take me off this job, then I'll have time to stretch out on the Word?" And the Lord answered our prayer, we got lazy, choosy and picky. The problem is we are lukewarm and conforming with the times. Before we had vision of great exploits, and now we are exploited out of the vision. This study guide will show how the Church has forced the last 2000 years and their character. Jesus gave us parables in St Matthew the 13th chapter that enlighten us on the Kingdom of heaven and the Church.

LAODICEA'S: DISPENSATION, CHARACTERISTICS, AND HISTORICAL TIME LINE

AD 30	AD 100	AD 300	AD 500	AD 1500	AD 1700	AD 1900
Ephesus	**Smyrna**	**Pergamos**	**Thyatira**	**Sardis**	**Philadelphia**	**Laodicea**
Desirable	Crushed	Married	Continual	Remnant	Brotherly love.	Rights or ruled of the people. Lukewarm
Apostolic	Persecuted	Worldly	sacrifice.	Reformati	Revival,	Tolerant
Church	Church	Imperial	Pagan Papal	on church	Missionary	Ecumenical Church
		Church	Church		Church	
Sower	Wheat & Tares	Mustard Seed	Leaven	Treasure Hid	Pearl	Dragnet
St. Matt. 13:3-9	St. Matt. 13:24-30	St. Matt. 13:31 –32	St. Matt. 13:33-35	St. Matt. 13:44	St. Matt. 13:45-46	St. Matt. 13:47-50
Rev. 2:1-7	*Rev. 2:8-11*	*Rev. 2:12-17*	*Rev. 2:18-29*	*Rev. 3:1-6*	*Rev. 3:7-13*	*Rev. 3: 14-22*

And unto the angel of the church of the Laodiceans write; These things saith the Amen, the faithful and true witness, the beginning of the creation of God; I know your works, that you are neither cold nor hot. I wish you were either one or the other! So, because you are lukewarm and neither cold nor hot-I am about to spit you out of my mouth. You say, 'I am rich; I have acquired wealth and do not need a thing.' But you do not realize that you are wretched, pitiful, poor, blind and naked. I counsel you to buy from me gold refined in the fire, so; you can become rich; and white clothes to wear, so you can cover your shameful nakedness; and salve to put on your eyes, so you can see. Those whom I love I rebuke and discipline. So be earnest, and repent. Here I am! I stand at the door and knock. If anyone hears my voice and opens the door, I will come in and eat with him, and he with me. To him who overcomes, I will give the right to sit with me on my throne, just as I overcame and sat down with my Father on his throne. He who has an ear, let him hear what the Spirit says to the churches.

(Revelation 3:14-22)

Important Points About Laodicea

1. Neither cold nor hot
2. Lukewarm, sickening
3. Wretch, in the Greek, talaiporos – enduring toil
4. Miserable, in the Greek, eleeinos- pitiable
5. Poor, in the Greek, ptochos – a beggar
6. Blind, in the Greek, tuphlos – blind in hearing, seeing and thinking
7. Naked, in the Greek, gumoros – stripped of arms, defenseless

God's creation and beginning is far different from man's current state. The Church starts out a desirable body made in the image of God with Jesus Christ as our example. But leave anything too long in the hands of mankind, and after awhile, as syndromes go, it will develop wavering patterns of misusage and humanist characteristics. We must return to God. The state of spiritual backsliding with a lukewarm sensation was not new.

The church at Laodicea started out on fire, and then the Lord blessed them and supplied their needs so that they had no worries. At that point the Church stopped seeking and growing. The flow coming from God's anointing was sealed up with an "It don't take all that no more" attitude. Pretty soon Laodicea stopped leading the charge. Instead, they needed a charge. Jesus said to them, *"I know thy works that thou art neither cold nor hot: I would thou wert cold or hot. So then because thou art lukewarm, and neither cold nor hot, I will spew thee out of thy mouth"* (Revelation 3:15-16).

Listen, Jesus said, *"...I will spew them out of my mouth"* meaning, *"I do not enjoy the relationship. I take back what I have given. They are not mine anymore."* This was a severe statement. *"I will strip you of my anointing, take away the authority and draw back my Spirit from you."* After God used Philadelphia, it seems that man chose the way of Laodicea.

Jesus told them,
I counsel thee to buy of me gold tried in the fire, that thou mayest be rich; and white raiment, that thou mayest be clothed, and that the shame of thy nakedness do not appear; and anoint thine eyes with eyesalve, that thou mayest see.

(Revelation 3:18)

The Lord knew the danger of being a Comfort Zone Christian. He told the Laodiceans, *"I counsel thee."* In other words, "Here is what you need to do to stay hot. Open up the door, and I will come in to you and fellowship. I will spend time with you for your spiritual benefit." Jesus further told the Laodiceans, "You have problems and you know it." The Lord said, *"But I will counsel thee..."* Counsel means to advise; it offers a policy or plan of action or behavior. Jesus would be everything they had been trying to look like; He would show them how to bring it to pass, but on his terms.

"As many as I love, I rebuke and chasten" (Revelation 3:19). They were to be zealous, therefore, and know that Jesus was not out to get them, but to love and treat them like sons of His own birth line. He would correct them in the same way a father would correct the flawed pattern of his son's life. Because of the love and respect of the father, a son then would graciously accept chastisement. This was Jesus' purpose for the Laodicean church.

Behold, I stand at the door, and knock: if any man hear my voice, and open the door, I will come in to him, and will sup with him, and he with me.

(Revelation 3:20)

Now, we need to understand that all of the seven churches of Asia Minor were actual ongoing churches and ministries. These churches also may represent the seven dispensations of the church age. Therefore, Laodicea represents the last day or latter times ministry.

Regarding this type of ministry, Paul spoke to Timothy:

This know also, that in the last days perilous times shall come. For men shall be lovers of their own selves, covetous, boasters, proud, blasphemers, disobedient to parents, unthankful, unholy, without natural affection, truce-breakers, false accusers, incontinent, fierce, despisers of those that are good, traitors, heady, high-minded, lovers of pleasure more than lovers of God; having a form of godliness but denying the power thereof: from such turn away.

(2 Timothy 3:1-5)

Look at what Paul says about the character of the latter day church and understand the times of its dispensation. The big shocker is that the members have a form of Godliness. Allow me to repeat myself: "a form of Godliness." How Laodicean can you get? Looking, acting, and sounding like you have a godly relationship with Christ, but your actions, relationship, and motives are far from Him. There are eighteen manifestations of a lukewarm relationship mentioned here in 2 Timothy 3. All of them are manifested in most local churches of today.

EIGHTEEN MANIFESTATIONS
OF THE LAODICEAN CHURCH

1. **Lovers of themselves**: *philoutos*; fond of oneself, selfish. We testify that God is first in our lives, but when under pressure, we have a tendency to deny that we walked with Him.

2. **Covetous**: *philarguroi*; fond of money; desire for what's not yours. We are more afraid of the IRS and creditors than what happens when we rob God in tithes and offerings.

3. Boasters: *alazones*; brags on one's self. Many churches are living in the book of Numbers rather than the book of A.C.T.S. They boast on how many are in church, rather than on how many the church is truly in.

4. Proud: *huperephanoi*; self-exaltation; importance. We are proud of material things that will fade with time. Everything we think is good isn't necessarily of God or good in God's eyes.

5. Blasphemers: *blasphemoi*; Any contemptuous or profane act, to dishonor. I've seen in these last days church people talk against the move of God because it wasn't manifested in their denomination.

6. Disobedient to parents: *goneusin apeitheis;* unruly children that defile leadership. The Scripture says, *"Train up a child in the way he should go, and when he is older he will not depart far from it."* But if trainers are not trained, (or walking in obedience to the Word themselves) then how can they train their children to be obedient? The church must train parents to train their children in the Word of God.

7. Unthankful: *acharistoi*; unappreciative, ungrateful. The unthankful will always be church hopping and never satisfied with the ministry and authority they are under. Also, unthankful people try to get more and more without sowing anything themselves.

8. Unholy: *anosioi*; without holiness, no righteousness. The Church must remain a tower of holiness. We must not compromise with the world. The Church must draw the world, not become the world.

9. Without natural affection: *astorgoi;* homosexuals; sodomites, unclean. The gays came out of the closet. That's good—now we know who they are. Let's win them to Christ so that He will give them Godly affection.

10. Trucebreakers: *aspondoi;* never keep their word. Your credit is a written expression of your word. Church members must pay their bills and keep their commitments to the World and their church.

11.**False accusers**: *diaboloi*; just like the devil, slanderers and liars. Behind every accusation there is a motive. A false accuser has evil motives and no regard for the truth.

12.**Incontinent**: *akrateis*; no control of one's self, attitudes, sex drive, or appetites. This can affect anyone. I've seen it in pastors, deacons, and members. It manifests itself in many ways—some obvious and some not so obvious.

13.**Fierce**: *anemeroi*; uncontrollable, beastly attitudes. Sometimes this spirit manifests itself in religious doctrine and denominationalism. The Church must be fierce in the war against Satan, not one another. "We wrestle not against flesh and blood."

14.**Despisers of good**: *aphilagathoi* hate the righteousness of God and despise God's people. It is when people get set in their ways and refuse to change.

15.**Traitors**: *prodotai*; betrayers. Young people today call this, "selling out". Are you selling out on God? Every time you deny Him you are crucifying Christ again. That's selling out.

16.**Heady**: *propeteis*; reckless and headstrong. How many times have I heard members say, "I can hear God myself, I don't need a preacher." Then they go out and wreck their life. It's not about hearing God, it's about rebellion and authority.

17.**High-minded**: *tetuphomenoi*; thinking one is better; conceited. This is a similar manifestation of the heady group.

18.**Lovers of pleasures**: whatever pleases the flesh. Preferring the flesh over the Spirit. These are people who prefer a BBQ to a prayer service, or football games to a revival crusade. When the thrill is gone, Satan will give you something to ease the pain.

These symptoms are why a large portion of the so-called Church of the new millennium is wretched, miserable, poor, blind and naked in the presence and glory of God. We are manifesting but a small percentage of what we preach. We resort to gimmicks, games, picnics and programs to draw people.

Woe unto you, scribes and Pharisees, hypocrites! For ye compass sea and land to make one proselyte, and when he is made, ye make him twofold more the child of hell than yourselves.

(Matthew 23:15)

It is very seldom, if at all, that we hear a minister preach on suffering, sin, and sonship through the blood of Jesus. Holiness is considered a fanatical, uneducated, left-field, primitive lifestyle that can get you fired as a pastor, silenced as a minister and excommunicated as a member. To some men the form is more important than the substance. There are more conferences, colleges, seminaries, seminars, and more books about the Bible than ever in the history of mankind. And still, most churches are bankrupt of God's presence. We are guilty of moving from His glory to a man-made story from Shiloh to Ichabod, which is going from the very presence of His Glory to the departed presence of His Glory. Most ministers are dwelling where God's manna was yesterday, instead of reigning in His immediate Shekinah Glory. But in spite of this apostate attitude, Jesus is standing at the door and knocking. We must not keep Him knocking too long. He possesses all power in heaven and on earth. I firmly believe that He can get whatever He wants. As many as He loves, He rebukes and chastises.

Jesus' love for the Laodicean Church (or Last Day Church) is so great that He will do whatever it takes to make it the Church without spot or wrinkle. The best way to get out wrinkles is through fire, with a hot iron or hot steam.

John the Baptist says concerning Jesus,

I indeed baptize you with water unto repentance: but he that cometh after me is mightier than I, whose shoes I am not worthy to bear: he shall baptize you with the Holy Ghost, and with fire.

(Matthew 3:11)

There is a cleansing process of baptizing with fire. The Lord is knocking at the door, and He wants to baptize you with fire

245

which I believe will get your attention. John goes on to say,

> *Whose fan is in his hand, and he will thoroughly purge his floor, and gather his wheat into the garner; but he will burn up the chaff with unquenchable fire.*
>
> (Matthew 3:12)

The Laodicean Church is full of chaff—so closely connected with the wheat that it will take a process of spewing out.

Paul spoke to the Corinthians,
Every man's work shall be made manifest: for the day shall declare it, because it shall be revealed by fire; and the fire shall try every man's work of what sort it is.
(1 Corinthians 3:13)

What the Church does shall come to light. Time tells the whole story whether you want it to or not. Good or bad, there is a reward. We reap what we sow. *"If any man's work abide which he hath built thereupon, he shall receive a reward"* (1 Corinthians 3:14). The reason that Jesus counsels the Church is because He loves to give rewards. It is not the will of God that we perish, but have life and have it more abundantly.

"If any man's work shall be burned, he shall suffer loss: but he himself shall be saved; yet so as by fire" (1 Corinthians 3:15).

The true Church will be saved whether its works are burned or rewarded, because Jesus is knocking at the door. There are works of the flesh and works of the Law. The Laodicean Church was caught up in both manifestations. Paul pointed out that God...

> *Hath saved us, and called us with an holy calling, not according to our works, but according to his own purpose and grace, which was given us in Christ Jesus before the world began.*
>
> (2 Timothy 1:9)

The best way to break a habit is to stop doing what makes it enjoyable. We, as Americans, have a terrible habit of thinking that God is pleased with our every move. We start this great country with prayer and a hunger for God; now we have voted God out of government and have a hunger for drugs, violence, sex and the psychics. Let's break these habits.

I love all of God's people and creation, but I know personally the struggle of the underprivileged. I'm an American, I'm a preacher, I'm a black man, and I'm sometimes disappointed, upset and troubled, just to name a few of my challenges. It's difficult when you meet ministers of different colors and they admire and desire your anointing, but they're afraid of you. When they visit your church you welcome them to the pulpit, or honor their presence, but when you visit them, they don't even recognize you, not that you're looking for it. Let's break the barriers; it will keep us in Laodicea. We all believe that we're going to heaven and live with the Lord, but every Sunday we separate and divide ourselves.

Some of us feel uncomfortable about racial issues. We wish it would just go away. It has no place in our religion. This is a part of Spiritual Warfare that troubles leadership. We all can't serve God in our own personal way, and when we get to heaven we will let God place us in the part of heaven He wants us to live in. Don't be surprised if the Lord says, "I never knew you." God is a spirit and they that worship Him must worship in spirit and truth (The spirit has no color and the truth isn't divided). Jesus is coming back for a Church without a spot or wrinkle. Confess to the Lord that you have a problem repent and bring gifts (love) that are worthy. To hate your brother whom you see and say you love and serve God whom you don't see is HYPOCRITICAL. Try serving your brother and loving the Jesus in him. Then you will make God smile on you and say, *"My son, My son, you look just like me."* Remember the parable of the net in St. Matthew 13:47-50.

We, as a whole, will defeat Satan. I've been in meetings and conferences with major ministry leaders, and I pray to God for them because I believe they're targets. But what gets to me is that we believe size is God, the bigger the church, the bigger the God. I once heard a preacher at a large church say, "All the storefronts should close down and come to this church because this is the Holy Ghost Headquarters." I said within myself, "If God ever blesses my ministry to be an overseer of thousands, I'll help the smaller ministry because they do a personal job one-on-one." How many times have we gotten big, just to turn lukewarm after we get noticed? There's a great move of God in the midst of Laodicea. God is raising up leaders who will not compromise or conform to their surroundings.

CHAPTER THIRTEEN

The Ichabod Syndrome:
Sin Now, Pay Later

Do whatever and whenever the Lord instructs you to do. We sometimes get caught up in the circumstances and situations that seem at the time to be overpowering our will to submit to God. This is a syndrome—a set of symptoms characterizing a disease. The disease is sin, and the symptoms are self-will, compromise, lust, envy, strife, etc.. Warning always comes before destruction when we have a good connection. When the Lord speaks we may not understand, perceive or sense the reason why we should comply, but God is sovereign. He sees all and knows all. There's nothing hidden from God at any time. I don't know how many times in my walk with God He has spoken a word in my spirit about someone or something and there was no way I thought that this would happen. It didn't make sense. Logic wouldn't allow this. But I listened and took heed, because I knew it was the Lord speaking.

God has a sense of humor, which blows my mind. When He speaks, all the logic in the world can't oppose the situation. Sometimes I just shake my head, lift my hands and say, "Lord, have mercy." Then my wife will say "Nobody but the Lord."

Over the years, I have learned to move whenever the Lord has said, "move." Most of the time He speaks when I'm broke and tells me to buy things. He knows I don't have any money. Sometimes I joke with the Lord and say, "In order for me to get that, I need a ski mask, fast car, and a gun." The Lord will then reply, "You will have a prison ministry. But I have a better way than your sacrifice, and that way is obedience. Do exactly as I tell you. Move the second I tell you, and speak My Word to the letter."

Every time I obey God, I'm blessed and rewarded. But let me tell you the whole truth—I have tried to obey God in every situation. There was a time when God and I didn't see eye to eye. I had issues and to me it took God too long to respond. So when it seemed like God was slow, I helped out. I did it religiously. Nevertheless I thought God needed my help. I was once asked, what to do when the bottom falls out. The right answer is to climb closer to the top. But because it was God who caused the bottom to blow out, He greased the sides so I couldn't climb any higher. When the bottom falls out, I'm in the mess. Then I cry like Jonah for my deliverance. God is so good that after He allows me to stay for a season in the mess I created, He brings me out with praise on my lips. Disobedience is sin, and God hates sin because it represents Satan's Inward Nature (S.I.N), which is iniquity. The Bible teaches that the wages of sin is death. Sin today pays tomorrow. Some sins linger through generations. Sin is a cancer that must be dealt with immediately. The best and only cure for sin is the cross of Calvary, the blood that Jesus shed for our redemption. Sin must be confessed, repented and cleansed. It's a killer and has no respect of persons.

The Ichabod syndrome reveals how the disobedience of some can have a lasting effect upon the lives of others. Ichabod was the victim of an ungodly circumstance. He had nothing to do with his father and uncle's behavior, or his grandfather's lack of control in their lives. He was a child born in a world of sin, and in a family of ministers who lived in their comfort zones. Compromising today could be the cause of your family's destruction tomorrow.

Is it possible that if Ichabod was stillborn he had a better future than being born without the Spirit of the Lord overshadowing his life? To live a life without the Spirit of God is like a mummy out of the tombs. You're walking and talking, but you're totally dead on the inside. Again I say that the wages of sin is death. Eli's sons Hophni and Phinehas worked very hard at committing sin, and Ichabod received the prize of the living dead.

And when the people were come into the camp, the elders of Israel said, 'wherefore hath the LORD smitten us today before the Philistines? Let us fetch the ark of the covenant of the LORD out of Shiloh unto us, that, when it cometh among us, it may save us out of the hand of our enemies.' So the people went to Shiloh, that they might bring from thence the ark of the covenant of the LORD of hosts, which dwelleth between the cherubims: and the two sons of Eli, Hophni and Phinehas, were there with the ark of the covenant of God. And when the ark of the covenant of the LORD came into the camp, all Israel shouted with a great shout, so that the earth rang again.

And when the Philistines heard the noise of the shout, they said, 'What meaneth the noise of this great shout in the camp of the Hebrews?' And they understood that the ark of the LORD was come into the camp. And the Philistines were afraid, for they said, 'God is come into the camp.' And they said, 'Woe unto us! For there hath not been such a thing heretofore. Woe unto us! Who shall deliver us out of the hand of these mighty Gods? These are the Gods that smote the Egyptians with all the plagues in the wilderness. Be strong, and quit yourselves like men, O ye Philistines, that ye be not servants unto the Hebrews, as they have been to you: quit yourselves like men, and fight.' And the Philistines fought, and Israel was smitten, and they fled every man into his tent: and there was a very great slaughter; for there fell of Israel thirty thousand footmen. And the ark of God was taken; and the two sons of Eli, Hophni and Phinehas, were slain. And there ran a man of Benjamin out of the army, and came to Shiloh the same day with his clothes rent, and with earth upon his head. And when he came, lo, Eli sat upon a seat by the wayside watching: for his heart trembled for the ark of God. And when the man came into the city, and told it, all the city cried out. And when Eli heard the noise of the crying, he said, 'what meaneth the noise of this tumult?' And the man came in hastily, and told Eli. Now Eli was ninety and eight years old; and his eyes were dim, that he could not see. And the man said unto Eli, 'I am he that come out of the army, and I fled today out of the army. And he said, 'What is there done, my son?' And the messenger answered and said, 'Israel is fled before the Philistines, and there hath been also a great slaughter among the people and thy two sons also, Hophni and Phinehas, are dead, and the ark of God is taken.' And it came to pass, when he made mention of the ark of God, that he fell from off the seat backward by the side of the gate, and his neck brake, and he died: for he was an old man, and heavy. And he had judged Israel forty years, And his daughter-in-law, Phinehas' wife, was with child, near to the delivered: and when she heard the tidings that the ark of God was taken, and that her father-in-law and her husband were dead, she bowed herself and travailed; for her pains came upon her. And about the time of her death the women that stood by her said unto her, 'Fear not; for thou hast born a son.' But she answered not neither did she regard it. And she named the child Ichabod, saying, 'The glory is departed from Israel:' because the ark of God was taken, and because of her father-in-law and her husband.

(1 Samuel 4:3-21)

How do we start at Shiloh and end at Ichabod? Shiloh is the place of His glory and honor, a place to worship, give thanks. We can testify and dance at Shiloh. Also, there were great religious festivals and pilgrimages were held at Shiloh (Judges 21:19-21), as well as special meetings of the tribes to settle difficult matters (Joshua 22:12). Shiloh was distinguished as the place where the tabernacle of the Ark of the Covenant rested. After the ark was seized in battle by the Philistine overlords (1 Samuel 4:11), Shiloh lost its prominence. Shiloh is also a prophetic name for Christ:

"The sceptre shall not depart from Judah, nor a lawgiver from between his feet, until Shiloh come" (Genesis 49:10).

When we are at Shiloh, our ministry is thriving in the perfect will and timing of God. Sometimes, we get too comfortable at Shiloh and begin to take things for granted. Because God is

252

blessing us, we don't think He requires us to answer for sin and disobedience.

I told a young man not to long ago that because we are saved by faith, it doesn't give us a license to sin and doesn't shield us from the penalties of our past lives as far as the natural body is concerned. You see, he was HIV positive. It happened before he was saved and was discovered after he confessed Jesus as Savior. If God didn't heal him, he had his salvation. But there are consequences to our actions. Ask Eli and his sons. They were at Shiloh in the glory days, strolling down "Blessed boulevard." Maybe there was a little compromise here and there at first. Then there were mistakes that were over looked. Perhaps Hophni caught Phinehas doing something wrong and said, "Don't worry, I've made the same mistake before, and God didn't kill me. We're only human. God made us to be this way. Besides, our father allows us to minister in the temple."

Unconfessed sin will give you a false sense of security. You begin to think nobody will find out what you're doing. As long as you don't hurt anyone it will be okay to do it in secret. It's a private matter! These are the lies Satan tells bishops, presidents, judges, policemen, etc. And within a short period of time, your name, picture and position are blasting over the 6:00 p.m. news. There are reporters camped on your front yard with cameras. The F.B.I., C.I.A., N.S.A., and the metermaid are chasing you all over town. They call this pay-up time. You did the crime, now do the time. And where is Satan? He's laughing, "You fool, you fool."

The ark was a box made of acacia wood overlaid with gold and crowned with two golden cherubim bending over the cover, or mercy seat. It contained two tablets of the law that Moses brought down from Horeb, a golden pot of manna, and Aaron's rod that blossomed. The ark was used in battle with the cry, *"Arise, O Lord, and let thy enemies be scattered"* (Num. 10:33-36). The Levitical priests carried it when they opened the Jordan River to allow Israel to pass through (Joshua 3). It was used to bring down the walls of Jericho (Joshua 6). And it was sent back to Israel on an ox cart.

When in the hands of the enemies of Israel, the Philistines found the ark too hard to cope with because they were afflicted with boils, and their god Dagon fell flat on his face in Ashdod.

With Eli at ease in Zion and not properly chastening his sons, the fire went out in the temple. And people wonder what is wrong with the Church!

Eli's Problems

Now why had the "glory departed" as Ichabod means? Because the fire had gone, compromise and complacency had set in. Eli had become too old and out of shape (spiritually and naturally) to fulfill his proper calling. Greed and lust had his sons bound. At this point, Eli was not going to church; he had retired.

> *Now Eli was very old and heard all that his sons did unto all Israel; and how they lay with the women that assembled at the door of the tabernacle of the congregation. And he said unto them, "Why do ye such things? For I hear of your evil dealings by all this people.*
> (1 Samuel 2:22-23)

In other words, everybody's talking about the dirt you do!

"Nay, my sons; for it is no good report that I hear: ye make the Lord's people to transgress" (1 Samuel 2:24).

These were spiritual pimps in the church! Eli's sons were not about doing God's will, but about enjoying the pleasures of life. They were not presenting their bodies as a living sacrifice, but to adultery and uncleanness.

> *And this shall be a sign unto thee, that shall come upon thy two sons, on Hophni and Phinehas; in one day they shall die both of them. And I will raise me up a faithful priest, that shall do according to that which is in mine heart and in my mind: and I will build him a sure house; and he shall walk before mine anointed forever... And therefore I have sworn unto the house of Eli, that the*

iniquity of Eli's house shall not be purged with sacrifice nor offering for ever.

(1 Samuel 2:34-35; 3:14)

When we don't pay the price of seeking God, we can easily move to the Ichabod Syndrome where we were: Better off Born Dead.

And she named the child Ichabod, saying, 'The glory is departed from Israel:' because the ark of God was taken, and because of her father-in-law and her husband. And she said, 'The glory is departed from Israel: for the ark of God is taken.'

(1 Samuel 4:21-22)

God's man of the hour would not deal with the sin problems of his house, so it affected (or infected) the entire kingdom and nation. Sin is a cancer that if not destroyed at the root, will destroy everything in its path.

The act of abortion is despicable and is wrong. Before you have a one-night stand with sin, know that it can kill and destroy your future with God. If you have failed already, there are some important matters you must deal with. Quickly confess your sins and shortcomings. Lay aside the weight and ask God for spiritual cleansing. And please do not return to the scene of the crime. I believe the presence of God has left many Eli's of today.

WHAT TO DO ABOUT SIN!

Sin is easy to get involved in because it offers the lust of the flesh, lust of the eyes, and the pride of life. Hophni and Phinehas enjoyed sex on the steps of the temple, and Eli's administration became scandalous because he didn't chastise his sons. When you know to do good and don't, when you can stop bad things and don't, it's sin unto God and you. But with some people it is easier to sit still and be quiet. They don't want to make waves or cause friction. In today's media we see victims of "Bishops abuse" in the Catholic Church, grown men, mature adults of the cloth who misuse their position and power. I don't profess to know how many of these Bishops are guilty.

To hide, overlook and even reward habitually sick-minded men is a shame before God. Somebody is going to pay up in the courts of this land, the courts of public opinion and on judgment day. I believe this is only a small ripple in the religious garments of an apostasy in the church, a Laodicean manifestation. Within the next year or two, their headquarters will have a great shaking and some top leaders will be jailed because they knew what happened years ago and refused to chastise their brothers. However, God is no respecter of persons. There are some Godly people in organizations who's praying for restoration. The prayers of the righteous availeth much. So we must also keep praying for the Church at large.

We know offenses must come, we know there's going to be a great falling away, but let it not be you. Pray for your leaders; don't be afraid to question things that don't fall in line with the Word of God. Don't become an accuser of the brethren, but cry loud, spare not, call sin, sin. When a brother is overtaken in a fault, ye which are spiritual, go to them, fast, pray, and have mercy, but don't condemn, compromise or excuse them to continue. Also, consider how you would handle this situation if it were you. No more business as usual. It used to be a time that God winked on our ways and it seems like He allows us ample time to pay the price and get back to the place where we left off, swiftly. But in these last days, destruction seems to come just as swiftly as we commit the offenses. Time is winding up, the daylight is further away and the evening is upon us, night will set in soon. Hurry, hurry finish your work. Stop playing religious games, ignite the warfare, and let's kick some devil's butt! This is what we need to do regarding sin.

Consider Ichabod, the son of Phinehas and grandson of Eli, priest of the shrine at Shiloh. Because of the power of the seed, all that was in Eli and Phinehas rested upon Ichabod. Let us note what happens when we stop pursuing a relationship with God, and allow sin to run rampant in the corridors of our spirit. The results are devastating. What about sin?

ELEVEN WAYS TO AVOID THE ICHABOD SPIRIT
(CONSEQUENCES)

1. Bad advice—Don't Listen to the Devil

Now the serpent was more subtil than any beast of the field which the Lord God had made. And he said unto the woman, 'Yea, hath God said, "Ye shall not eat of every tree of the garden?"' And the woman said unto the serpent, We may eat of the fruit of the trees of the garden: But of the fruit of the tree which is in the midst of the garden, God hath said, 'Ye shall not eat of it, neither shall ye touch it, lest ye die.'" And the serpent said unto the woman, 'Ye shall not surely die: For God doth know that in the day ye eat thereof, then your eyes shall be opened, and ye shall be as gods, knowing good and evil.' And when the woman saw that the tree was good for food, and that it was pleasant to the eyes, and a tree to be desired to make one wise, she took of the fruit thereof, and did eat, and gave also unto her husband with her; and he did eat. And the eyes of them both were opened, and they knew that they were naked; and they sewed fig leaves together, and made themselves aprons."

(Genesis 3:1-7)

Both Adam and Eve listened to the devil, and we have been paying for it ever since.

2. Watch What You Give – "Jealousy" (Cain)

And in the process of time it came to pass, that Cain brought forth of the fruit of the ground an offering unto the Lord. And Abel, he also brought of the firstlings of his flock and of the fat thereof. And the Lord had respect unto Abel and to his offering: But unto Cain and to his offering he had not respect. And Cain was very wroth, and his countenance fell. And the Lord said unto Cain, 'Why art thou wroth? And why is thy countenance fallen.'

(Genesis 4:3-6)

257

Cain's parents were not present at the murder scene but the results of their disobedience allowed sin to enter into Mankind. Some of the first manifestations were pride, deceit, selfishness and then murder. The wages of sin is death, and from that time on how many lives have been lost because of sin?

3. Choose the Right Place to Live (Lot)

And Lot also, which went with Abram, had flocks, and herds, and tents. And the land was not able to bear them that they might dwell together: for their substance was great, so that they could not dwell together. And there was a strife between the herdsman of Abram's cattle and the herdsmen of Lot's cattle: and the Canaanite and the Perizzite dwelled then in the land. And Abram said unto Lot, 'Let there be no strife, I pray thee, between me and thee, and between my herdsmen and thy herdsmen; for we be brethren. Is not the whole land before thee? Separate thyself, I pray thee, from me. If thou wilt take the left hand, then I will go to the right. Or if thou depart to the right hand, then I will go to the left.' And Lot lifted up his eyes, and beheld all the plain of Jordan, that it was well watered every where, before the Lord destroyed Sodom and Gomorrah, even as the garden of the Lord, like the land of Egypt, as thou comest unto Zoar. Then Lot chose him all the plain of Jordan; And Lot journeyed east: and they separated themselves the one from the other. Abram dwelled in the land of Canaan, and Lot dwelled in the cities of the plain, and pitched his tent toward Sodom. But the men of Sodom were wicked and sinners before the Lord exceedingly.

(Genesis 13:5-13)

And the men said unto Lot, 'Hast thou here any besides? Son-in-law, and thy sons, and thy daughters, and whatsoever thou hast in the city, bring them out of this place: For we will destroy this place, because the cry of them is waxen great before the face of the Lord; And the Lord hath sent us to destroy it.' And Lot went out, and spake unto his sons-in-law, which married his daughters, and said, 'Up, get you out of this place; for the Lord will destroy this city,' but he seemed as one that mocked unto his sons-in-law. And when the morning arose, then the angels hastened Lot, saying, 'Arise, take thy wife, and thy two daughters, which are here; lest thou be consumed in the iniquity of the city.' And while he lingered, the men laid hold upon his hand and upon the hand of his wife, and upon the hand of his two daughters; the LORD being merciful unto him: And they brought him forth, and set him without the city.

(Genesis 19:12-16)

Lot's choice was based upon what seemed good to Lot. Now he was choosing against Abram, the uncle who chose to give him a better life and bless him along the way. Maybe it would have been better for Lot to say to Abram, "You choose first because you're my elder, and I'll accept the decision you make." Lot soon learned that everything that looks good isn't of God. Your choices will affect your family's future.

4. Bad Relationship (Samson & Delilah)

Then went Samson to Gaza, and saw there an harlot, and went in unto her. And it came to pass afterward, that he loved a woman in the valley of Sorek, whose name was Delilah, And the lords of the Philistines came up unto her, and said unto her, 'Entice him, and see wherein his great strength lieth, and by what means we may prevail against him, that we may bind him to afflict him. And we will give thee every one of us eleven hundred pieces of silver'.

(Judges 16:1,4-5)

Samson should have listened to his parents and their wise counsel. Instead, he followed his fleshly desires and laid his head in the wrong lap. There are some people you just don't get involved with. Beauty is only skin deep. It's what is in the spirit and heart that make for true love and companionship. Your involvement with others will build or destroy your future.

5. Runaway Lust (David & Bathsheba)

And it came to pass in an eveningtide, that David arose from off his bed, and walked upon the roof of the king's house: and from the roof he saw a woman washing herself; and the woman was very beautiful to look upon. And David sent and enquired after the woman. And one said, 'Is not this Bathsheba, the daughter of Eliam, the wife of Uriah the Hittite?' And David sent messengers, and took her; and she came in unto him, and he lay with her; for she was purified from her uncleanness: and she returned unto her house. And the woman conceived, and sent and told David, and said, 'I am with child.'

(2 Samuel 11:2-5)

David should have been in battle. This was the season that kings went out to war with their armies. His failure to be in the right place cost him his throne for a season. Lust will cost you in a tremendous way. Families, jobs, titles, homes, kingdoms and even lives have been lost to lust. Lust doesn't say, "I'll destroy you." It says, "I'll make you feel good." Lust is from Satan, and it has the ability to draw. The spirit of lust is a taker, not a giver.

6. Too Many Choices (Solomon)

But king Solomon loved many strange women, together with the daughter of Pharoah, women of the Moabites, Ammonites, Edomites, Zidonians, and Hittites; of the nations concerning which the LORD said unto the children of Israel, 'Ye shall not go in to them, neither shall they come in unto you: for surely they will turn away your heart after their gods:' Solomon clave unto these in love. And he had seven hundred wives, princesses, and three hundred concubines: and his wives turned away his heart.

(1 Kings 11:1-3)

Narrow your choices and you will be less likely to make a mistake. It's hard to choose when you allow yourself to be influenced by too many situations. It causes a clear view to become cloudy and an easy decision to become complex. Solomon had all the wisdom for others but he did not listen to the Lord concerning himself.

7. Go the First Time (Jonah)

Now the word of the LORD came unto Jonah the son of Amittai, saying, 'Arise, go to Nineveh, that great city, and cry against it; for their wickedness is come up before me.' But Jonah rose up to flee unto Tarshish from the presence of the LORD. and went down to Joppa; and he found a ship going to Tarshish: so he paid the fare thereof, and went down into it, to go with them unto Tarshish from the presence of the LORD. But the LORD sent out a great wind in to the sea, and there was a mighty tempest in the sea, so that the ship was like to be broken...So they took up Jonah, and cast him forth into the sea: and the sea ceased from her raging. Then the men feared the LORD exceedingly, and offered a sacrifice unto the LORD, and made vows. Now the LORD had prepared a great fish to swallow up Jonah. And Jonah was in the belly of the fish three days and three nights.

(Jonah 1:1-4; 15-17)

As Jonah found out, it's easier to obey the Lord and do the right thing quickly. This way you save yourself from the pain and discomfort of chastisement. God's plan will be done, whether by you or some obedient servant. Disobedience can cost you time, money and effort. Don't procrastinate or hesitate in your obedience to God because it frustrates the grace of God.

8. Learn From a Weak-minded Man Married To a Dominant Woman (Ahab & Jezebel).

And it came to pass after these things, that Naboth the Jezreelite had a vineyard, which was in Jezreel, hard by the palace of Ahab king of Samaria. And Ahab spake unto Naboth, saying, 'Give me thy vineyard, that I may have it for a garden of herbs, because it is near unto my house: and I will give thee for it a better vineyard than it;

or, if it seem good to thee, I will give thee the worth of it in money.' And Naboth said to Ahab 'The LORD forbid it me, that I should give the inheritance of my fathers unto thee.' And Ahab came into his house heavy and displeased because of the word which Naboth the Jezreelite had spoke to him: for he had said, 'I will not give thee the inheritance of my fathers.' And he laid him down upon his bed, and turned away his face, and would eat no bread.

(1 Kings 21:1-4)

And the men of his city, even the elders and the nobles who were the inhabitants in his city, did as Jezebel had sent unto them, and as it was written in the letters which she had sent unto them. They proclaimed a fast, and set Naboth on high among the people. And there came in two men, children of Belial, and sat before him: and the men of Belial witnessed against him, even against Naboth, in the presence of the people, saying, 'Naboth did blaspheme God and the king.' Then they carried him forth out of the city, and stoned him with stones, that he died. Then they sent to Jezebel, saying, 'Naboth is stoned, and is dead.' And it came to pass, when Jezebel heard that Naboth was stoned, and was dead, that Jezebel said to Ahab, 'Arise, take possession of the vineyard of Naboth the Jezreelite, which he refused to give thee for money: for Naboth is not alive, but dead.' And it came to pass, when Ahab heard that Naboth was dead, that Ahab arose up to go down to the vineyard of Naboth the Jezreelite, to take possession of it. And the word of the Lord came to Elijah the Tishbite, saying, 'Arise, go down to meet Ahab king of Israel, which is in Samaria: behold, he is in the vineyard of Naboth, whither he is gone down to possess it. And thou shalt speak unto him, saying, "Thus saith the LORD, 'Hast thou killed, and also taken possession?' And thou shall speak unto him, saying, Thus saith the LORD, "In the place where dogs licked the blood of Naboth shall dogs lick thy blood, even thine."' And Ahab said to Elijah, 'Hast thou found me, O mine enemy?' And he answered,

'I have found thee: because thou hast sold thyself to work evil in the sight of the Lord. Behold, I will bring evil upon thee, and will take away thy posterity, and will cut off from Ahab him that pisseth against the wall, and him that is shut up and left in Israel, and will make thine house like the house of Jeroboam the son of Nebat, and like the house of Baasha the son of Ahijah, for the provocation wherewith thou hast provoked me to anger, and made Israel to sin.' And to Jezebel also spake the LORD, saying, "The dogs shall eat Jezebel by the wall of Jezreel. Him that dieth of Ahab in the city the dogs shall eat; and him that dieth in the field shall the fowls of the air eat.'

(1 Kings 21:11-24)

It's often said that Ahab was a good man married to the wrong woman. Now, I personally don't agree with that. At the same time, Jezebel was definitely a bad influence on him. She was wicked to the core, self-centered and dominant. When choosing a spouse, let the Lord lead you, and He will give you someone with a compatible spirit and personality.

9. Be Careful With Your Partners and Relationships (Jehoshaphat)

Howbeit the high places were not taken away: for as yet the people had not prepared their hearts unto the God of their fathers. Now the rest of the acts of Jehoshaphat, first and last, behold, they are written in the book of Jehu the son of Hanani, who is mentioned in the book of the kings of Israel. And after this did Jehoshaphat king of Judah join himself with Ahaziah king of Israel, who did very wickedly: And he joined himself with him to make ships to go to Tarshish: and they made the ships in Eziongaber. Then Eliezer the son of Dodavah of Mareshah prophesied against Jehoshaphat, saying, 'Because thou hast joined thyself with Ahaziah, the LORD hath broken thy works.' And the ships were broken, that they were not able to go to Tarshish.

(2 Chronicles 20:33-37)

263

So many times the saints of God look at worldly opportunities and think that the Lord will bless whatever they lay their hands to. They often believe that the relationships they are in are a blessed union because they are in them. We must learn that the people of God are holy, and they represent the very presence of God Himself. Of course, there are times when we associate to draw people to Christ, but that's not what I am referring to. You can't serve God and mammon.

10. The Gate of Sediton (Absalom Undermines David)

And it came to pass after this, that Absalom prepared him chariots and horses, and fifty men to run before him. And Absalom rose up early, and stood beside the way of the gate: and it was so, that when any man that had a controversy came to the king for judgment, then Absalom called unto him, and said, 'Of what city art thou?' And he said, 'Thy servant is of one of the tribes of Israel.' And Absalom said unto him, 'See, thy matters are good and right; but there is no man deputed of the king to hear thee.' Absalom said moreover, 'Oh that I were made judge in the land, that every man which hath any suit or cause might come unto me, and I would do him justice!' And it was so, that when any man came nigh to him to do him obeisance, he put forth his hand, and took him, and kissed him. And on this manner did Absalom to all Israel that came to the king for judgment: so Absalom stole the hearts of the men of Israel.

(2 Samuel 15:1-6)

Satan has filled the heart of Absalom with a desire to destroy his father's place in the kingdom. David should have watched his gates more carefully and not allowed those that didn't have his best interest at heart to serve in important places. If you open your gates to sin, death will walk in and take you out.

11. Not Enough Oil in Your Lamp (Five Foolish Virgins)

Then shall the kingdom of heaven be likened unto ten virgins, which took their lamps, and went forth to meet the bridegroom. And five of them were wise, and five were foolish. They that were foolish took their lamps, and took no oil with them: But the wise took oil in their vessels with their lamps. While the bridegroom tarried, they all slumbered and slept. And at midnight there was a cry made, 'Behold, the bridegroom cometh; go ye out to meet him.' Then all those virgins arose, and trimmed their lamps. And the foolish said unto the wise, 'Give us of your oil; for our lamps are gone out.' But the wise answered, saying, 'not so; lest there be not enough for us and you: but go ye rather to them that sell, and buy for yourselves.' And while they went to buy, the bridegroom came; and they that were ready went in with him to the marriage: and the door was shut. Afterward came also the other virgins, saying, 'Lord, Lord, open to us.' But he answered and said, 'Verily I say unto you, I know you not.' Watch therefore, for ye know neither the day nor the hour wherein the Son of man cometh.

(Matthew 25:1-13)

There are many more, but time will not permit to list them all. Ichabod was just born in a family that compromised and walked away from the important things in life.

CHAPTER FOURTEEN

The Saul Syndrome
Obedience is Better than Sacrifice

I remember awhile ago we were house shopping. I took my family to visit a particular house. We were a few minutes early, and the realtor was on her way to show us this beautiful home that had many flowers and trees in the yard. Audrey and I were standing about six feet away from my oldest daughter Teri. With a calm voice, my wife said, "Teri come here." Now understand we have two beautiful obedient kids. Teri stood there and asked, "What?" "What?" Her mom said, slightly raising her voice. "Just come here," and immediately my daughter responded. That's when we all got the revelation there was a snake in the flower bed by her feet. What if Teri was a disobedient and hard-headed child? The snake probably would have bitten her. What if her mother had not reacted wisely? Teri could have panicked and hurt herself. The moral of the story is to train your children to obey the first time you call them. They may not get a second chance.

There is another lesson God taught me when I had what I call a flash-vision. This is when something flashes before you and the details come later through lessons and illustrations.

I saw this father with a son; he was so proud. As fathers do, he bragged on him and told cute little stories on how great of an athlete he was going to be some day. But, he failed to properly discipline this child. Every time he would call for the child, the boy would take forever to answer, if he decided to respond at all. When together, the child would tell the father what he wanted and if he didn't get what he wanted, he would have temper-tantrums and embarrass his father.

One day in the supermarket this very thing happened at the check-out counter. The child wanted candy, but the father said "no." The child began to kick and scream at the father and demanded some candy at once. A little old lady came from the rear of the line and told the father to hold his ground. She said, "If you let the child win now, he will grow up to be a loser." But pride rose up in the father. He said, "Nobody is going to tell me how to discipline my boy," and he gave in to the child's wishes. The little boy was so happy that he ran out of the store ahead of his father into the parking lot with his candy. Immediately the father heard tires streaking in the parking lot and people crying out, "Oh my Lord." The father knew then it was his child seriously injured, lying lifeless on the cold pavement. As he walked toward the body, he heard the Lord say, "Obedience, obedience, obedience."

Saul was chosen by God to be the first king of Israel. He was a Benjamite and the son of Kish who was a man of power. Though Saul came from the smallest tribe in his family, he may have been highly recognized in the Hebrew community. He was head and shoulders above the men of his tribe and had the stature of a great warrior. Saul's name means "Asked of God." Saul was about forty years old when the prophet Samuel anointed him king. Because of his physique, almost seven feet tall, he was thought to be a young man.

Through unforeseen circumstances, years earlier, Saul is sent to search for his father's lost donkeys. God had spoken the day before concerning Israel's next king. Saul has no idea that obeying his earthly father would place him in the will of his Heavenly Father. Samuel was on a mission from God, and Saul was on a mission for his father. Understand this simple truth—the father knows best and expects total obedience, today, tomorrow and forever.

For the rest of Saul's life, as long as he obeyed God, everything went according to the plan of God. As time went on, Saul began to shy away from obedience to God. He started to look at himself and forsake God. Maybe the challenges of the throne, the war with the Philistines, the battles with Goliath in his life, the praises of a younger warrior like David all took a toll. Somewhere, Saul picked up an evil spirit. The end result was that Saul forsook obeying God. This would cause him to lose his crown to another.

> *And he sent, and brought him in. Now he was ruddy, and withal of a beautiful countenance, and goodly to look to. And the Lord said, 'Arise, anoint him: for this is he. Then Samuel took the horn of oil, and anointed him in the midst of his brethren: and the Spirit of the LORD came upon David from that day forward. So Samuel rose up, and went to Ramah. But the spirit of the LORD departed from Saul, and an evil Spirit from the LORD troubled him.*
>
> (1 Samuel 16:12 –14)

When the spirit leaves, an evil spirit or spirits replace the empty space. Don't expect things to operate the same way when God has rejected your life. The outward man may look the same, but inwardly there is confusion.

It's very sad to know that Saul started out with God's anointing. But disobedience and greed cost him his anointing, relationship, kingdom, and ultimately his life.

> *Now the LORD had told Samuel in his ear a day before Saul came, saying, 'Tomorrow about this time I will send thee a man out of the land of Benjamin, and thou shalt anoint him to be captain over my people Israel, that he may save my people out of the hand of the Philistines: for I have looked upon my people, because their cry is come unto me.' And when Samuel saw Saul, the LORD said unto him, 'Behold the man whom I spake to thee of! this same shall reign over my people.'*
>
> (1 Samuel 9:15-17)

Remember, "anoint" is symbolic of the Spirit of the Holy Ghost. God had a plan for Saul's life even before Saul recognized his purpose on the earth. The anointing is God's way of saying, "He will smell like Me, have My aroma, we will spend time together in fellowship. I'll sup with you, I'll lead you and reveal Myself through you."

God uses His anointed prophet Samuel to begin the process.

Then Samuel took a vial of oil, and poured it upon his head, and kissed him, and said, 'Is it not because the LORD hath anointed thee to be captain over his inheritance?'

(1 Samuel 10:1)

After receiving marching orders, Saul was going to enter a deeper manifestation of prophecy.

After that thou shalt come to the hill of God, where is the garrison of the Philistines: and it shall come to pass, when thou art come thither to the city, that thou shalt meet a company of prophets coming down from the high place with a psaltery, and a tabret, and a pipe, and a harp, before them; and they shall prophesy: and the Spirit of the LORD will come upon thee, and thou shalt prophesy with them, and shalt be turned into another man.

(1 Samuel 10:5-6)

Praise the Lord! It went just as the prophet Samuel had told him. After a series of events, Saul became Israel's first king. You can read several other times in Scripture how the Spirit of God came upon Saul (1 Samuel 10:10; 11:6). As long as Saul obeyed the prophet and the Lord, the Spirit of God prospered him. When Saul did it his own way, trouble and disruption immediately followed. Saul decided one day that being king was not enough. He wanted to hold the office of priest.

And Saul said, 'Bring hither a burnt offering to me, and peace-offerings.' And he offered the burnt offering. And it came to pass, that as soon as he had made an end of offering the burnt offering, behold, Samuel came; and Saul went out to meet him, that he might salute him. And

270

Samuel said, 'What hast thou done?' And Saul said, 'Because I saw that the people were scattered from me, and that thou camest not within the days appointed, and that the Philistines gathered themselves together at Michmash; Therefore said I, "The Philistines will come down now upon me to Gilgal, and I have not made supplication unto the Lord:" I forced myself therefore, and offered a burnt offering.'

(1 Samuel 13:9-12)

When we override the Spirit of God and rely on our own intellectual capacity of human reasoning, we are in big trouble. It makes us self-willed, self-centered and the master of "I." Saul said, "I will do this without proper authority because I am king, I rule, I am God's man of the hour so I force myself ... and offered a burnt offering." Somewhere along the way, Saul forsook the Lord. We need to know that even when the Lord calls us, appoints us and anoints us, we must remain totally surrendered to Him, or face the penalty of rejection.

And Samuel said to Saul, 'Thou hast done foolishly: thou hast not kept the commandment of the LORD thy God, which he commanded thee: for now would the LORD have established thy kingdom upon Israel for ever. But now thy kingdom shall not continue: the LORD hath sought him a man after his own heart, and the LORD hath commanded him to be captain over his people, because thou hast not kept that which the LORD commanded thee.'

(1 Samuel 13:13-14)

Here we see the first impeachment of an Israelite ruler. Saul moves from the favor of God to the rejection of God. Just like an impeachment process, leaders are sometimes left in office. God allows Saul to stay king for a season. God is so good that He allows us time for redemption, in spite of our stupidity.

This is one of the reasonings for rejection:

Samuel also said unto Saul, 'The LORD sent me to anoint thee to be king over his people, over Israel: now therefore hearken thou unto the voice of the words of the LORD. "Thus saith the LORD of hosts, I remember that which Amalek did to Israel, how he laid wait for him in the way, when he came up from Egypt. Now go and smite Amalek, and utterly destroy all that they have, and spare them not; but slay both man and woman, infant and suckling, ox and sheep, camel and ass.'

(1 Samuel 15:1-3)

Saul had direct orders from the prophet Samuel on what to do in order to be pleasing and successful before God. As it was, Saul was still stuck on I and me, and what was suitable in his own mind. Saul had the prince of this world in him, iniquity, pride, and self-centeredness. He couldn't obey God because he lost the Spirit of God. Saul loved the world. I John 2:15-17 is the place where Saul dwelt.

And Saul said unto the Kenites, 'Go, depart, get you down from among the Amalekites' ... And Saul smote the Amalekites from Havilah until thou comest to Shur, that is over against Egypt. And he took Agag the king of the Amalekites alive, and utterly destroyed all the people with the edge of the sword. But Saul and the people spared Agag, and the best of the sheep, and of the oxen, and of the fatlings, and the lambs, and all that was good, and would not utterly destroy them: but every thing that was vile and refuse, that they destroyed utterly.

(1 Samuel 15:6-9)

It was a custom that kings would sometimes spare the lives of other kings. The price would be the loss of their kingdoms, yet the king was able to live in exile until death. Saul probably was following the world's customs.

Notice the SAUL SYNDROME at work again, "me, myself, and I." Saul got a word from the Lord and refused to fully obey. It disgusts and grieves the Spirit of the Lord when we disobey Him and do not accept His Word of command. God is all knowing, all-seeing and everywhere. He had a reason for what He told Saul to do—He wanted His people to trust Him and be blessed. What we think about a situation maybe millions of miles away from the truth—and from the plan of God.

Isaiah says:

Let the wicked forsake his way, and the unrighteous man his thoughts: and let him return unto the LORD, and he will have mercy upon him; and to our God, for he will abundantly pardon. "For my thoughts are not your thoughts, neither are your ways my ways," saith the LORD. 'For as the heavens are higher than the earth, so are my ways higher than your ways, and my thoughts than your thoughts.'

(Isaiah 55:7-9)

Man's ways are the methods of the world. They are the enmity of God, they deal with the pride of life, lust of the eyes and the flesh. Remember, men love darkness not light.

God came to the end of His rope with Saul. Enough is enough.

Then came the word of the Lord unto Samuel, saying, 'it repenteth me that I have set up Saul to be king: for he is turned back from following me, and hath not performed my commandments.' And it grieved Samuel; and he cried unto the LORD all night.

(1 Samuel 15:10-11)

Samuel is no stranger to rejection. As we have seen already, years earlier his spiritual father, Eli, had not chastised his sons Hophni and Phinehas (1 Samuel 2), with the result that Eli's family and all of Israel were rejected. After the rejection, there had always been destruction and Ichabod ("The Glory has departed"). When the Spirit of the Lord departs, an evil spirit will enter in and set up his throne like the most high and exalt himself over the stars of God. S.I.N. is at work.

Now study the rest of 1 Samuel 15. You will find many things, including:

Eight Points About the Saul Syndrome

1. Saul lies to Samuel: *"And Samuel came to Saul: and Saul said unto him, 'Blessed be thou of the LORD: I have performed the commandment of the LORD'... And Saul said unto Samuel, 'Yea, I have obeyed the voice of the LORD, and have gone the way which the LORD sent me, and have brought Agag the king of Amalek, and have utterly destroyed the Amalekites.'"* (1 Samuel 15:13-20)

Satan filled Saul's heart to lie to the man of God as he did with Ananias in Acts 5. When you lie to God's messenger you lie to God Himself and there's a price to pay for your actions. The devil never helps pay the price even though he's responsible for man's destructions.

2. Samuel hears the factual truth: *"And Samuel said, 'What meaneth then this bleating of the sheep in mine ears, and the lowing of the oxen which I hear?'"* (1 Samuel 15:14)

Satan will trick you and expose your secrets. The very thing he helps you in plotting, he will turn and shame you with.

3. Samuel preaches, "to obey is better than sacrifice:" *"For rebellion is as the sin of witchcraft and stubbornness is as iniquity and idolatry. Because thou hast rejected the word of the LORD, he hath also rejected thee from being king"* (1 Samuel 15:23). Disobedience will cost you your anointing and position; ask Adam and Eve, they had it made. They had perfect conditions for good country living until they listened to Satan and got evicted. From that point on life was hard to handle.

4. Saul confesses: *"And Saul said unto Samuel, 'I have sinned: for I have transgressed the commandment of the LORD, and thy words: because I feared the people, and obeyed their voice. Now therefore, I pray thee, pardon my sin, and turn again with me, that I may worship the LORD'"* (1 Samuel 15:24-25).

Note: Saul feared the people and obeyed their voices rather than fearing and obeying God. But as we see elsewhere in Scripture: *"Fear them not therefore: for there is nothing covered, that shall not be revealed, and hid, that shall not be known... And fear not them which kill the body, but are not able to kill the soul: but rather fear him which is able to destroy both soul and body in hell"* (Matthew 10:26-28).

5. Samuel rebukes: *"And Samuel said unto Saul, 'I will not return with thee: for thou hast rejected the word of the LORD, and the LORD hath rejected thee from being king over Israel.' And as Samuel turned about to go away, he laid hold upon the skirt of his mantle, and it rent. And Samuel said unto him, 'The LORD hath rent the kingdom Israel from thee this day, and hath given it to a neighbor of thine, that is better than thou. And also the Strength of Israel will not lie nor repent: for he is not a man, that he should repent'"* (1 Sam. 15:26-29). Eventually, the truth comes out. And many times we are not prepared for the results; there's a price for living a lie, and falsifying the truth. Your actions are a reflection of what's happening—the Spirit realm. Saul renting the mantle was a demonstration of what was happening, the natural manifestation of a spiritual happening.

6. Saul pleads for honor: *"Then he said, 'I have sinned: yet honour me now, I pray thee, before the elders of my people, and before Israel, and turn again with me, that I may worship the LORD thy God.' So Samuel turned again after Saul; and Saul worshipped the LORD"* (1 Samuel 15:30-31). Take a real look at the religious pride Saul demonstrated. Saul's desire was to look good before the people. What he asked for was for Samuel to honor him, even after he dishonored himself and God—in other words, "help me look the part." Samuel had the people of God at heart so he went with him. But Saul had himself at heart. From his youth Samuel loved the people of God and hated disobedience.

7. Samuel finishes Sauls' job: *"Then said Samuel, 'Bring ye hither to me Agag the king of the Amalekties.' And Agag came unto him delicately; And Agag said, 'Surely the bitterness of death is past.' And Samuel said, 'As thy sword hath made women childless, so shall thy mother be childless among women.' And Samuel hewed Agag in pieces before the LORD in Gilgal. Then Samuel went to Ramah; and Saul went up to his house to Gibeah of Saul.*

And Samuel came no more to see Saul until the day of his death: nevertheless Samuel mourned for Saul: and the LORD repented that he had made Saul king over Israel" (1 Samuel 15:32-35). I wonder how many times God has had to send someone else to finish what we started; how many projects have gone unfinished; how many souls will be lost, lives destroyed, dreams unfulfilled because of our disobedience to God's Word.

8. *"So Saul died for his transgression which he committed against the Lord, even against the word of the Lord, which he kept not, and also for asking counsel of one that had a familiar spirit, to enquire of it; and enquired not of the Lord: therefore he slew him, and turn the kingdom unto David the son of Jesse."* (I Chronicles 10:13-14)

The result of Saul's disobedience led to premature death. He may have died at the hands of his enemies, but it was the Lord who killed Saul. Saul went beyond the limits of grace. Saul disobeyed the Lord, the prophet, and God's spokesman, the Word of the Lord. And to add insult to injury, he sought counsel from a witch, voodoo doctor and physic. When God's chosen choose not to honor God, it's an abomination. How many Sauls have you met lately who will turn their backs on God after He has chosen them and set them up to be successful? There are blessed people who have started out poor, living in ghettos and dumpster-diving for a decent meal, but God has picked them up and given them an idea or invention; overnight things have turned around. They are ashamed of their past and afraid to acknowledge it. I don't know where they would be if it hadn't been for the Lord.

What about the professors, doctors, lawyers, athletes, movie stars and our religious leaders who bought in on the big fat lie that it's not professional or popular to acknowledge Jesus Christ in public? It must be a private matter. How many Christians does God wake up in the morning and the first thing they do is read their horoscopes (Horror- scope). Christianity mixed with physic activities lead to rebellious behavior. Horoscopes are the love letters from demons and familiar spirits. They don't know the future but they are familiar with coming activities because their master is the prince of this world. He planned things and sent memos to the different regional hierarchy and they passed it along to the foot soldiers, foul spirits, imps, etc. Saul was killed because he was Israel's king—God's chosen people shouldn't be led by a disobedient transgressor. The Kingdom was turned over to David, a man after God's own heart. When David transgressed, remember God punished him, but David knew how to repent.

Obedience is better than sacrifice because we serve an omniscient all-knowing, omnipresence, omnipotence all-seeing, all-mighty God. His plans for our life are perfect, victorious, and eternally rewarding. When we disobey or delay the will of God by procrastinating, it takes us out of God's perfect timing for miracles, signs, and wonders, which also means that souls can be lost to Satan. Obedience sets up the timing of events that may alter decisions and determine the destiny of people for eternity.

Our obedience is very important in these last days because time is short. We don't have the time to play religious games. Satan is on the rampage, seeking whom he may destroy. This battle is fierce enough without the Church doing things their way and being out of the will of God.

Imagine a church that's afraid to obey the flow of God—a church that decides it's not proper to call sin, sin. A church that has to "wait and see" what a proper attitude is. A church where ministries use ungodly techniques to raise funds, then will misuse funds for personal use, and invest God's monies in the world system, and after the return not build the Kingdom. This is what we must fight. We must ignite the warfare and kick some devil's butt.

Disobedience will cause us to lose our anointing, our relationship, and abort our mission for worldly fame and honor. This world and its establishment will fail. The stone hewed out of the mountain will crush it. God's Kingdom will last forever. Don't give up on the Hero (God) and accept the lies of a (0) zero (Satan). There is a song that we sing sometimes that says, "Serving the Lord will pay-off after a while." Sometimes in life things that happen to us don't seem fair or right. There are some days when we just want to catch a break. This is the "in-between period" when you are in between the promise and the fulfillment. You want to do right, but it seems so much more simple and easy to give a sacrifice. But a sacrifice isn't necessary, it won't do the job. God is sovereign. He sees all, knows all and is looking out for your best interest. That's why he requires total obedience (100%).

Can You Walk Away From It?

It was in Orlando, FL., one Sunday morning that God gave me this powerful message. I was preaching at Rhema Life Ministry where the Bishop Gary and Prophetess C Jefferson were pastors. As many of their services are, this one was awesome! God dealt with me about Abraham and his love for Isaac, the child of promise and the son of his old age. What happens when God asks or commands you to give up something you've waited a lifetime for, something that has fulfilled void in your life? The missing link between you and the legacy that will carry on after you're dead and long gone. What if God said to give it up, turn it over to another or kill it? Have mercy!

This is what Abraham was facing. He also had to tell Sarah, his wife, what God said. Sometimes we find it easier to fall into the hands of an angry God, rather than to live with an angry woman. I can't imagine what he had to say to Sarah or if he told her up front, but Abraham's total obedience was required.

As Abraham and the lad went up the front side of the mountain, the ram came up the backside of the mountain. Abraham trusted God, but he didn't know how this would unfold. As God would have it, obedience was better than sacrifice. A week later I realized God was talking to me in that message one day while I was in prayer. He began to minister to me about totally trusting in Him, following Him blindly and asking for no explanations. I'm very nervous when I'm blindfolded and get the jitters when I'm in the dark. That's why I said God ministered to me. I needed some help with what God was about to say to me. First, He told me to turn my church over to one of my sons and daughters in the Gospel, Pastors Ronnie and Zhenee Thompson. Now Prophetess and I started this church in the livingroom of our home and groomed it until we now had several buildings, and a staff of twenty plus ministers, ten to fifteen teachers, and a several hundred thousand dollar budget. We pay all of our bills on time and are 98% debt free (we'll get the other 2% when you buy this book).

God said, "Turn it over and walk away from it." The Lord also said to move away to the next county and purchase a large, beautiful home. I said, "Lord, how will I pay for a home with no job, no church, and what about an INCOME?" God said, "I'm your source, just do what I tell you." Now my credit was good because I believed and have taught that saints should pay their bills fully and on time. Your credit is your word and reputation.

I believe I arrived at this point in my ministry by standing on the promises of God and by obeying His Word. But to start over after twenty years as pastor after thirty years of preaching with a daughter on her way to college, two very nice cars and a new mortgage was a challenge. Again, this is why I say God ministered to me. Remember the preface, "Finding Strength in the Struggles" written by my wife? Well I still have flashbacks of those days. I don't want to go backward after all this time. Maybe in some areas I've become comfortable or maybe I didn't know just how much I trusted God who has provided my daily bread. I don't think it's a sin or you're selling out when you apply the faith with works and God blesses you to live in the best of homes, drive the best of cars, and eat the best foods. I'm a King's kid, and a member of the royal family, and my Heavenly Father owns all of this.

I realized at this point God was shifting me to a new place in His will for my life. He ministered to me to help me to flow with what He is presently doing in my life. I couldn't remain in the same place or position, my position as an apostle and a mentor to those who operate in the five fold ministries. God said, "My leaders need ministering to also." I will preach to the church but my ministry is to pastor leaders. In reality I walked away from Isaiah to help Abraham and Sarah. Please pray for me as I help leaders because this isn't easy. I have found that some leaders will look over the anointing in you, and the gift God has given them in a mentor. Their agenda or interest is only based on "How you can get me to my next appointment, or how many doors you can open for me." Those that allow the spirit of pride causes them to compare themselves to you in ways such as, "Is your degree higher than mine?" "Can I really trust a black or white preacher?" I say to this preacher, "Lay down your pride, prejudice, ignorance and walk away from it." I keep myself focused by remembering that God said to me that pastoring the church was only a part of my ministry, the total sum of ministry is to stay in the perfect will of God!

CHAPTER FIFTEEN

The Perfected Will

One evening after I returned from a ministry scouting trip, it was late, and I was tired from a long drive. As my beautiful wife and I settled in at home, the Lord began to talk to me about how it disappointed Him that we the believers don't take advantage of His gifts and benefits. It was as though He was saying,

"I have given them everything that they need to be happy, blessed and successful, but they struggle with carnal matters and are so easily distracted by the cares of life. These cares aren't here to sidetrack the believer but to enhance their faith in Me. But instead, they allow the opposite effect upon their walk with Me. I want to commune with them as I did Enoch and others. Their walk is filled with complaints, grumbling and negative mindsets. I've given them abundance, but they can't see the forest from the trees. Their hearts are far from Me. Tell them one of the greatest blessings of warfare is to understand, trust and give thanksgiving for My divine supply. Look to Me. Search diligently for Me. I'm everywhere and in every place in all time zones, constantly supplying, providing and directing. Choose first to bless My Name, choose first to praise Me, choose first to trust My Word, choose first to seek Me and allow no second nor third to cause doubt. I'm bigger than all your cares. I love you more than all your mistakes. I'm happy to make you happy. It gives Me joy to make you smile. And I feel your sorrow when you're sad. Jesus died not only for you, but for My joy in reconciling the world to Me."

When the Lord ministered this to me, I can't tell you the awesome force that came with this revelation. I learned how God feels when we don't trust His perfect provision...Jesus the Christ our Lord and Savior. When we learn how much God cares, the devil is in trouble. When we get to know Him as El-Shaddai; the Almighty God, the enemy is headed for defeat.

Hebrew: <u>Shaddiy</u> – the Almighty this title indicates the fullness and riches of God's grace, and would remind the Hebrew reader that from God comes every good and perfect gift – that He is never wary of pouring forth His mercies on His people, and that He is more ready to give than they are to receive.

<u>Shadad</u> – powerful (pass impregnable).

Greek: pantokrator – <u>pas</u>; all, any, every. Kratos: vigor (great) force, strength, might more especially manifested power, God is all-great, all-strength, every might, the Shadad, all powerful One, impregnable.

Our father which art in heaven, Hallowed be thy name. Thy kingdom come. Thy will be done in earth, as it is in heaven. Give us this day our daily bread. And forgive us our debts, as we forgive our debtors. And lead us not into temptation, but deliver us from evil: for thine is the Kingdom, and the power, and the glory, forever, Amen.
(Matthew 6:9-13)

This is the model prayer of Jesus that the body of Christ uses to submit their will and destiny to the fulfillment of God's will and purpose for their lives.

When we walk in His perfected will, that means we have sought God diligently with all our spirit, soul and body, and now we are demonstrating His will for our lives. First, acknowledge His sovereign ability. He is in heaven, ruler of all and everything. His name is to be honored, praised, understood, and worshipped. The Kingdom comes whenever and wherever there's a believer representing the King and ruler. His Kingdom resides in the believers. Wherever we go in obedience, His will shall be done in the earth as it is done in the heaven. It is very important for the Body of Christ to submit to their headship. We can have heaven on earth and rule with authority. Remember whenever the

282

righteous are in authority, the people rejoice, but when the wicked beareth rule, the people mourn.

The world is in turmoil because the manifested sons of God have not ignited the warfare.

Then cometh the end, when he shall have delivered up the kingdom to God, even the Father; when he shall have put down all rule and all authority and power.

(I Corinthians 15:24)

As Jesus is, so are we to this world. The kingdoms of heaven and earth belong to God and it's up to His sons to bring order in the earth as it is in heaven. We are equipped and gifted to fulfill the task. It's time to stop playing religious games and seek the perfected will of God for our lives. Let's take the territory by any means necessary.

The earth is the Lord's and the fullness thereof, the world and they that dwell therein.

(Psalm 24:1)

What shall we say then? Is there unrighteousness with God? God forbid, for he saith to Moses I will have mercy on whom I will have mercy, and I will have compassion on whom I will have compassion. So then, it is not of him that willeth, nor of him that runneth, but of God that sheweth mercy. For the Scripture saith unto Pharaoh, even for this same purpose have I raised thee up, that I might shew my power in thee, and that my name might be declared throughout all the earth. Therefore hath he mercy, and whom he will have mercy, and whom he will he hardenth.

(Roman 9:14-18)

This is God's earth and kingdoms. He controls and crowns whom He will. He made Pharaoh and Moses and set the events of their lives in action to prove to both that He is God, the Great I Am. The power and the glory belong to God at all times and He has chosen men to take authority over angels, demons and lastly Satan. It's time to stop playing religious games. Real power is in the will, the might and the purposes of God. It's already proven God is sovereign. His perfect will shall be done. Read the back of the book. We will win and reign with God forever. The book of Revelation says so.

Remember, the kingdom of heaven suffereth violence, and the violent take it by force. (St. Matthew 11:12)

This violent force (viazo) means to force one's way into a place. Before Jesus came on the scene it used to be that the Kingdom was only a view, or an image in one's mind. Then John the Baptist preached it, and Jesus opened it up by demonstration. Mankind began to press into the Kingdom with such desperation; it resembled a violent act or stampede. It appeared they would seize it by force. This kind of frenzy expressed the earnestness that mankind must have in getting rid of all the satanic strongholds and sin in their lives. Jesus knew that in order for man to win the real battle, and have communion with God, mankind would have to be confronted. Not an easy task.

Thou therefore endure hardness, as a good soldier of Jesus Christ. No man that warreth entangleth himself with the affairs of this life; that he may please him who hath chosen him to be a soldier... I have fought a good fight, I have finished my course, I have kept the faith.
(2 Timothy 2:3-4; 4:7)

Stop connecting with losers; the affairs of this world are for losers. Seek the perfect will of God; it's the safest place to dwell.

To understand the basics of everything dealing with life and death, you must first grasp the before life, after death and present spiritual surroundings. These things hold the keys to open, uncover and expose the true facts about life and how to live, how to defeat death, have victory over it, and present situations too. It is time to stop playing religious games. The stakes are too high. Souls can and will be lost if we do not get a grip on the purpose and plan of God.

The Apostle Paul understood the warfare involved even in his day. Paul recognized those men who had a form of godliness, "but denied" the power thereof. Paul said to Timothy, *"from such turn away"* (2 Timothy 3:5). The traditional Church believes it's more important to be a good citizen and neighbor than to seek the Kingdom of God and pursue the will of God in the earth. That's what happened in Jesus' day, but someone got tired of business as usual. History will repeat itself. This Church must pursue God again or lose its members to false religions. There's churches without walls, independent non-denominational ministries that are not afraid to kick some devil's butt.

The rejection of this notion has allowed such people to creep into the traditional churches and lead uninformed and misinformed people astray. But when dynamite explodes, its power exposes the core of a situation. It exposes things that were not seen before. These demonically-inspired people do not want to be exposed or revealed. When lights come on, darkness must leave. Have you ever seen an explosion that was dark? Every time dynamite is lit and blows up, there is a tremendous light that follows.

Paul said that man is learning, but never able to come to the full knowledge of the truth. If a man learns, but still does not know the truth, then there is a problem in what he is being taught. If there is a problem in what he is being taught, then there is perhaps a problem with his teacher. Remember, having a form of godliness, but denying the power thereof doesn't cut it. How many teachers or preachers do you know, how many churches or denominations have you been a part of that neither teach nor minister the full Gospel message, or demonstrate the power of God? God will expose them. They're sleeping dogs in the bed of iniquity. Isaiah 56:10-11

> *They shall proceed no further, for their folly shall be manifest unto all.*

> (2 Timothy 3:9)

The covers of sin, the blankets of iniquity and sheets of disobedience will be exposed when we preach the Gospel and walk in the demonstration of the power of God. Remember, the time for games is over! It's dangerous to play with dynamite!

MORE GAMES: SIMON, THE SORCERER (ACTS 8:9-24)

Trouble or persecution can bring some of the most amazing changes to the Church. Every time we get into a comfort zone, God will stir the nest. When God stirs the nests of our ministry, there is a Philip waiting to be propelled. Philip was what some called "a layman" (Acts 6:5), yet he became one of the first great evangelist propelled beyond the church walls. Philip preached and ministered the saving grace of Jesus. Philip was a mature, serious soldier who did not mind leaving the comforts of home to promote the most powerful message of love, joy, and deliverance. Since the day of Pentecost, many cities and towns had never heard the Gospel. The Samaritans were outcast, second-class citizens according to most Jewish customs, and tradition did not allow good Jewish boys to speak with such unclean heathens. Can you imagine the souls of the Samaritans, so hungry for a spiritual renewal that they would settle for Simon the Sorcerer?

A prime example in the Scriptures of religious game playing was Simon of Samaria. Before Philip got to Samaria, Simon was the religious icon, a false spiritual leader. He merchandised the people, he had a form of godliness, but no real power, so he pursued witchcraft. You could dial 1-900-55-Simon and get your free 3-minute psychic update—$9.95 a minute after you hear the 3-minute tone buzzer. Get the picture? Simon had a blessing plan so even the poorest of the poor could financially "Buy here, pay here."

Everything was going just fine until the prayerful, devout, Holy Ghost-filled deacon (not a stiff-necked, hellish demon, but a man of prayer, fasting, and no compromise) entered the city. Yes, Philip was one of those scattered because of persecution, but the Holy Ghost works best when man says, "I'll stop you at all costs." *"Therefore they that were scattered abroad went everywhere preaching the Word. Then Philip went down to the city of Samaria and preached Christ unto them."* It was evident that Simon had been teaching something, but not the Gospel of Jesus, because the gospel exposes sin.

And the people with one accord gave heed unto those

*things which Philip spake, hearing and seeing the
miracles which he did. For unclean spirits, crying with
loud voice, came out of many that were possessed with
them: and many taken with palsies, and that were lame,
were healed. And there was great joy in that city.*

(Acts 8:4-8)

The power of the Holy Ghost, and the preaching of Jesus in
that city, caused explosions that got everybody's attention and
changed their way of thinking. It began an awakening that
created great joy in Samaria. Notice, because of persecution at
home (comfort zone), Philip went out and started a major
commotion in freeing victims of Satan's kingdom. They left the
false hope satanic ambition had offered, and psychic lies, because
they were introduced to the Kingdom of Jesus Christ. No wonder
the city had great joy! Philip was not promoting a denomination,
but a demonstration of Kingdom living and revelation. So often,
man gets a revelation, then builds a denomination. When the
revelation changes because of God's times and seasons, he is stuck
with a denomination, an old revelation that will never bring forth
a demonstration of the move of God. Thank the Lord; Philip was
a man of prayer and submission who was willing to change.

Meanwhile, Simon heard about the revival. It must have
puzzled him that Samaritans would go out and listen to a Jewish
preacher. Not only was this evangelist preaching about a man
who had been crucified sometime earlier, but Philip was healing
without a medical permit, doing surgery without anesthesia, and
freeing the psychologically unbalanced without therapy or shock
treatments. Lastly, he was accurately pinpointing in his psychic
predictions, and yet, was not charging for his services. He had no
crystal ball, charms, or chants, but spoke a funny sounding
gibberish when he praised God. Simon had lost all of his psychic
church hotline business, and decided it was time to join 'em if you
can't beat 'em. Simon figured he would hide out among the
anointed rather than be exposed as a fake. However, the truth
always exposes and reveals the intents, secrets and motives of the
heart, soul and spirit.

Now when the apostles which were at Jerusalem heard that Samaria had received the Word of God, they sent unto them Peter and John: Who, when they were come down, prayed for them, that they might receive the Holy Ghost: (For as yet he was fallen upon none of them: only they were baptized in the name of the Lord Jesus.) Then laid they their hands on them, and they received the Holy Ghost. And when Simon saw that through laying on of the apostle's hands the Holy Ghost was given, he offered them money, Saying, 'Give me also this power, that on whomsoever I lay hands, he may receive the Holy Ghost.' But Peter said unto him, 'Thy money perish with thee, because thou hast thought that the gift of God may be purchased with money.'

(Acts 8:14-20)

Peter exposed what was in Simon's heart. He was self-centered, only focusing on himself (me, myself and I). When man says "I", then there is always trouble. But when God says "I", the blessing begins. The nerve of Simon to say, "Can I offer you money for your anointing?" I do not know how many "bless me to prosper" healing lines or pray-for-the-miracle prophetic ministers I have seen in my life. I know everyone of them was not a Simon, but it is scary when you look at some of the resemblances. Some of them started out great, just wanting souls to be saved, then because of financial pressure and greed, the spirit of sorcery crept in. Some pastors have revival after revival, conference after conference, anniversary after anniversary, taxing their flock and using high-powered evangelists just to raise offerings for projects that are not the will of God, but the "I will" of man. At least Simon wanted to give the people something.

Some of our leadership today will strip you, and then dare you to receive manna from anywhere else. Just like Peter told Simon,

Thou hast neither part nor lot in this matter: for thy heart is not right in the sight of God. Repent therefore of this thy wickedness, and pray God, if perhaps the thought of thine heart may be forgiven thee.

(Acts 8:21)

288

Peter is saying to everyone, "Stop playing religious games, or pay the penalty." What a true believer has from God cannot be bought or sold. Only substitutes have a dollar value. Satan will see how much it will take to get you.

Satan does not come directly at us and say, "I'm the devil and I want your anointing." He comes in subtly through misguided prophecies, man-doctrines and apostasies. Satan wants the Church to play church, practice church, and act church. In other words, look busy but not be real. Keep up with what's popular but don't press into Jesus. Avoid conflicts and please don't make waves. When we stop playing religious games, confess our sins, and seek the face of God, what an anointing God will place upon us!

God's anointing is His aroma and it's like nothing else in the world. It is an enjoyable, distinctive, pervasive, savory smell. Jesus is our sweet smelling Savior offered to God as the perfect sacrifice. Satan hates this smell. It reminds him of his defeat. When God anoints, it's like placing an expensive perfume upon you. It will not fade through the heat and sweat of the day and when you leave a room, there's an aroma that lingers in the air. People who have had fellowship with you know where you've been because the aroma of Jesus was left there.

When Satan smells the aroma of God on us he knows we've been with Jesus, and the game is over. Simon came to the reality that his game was over.

I once preached a message entitled, "Stop Playing Church." Sometime in my own life, I was more impressed with the job of preaching, than the purpose of preaching. When the techniques and deliveries are more important that the Rhema and Logos, that's "playing church". Let's examine what we do as preachers. Be wise in your allotted time dealing in God's business. What about when the power of God takes over the praise service and it's cutting into offering time, even yet our preaching time? We have a way to stop the flow of God by grabbing the microphone and singing a slow song to calm the people down. That's "playing church." Understand me clearly. There's a time and season for sifting the flow but that's not what I'm talking about. Now we are praying for a mighty move of God in our churches and when God does it, we try to hinder, control, and in some cases fight against it. How not to play church is to seek the Kingdom of God and walk in the perfected will of God. Whenever or wherever God moves don't hinder, but flow with God. Jesus said, "Upon this rock, I'll build my Church and the gates of hell shall not prevail." Jesus knows how to build and operate the Church, it's His ministry and this ministry will bring forth His Kingdom. Not only does God rejoice when men press into the Kingdom, but when we walk in the will of God, the Kingdom presses into the lives of men. To play is to pretend or act without God's direction. How many times have we pretended to do the will of God, but only in our own strength? That's "playing church."

There are things in life you don't play or pretend with. Worship, praise and submitting to God are at the top of the list. Souls can be lost, time wasted and you might feel the wrath of an angry God. We all have some repenting to do. We figure God will only deal with the sinners and heathens and those who commit open sins, but what about the pretenders, players and self-righteous preachers? You know one thing I learned about games; there are winners and losers. God can't lose. The devil can't win. So where are you?

God's will shall be done in the earth as it is in heaven. It does not matter whom, where, what or why. God is sovereign, and if He said it, then it becomes law. God's will shall never become stagnated, when we submit and obey His purposes in our lives. Because of man's will, God will sometimes allow His omnipotence to stand still for a season, because He knows the outcome. God's will is the best provision for mankind. It starts from the foundation of the world when God knew that the man He made would sin and disobey Him. But God, in His compassion, still made man, and in Genesis set him in a garden designed to meet his every need. Sin will cause a delay in God's will for us, but His will shall be done sooner or later. God will allow His will to take us to places and do things we never imagined.

290

In Genesis 2:18, *"And the Lord God said, 'It is not good that the man should be alone; I will make him a help mate for him.'"*

This was God's will and provision. The woman helped him to disobey and helped him to obey. The will always works for our good and God's glory.

Genesis 3:15, *"And I will put enmity between thee and the woman, and between thy seed and her seed; it shall bruise thy head, and thou shalt bruise his heel."*

This was the will of God working through the woman–the one Satan beguiled with a lie. The one God commanded, Adam, had submitted his will to the woman.

Thousands of years before Christ came on the scene, it was the will of God to defeat Satan on Calvary's cross. But the battle still rages between the seed of the woman and Satan. Even after Satan suffered defeat, he still believes he has a chance through the will of man. So let us see how man's "I will" differs from God's "I will." Man has a history of submitting to what comes out of him—a woman, ideals, invention, education, sin, lust and pride.

MAN'S "I WILL"

The fight over the will of man is the fiercest battle that will ever take place in the mind. It is a fight for control—control of territory, property, souls, health, and even life itself. God grants such respect to the human will that even He who has created it will not interfere in its final decision. It is one of the clearest images of God's love for mankind. Nothing or nobody can control God's love, but God. Nothing or nobody can control the will of man, but man. God made us freewill agents. By our will, we can live for Him, or by our will we can deny Him. You can choose the what, when and where. God gave Satan the same opportunity.

How art thou fallen from heaven, O Lucifer, son of the morning! how art thou cut down to the ground, which didst weaken the nations! For thou hast said in thine heart, 'I will ascend into heaven, I will exalt my throne above the stars of God: I will sit also upon the mount of the congregation, in the sides of the north: I will ascend above the heights of the clouds; I will be like the most High.' Yet thou shalt be brought down to hell, to the sides of the pit.

(Isaiah 14:12-15)

Like Satan did, you can also choose to submit to your own will and forfeit the privileges given by God. A person can submit his will to God or turn it over to Satan. Unlike God, Satan has no proper principles when it comes to the will of man. He will deceive, cheat, lie or steal whenever he can to get man's will under his control. The devil himself does not recognize that he longs for the love of God. This is why the will of man is so important to him (it reminds him of the love of God).

Without his submission, praise and obedience directed toward God, we recognize that the devil is a fallen angel and foul spirit. If there is one thing that intimidates Satan, it is a born-again believer with a strong will for fellowship with God. The devil remembers the moments of splendid glory that he spent in the presence of God, but he has a strong will to serve himself. He left God's presence and fell under self-control. He then became the most dangerous and out-of-control being in the universe. Satan fell to the capital "I". "I will exalt myself like the most high." "I will ascend above God." "I" is the door to self-will, self-control, and self-denial. Satan fights and lies to keep the "I" in all of our lives. "I control my will" seems so harmless and innocent, but the truth is, while it is my right, I am lost because "I" was born in sin and shaped in iniquity. In reality, "I" don't know anything; "I" don't see anything; "I" can't do anything; "I" am lost when "I" control my destiny; "I" is in big trouble; "I" destroys families, communities, churches, relationships, race, religions and worlds.

One of my children's favorite TV sitcoms is "Family Matters". The star of the show is Jaleel White, also known as Steve Urkel. After he makes a disaster, he says those famous words, "Did I do that?" It reminds me of how we mess up our lives every way imaginable, and with a funny look on our face ask, "Did I do that?" How many times do we tell God, "I" didn't want to do it, but "I" did it anyway?

What did Adam and Eve tell God in Genesis 3:8-11 after they had sinned, and God came for fellowship in the garden? First, they saw their own nakedness; "I" will strip us to the bone. Second, they covered up; "I" will try to disguise who we are. Third, they heard the voice of God. "I" will try to hide. Can you imagine Adam and Eve sitting in glory looking at mankind saying, "Did 'I' do that?" All because they listened to Satan, and their will was subdued under his control for a very short season. You do not have to submit your will to the enemy for long. Just out of God's control for a moment, and you can cause death, hell and destruction. How many good men and women in a moment of frustration, took a drink, embezzled money, smoked some crack, or took a second look at a secretary or co-worker with lust in their eyes?

When one has the seed of God, he cannot sin, but the seed is spiritual and this deals with the spirit of man. I am talking about your flesh. This spiritual seed is for an immortal, supernatural body, that is and will be manifested. However, your flesh is carnal and living. It must die daily. "I" must die in order for "I" to live. We used to sing a song, "If I die now I won't have to die no more." This song carried a great revelation of eternal life with Jesus Christ. Allow "I" to die now, and live a victorious life.

Most of us would agree that Jesus died on Calvary's cross. I want to go a little deeper to say that the process of death started before the manger, climaxed at the baptism and settled in the wilderness with fasting for forty days and nights. The night in the Garden of Gethsemane embalmed him, and Calvary laid Him to rest. In all of this Jesus says, "I" lay down my life and can pick it up. "Not my will but thy will be done," (Luke 22:42). He conquered death, hell and the grave when He rose the morning of the third day saying, "I" have all power of heaven and earth in my hands. This is the only justified "I" spoken among men.

CHAPTER SIXTEEN

"I" Must Die

Wherefore if ye be dead with Christ from the rudiments of the world, why, as though living in the world, are ye subject to ordinances, (Touch not; Taste not; Handle not; which all are to perish with the using) after the commandments and doctrines of men? Which things have indeed a shew of wisdom in will worship, humility, and neglecting of the body; not in any honor to the satisfying of the flesh.

(Colossians 2:20-23)

The rudiments of the world is a system and order contrary to our walk with Christ. The center of its purpose is to build the "I" in man. Every time man has built upon "I" there has been a collapse in his relationship with El-Shaddai, the Almighty God. We must learn to live in the world, but not of the world. He that is a friend to the world is an enemy toward God. The "I" in man is his ego, pride, and self-centeredness. "I" increases the hunger for P.M.S. (power, money and sex) and when this happens, we desire to handle, taste, and touch everything that the world has to offer.

SATAN is the culprit behind the "I" factor. His appeal is to draw you away from God by the lust of the flesh, the lust of the eyes, and the pride of life. He also tries to get you to trust the works of the flesh instead of the blood of Jesus. Your focus has been on yourself not God. Satan will use everything in his possession to attract your will. If he has to take you to the top of the mountain, the bell tower in the temple, or challenge you to turn stones into bread, he will do it. He is the author of temptation and frustration. From the Garden of Eden to the Garden of

295

Gethasame, Satan has been trying to promote the benefits of "I". He promises you Power, Money, and Sex (P.M.S.) and we hear how painful that can be (Lord have mercy!). The promises of sin don't cooperate with the walk of faith.

> *And the things that thou hast heard of me among many witnesses, the same commit thou to faithful men, who shall be able to teach others also. Thou therefore endure hardness as a good soldier of Jesus Christ. No man that warreth entangleth himself with the affairs of this life; that he may please him who hath chosen him to be a soldier.*
>
> (II Timothy 2:2-4)

Sometimes it's hard to deny the flesh and submit to God, but we are soldiers in the army of the Lord. If we keep our focus on the prize at the end of this life, we won't substitute a minute, hour, or a day of pleasure to satisfy the flesh...*And, let every one that nameth the name of Christ depart from iniquity* (II Timothy 2:19b).

We know that the Christian Judahlizers were trying to approach God by their ceremonies, customs and procedures, (taste not, touch not, handle not). They were teaching their religious methods as the answer to the Christian walk, but departing from iniquity is more than what you handle, touch and taste. To abstain from worldly pleasure doesn't guarantee that we have a Godly relationship, only discipline.

What credentials does a preacher need to "Ignite the warfare" and kick some devil's butt? Let's examine a few character changes that are necessary for the preacher to die from "I."

Jesus must increase, but I must decrease (St. John 3:30).

God places, at His will the preacher for the specific work of preaching the Gospel. The preachers play a duel role; they take in the truth from God, and give out that truth to mankind. The preacher can appeal to God on behalf of men, then deal with men on behalf of God. They must at all times be truthful to both. Dishonesty in either direction can cause broken fellowship.

Some other character changes that are necessary for the preacher to die from "I" include:

A. The preacher must have truth embedded in his character and personality. This is how credit-worthiness is established. When your credit is bad, neither God nor man has confidence in your word.

B. Every fiber of the person's moral and spiritual nature must be controlled by the truth. If it is not the truth, then it is a lie—and we know who controls liars: their father Satan, who knew not truth from the beginning.

C. The preacher must not be a mere machine, automatically performing duties. They must be real people, full of the Holy Spirit with feelings and understanding. Preachers must be able to cry and laugh, sing out in joy, gravely warn of destruction, authoritatively bind and loose, take in and cast out—all of this sometimes before breakfast.

D. The personality of the preacher impacts the effectiveness of the message. You must preach what you live, and live what you preach. Do not preach from the mountaintop and live in the basement. The message is the experience and the truth operating in your life.

E. Before he can proclaim it with convicting force in and through the sermon, the preacher must have experience in the truth. You cannot be a good driver by simply sitting in a driver's education class. You must have open highway experiences—even if it includes a few fender benders.

F. True preparation for the Gospel ministry does not consist of mere tricks in sermon making or delivery, but in the development of true character. Such persons in the pulpit will surely prove to be preachers who will reach the masses, as long as they allow God to be the speaker and they remain a vessel of honor.

G. A good preacher will preach anywhere there are men and women to hear it. John preached in the most uncomfortable places of his day, but the people who were hungry pressed their way to hear of the Kingdom of God.

The Preacher's Personality

Times change, seasons come and go, laws are made and laws are broken, but the preaching of the Gospel must stand the test of time. It is said that truth and personality are the fundamentals of all true preaching. Truth must be the truth of God as it is revealed in our Lord and Savior Jesus Christ. This is truth, which is fitted for every man and does not change with the passing of time. Regardless of the changes around our own instability, the Gospel transforms lives. The call of Jesus to make fishers of men, and shepherds of the lost sheep is the same yesterday, today, and until Jesus comes. Only complete trust in Jesus can make personalities approve, improve, and be proven. Jesus living and abiding in the Spirit and soul of man will cause Godly personalities and righteous ways. What's on the inside will come out at any time.

The Preacher Must Be Himself

The average preacher is actually almost anyone else except himself. He must learn that the perfect plan of God includes the true him, designed from the foundation of the world.

Every truth the preacher expresses and every message he delivers ought to be stamped with his own personality and should be expressed in his own way. Through methods, style, etc., your unique message can reach the lives given to your ministry, to bring them into the Kingdom. You're only the clay. The potter knows the how's, when's and where's, so allow Him to make you.

Many times a man will fail in this ministry, when otherwise he would have been a glorious success. This is simply because he was not willing to take himself as God made him. It is the Almighty's ministry, and when He called you He also qualified you.

Men who copy successful preachers around them almost always copy their shortcomings, downfalls, weaknesses, and sometimes their self-justified human faults, but often not their virtues. They always take this to the extreme. Copycat preachers do not want to go through the "valley" experiences that make good preachers, or wilderness boot camps that build and strip. They want instant success with no toiling. There's a process, procedures and purposes for all the hardships, trials, and tribulations of ministry. Success is total obedience.

How many men have found it impossible to extricate themselves from difficulties they have been drawn into by attempting to imitate others? When you put on another man's shoes, you may not be able to fulfill the destiny of his walk.

The preacher should be himself, his best self, his consecrated self, and his highest self. In so doing, he will best prove his sincerity, honor God, and become a means of greatest blessing to the people he ministers to. The goal is to hear the Lord say, "Well done thou good and faithful servant. Thou hast been faithful over a few things and now I will make you ruler over many."

Let us remember that God made no two faces or voices the same! Each individual will be rewarded for his own works. On the day of judgment and rewards, your works will speak for you. Maybe some of your works will be burned, but you will be saved (1 Corinthians 3:15). Rejoice more that your name is written down in the Lamb's Book of Life.

The Preacher Must Practice What He Preaches

The great, and often the only difference in many sermons is simply the difference in the character of the preacher. The end result should be salvation, prosperity, and deliverance.

What we are does indeed speak louder than what we say and it certainly is more effective in the long run. Become a living (epistle) word like Jesus: *"The Word was made flesh, and dwelt among us"* (John 1:14).

A hypocrite cannot remain undiscovered in a real word ministry. If the preacher is not living up to his preaching, the people will soon find out. Normally, his family is the first to know, and he loses respect in the home, then the church. Remember he never did have God's respect.

"Teaching us that, denying ungodliness and worldly lusts, we should live soberly, righteously, and godly, in this present world." (Titus 1:12)

The preacher must be clean in the habits of his life. Little foxes spoil the vines. He is to have no impure habits or secret vices. As we learn from Paul to mortify the deeds of the flesh and to die daily, there is always help when we stay on our knees in prayer, seeking the face of God.

"Flee youthful lusts." The preacher will be shorn of his power in the pulpit if he is not clean in his private life. He cannot face his people with confidence if he knows that his life is not as pure as it ought to be. The accuser of the brethren and familiar spirits will make sure all the dirt that can be exposed comes to light. Sin is a telling business, everything and everybody talks. Sin will tell on you. It will not allow you to keep it in the dark. It's conceived in the dark, but when it has a victim, sin wants to walk in the light.

The preacher must cleanse himself from all defilement of the flesh and spirit, perfecting holiness in the fear of the Lord. Remember, deal with the flesh problem controlling your spirit man. The flesh is the last place sin shows up, and the first place it is seen.

If a man therefore purge himself... he shall be a vessel unto honor, sanctified, and meet for the master's use and prepared unto every good work.

(2 Timothy 2:21)

The devil has nothing in you when you clean up. There is nothing he can identify that can be used to convict and bind you.

Exaggeration is lying, "modifying" the truth is lying, and a lie in the pulpit is worse than a lie anywhere else. The Gospel is truth and it is the power of God. A lie is an untruth and it is the deception of Satan.

I have therefore whereof I may glory through Jesus Christ in those things which pertain to God. For I will not dare to speak of any of those things which Christ hath not wrought by me, to make the Gentiles obedient, by word and deed, through mighty signs and wonders, by the power of the Spirit of God; so that from Jerusalem, and round about

unto Illyricum, I have fully preached the gospel of Christ.
(Romans 15:17-19)

A preacher must not do evil so that good may come from it. A good tree can only bring forth good fruit. An evil, corrupt tree can only bring forth bad fruit. Only God can change the results.

Similarly, piety in the pulpit must be accompanied by piety at home. The pulpit is a reflection of the home of God. It is His throne of love, judgment, and fellowship with His body.

The preacher must keep his vows. If he has promised to meet an obligation on a certain day, he must meet it. If he is unable to meet it at the proper time, then he must be a man and confess his inability to do so.

"For that ye ought to say, 'If the Lord will, we shall live, and do this, or that.'" (James 4:15)

The Preacher Must Be a Person of Honor and Integrity
Therefore seeing we have this ministry, as we have received mercy, we faint not; But have renounced the hidden things of dishonesty, not walking in craftiness, nor handling the word of God deceitfully.
(2 Corinthians 4:1-2)

There should be a difference between the methods of a cheap advertising agency promoting a circus, and an ambassador from the court of heaven. One popular advertiser says, "Style is everything." I say substance in your style can make the difference, because style, slang and jingles come and go, but the truth remains eternally.

One of the greatest fears a preacher should have is that he may grieve the Holy Spirit. Whether by foolish talking and jesting or by anything else, words are power weapons and can be used to kill, bring down walls, make ax heads float, divide Red Seas, speak worlds into existence, raise dead bodies, and cast out demons. Our words are precious in God's sight. They also represent the praise of God.

Beware lest any man spoil you through philosophy and vain deceit, after the tradition of men, after the rudiments of the world, and not after Christ.

(Colossians 2:8)

The Preacher Must Take Care of His Physical Health

Your body is a gift from God to your spirit. The Lord has allowed us to be made in His image and after His likeness so that we may enjoy all the glory and majesty of this world and the world to come. However, we have destroyed everything from the ozone layer to the bottom of the sea. We may also be destroying our bodies by being so spiritually-minded that we don't eat, sleep or rest properly. We forget about exercising, since we think that exercising is for the world. Ordinarily, a man must be a good steward of the natural before he can be a good spiritual preacher. I believe the two work together for the glory of God (spirit and body).

Know ye not that ye are the temple of God, and that the Spirit of God dwelleth in you? If any man defile the temple of God, him shall God destroy; for the temple of God is holy, which temple ye are.

(1 Corinthians 3:16-17)

They Must Manage Their Stress

The preacher should be in his best condition, because ministering can be stressful to the physical body. Even Jesus lost virtue when touched; He lost strength in the Garden of Gethsemane, and stumbled while carrying His cross to Calvary. Paul was whipped, stoned and shipwrecked.

But in all things approving ourselves as the ministers of God, in much patience, in afflictions, in necessities, in distresses, in stripes, in imprisonments, in tumults, in labours, in watchings, in fastings; by pureness, by knowledge, by longsuffering, by kindness, by the Holy Ghost, by love unfeigned, by the word of truth, by the power of God, by the armour of righteousness on the right hand and on the left, by honour and dishonour, by evil report and good report: as deceivers, and yet true; as unknown, and yet well known; as dying, and, behold, we live; as chastened, and not killed; as sorrowful, yet always rejoicing; as poor, yet making many rich; as having nothing, and yet possessing all things.

(2 Corinthians 6:4-10)

But I keep under my body, and bring it into subjection, lest that by any means, when I have preached to others, I myself should be a castaway.

(1 Corinthians 9:27)

A good physique is an attraction in the pulpit as well as the basis for good spiritual enjoyment. It shows discipline and self-appreciation, and besides, it looks healthy.

John said,
Beloved I wish above all things that thou mayest prosper and be in health, even as thy soul prospereth.

(3 John 2)

A change of diet is the first thing some Christians need to attend to in order to progress in sanctification. Most of the attacks on the physical body can be avoided before a spiritual attack takes place. Just having good health is a help when the time comes to spend time in praise, prayer and worship without having your mind on what's ailing, aching, or burning you out. In general, we need to keep ourselves healthy and happy God's way.

For God hath not called us unto uncleanness, but unto holiness. He therefore that despiseth, despiseth not man, but God, who hath also given unto us His Holy Spirit. But as touching brotherly love ye need not that I write unto you: for ye yourselves are taught of God to love one another.

(1 Thessalonians 4:7-9)

Don't hate the temple, minister healing to it by taking care of it by resting, exercising, and eating a proper diet.

PAUL'S DAY   21ST CENTURY

EVERY PREACHER MUST BE DRESSED

Put on the whole armour of God, that ye may be able to stand against the wiles of the devil.

(Ephesians 6:10)

The preacher must learn how to dress to fight effectively. He must fully dress for the battle. Without the Holy Ghost, no minister can wage a successful attack on the kingdom of darkness. The Holy Ghost is the fabric that our armor is stitched from. We must be clothed in the very presence of God's spirit, and we can keep the armor on through prayer, obedience, submission and praise. These are just a few of the things well-dressed soldiers do to stand against the wiles of the devils.

Satan has various plans, schemes, and traps to enslave us. He doesn't fight fair. He will cheat, lie and deceive you to accomplish his agenda. We must put on our armor daily through praise, prayer and obedience.

Wherefore, take unto you the whole armour of God that ye

may be able to withstand the evil day, and having done all, to stand.

(Ephesians 6:13)

We are commissioned to fight the good fight regardless of spiritual wickedness in high places. Being properly dressed, we can cast down the strongholds of Satan. Everything about you will be manifested and tested by Satan's kingdoms.

THE ARMOR OF THE SAINTS

Offensive and Defensive Armor

Our armor can be used offensively and defensively – offense for attack and defense for protection:

1. The Helmet of Salvation and Sword of the Spirit

a. The helmet of salvation (gr) perikephalaia for the head. When Satan accuses and whispers that you aren't saved or redeemed, that you've lost your anointing, that the power of God isn't real in your life, be careful. The devil will play with your mind; it's the battleground. So preacher, guard your mind and thoughts with the power of the Gospel and the helmet of salvation. It takes a well made-up mind to continue to praise and serve God when you've been under heavy attacks. Know in your mind that Christ has saved you. Trust the written Word and your confession of faith. Have a active relationship with Jesus through prayer, praise, study and worship (Romans 10:8-15).

b. The girdle – Greek - Zoma – for the loins to brace the armors closely to the body. Know the truth of God's Word when Satan appears with doubts and fears. Keep the Word hidden in your heart, study your Bible daily and eat, sleep and breathe the Word. The heart is the dwelling place of the spirit. By the natural heart giving life to the whole body of the spirit comes the issues of life (Prov. 4:23). So guard and keep the heart protected with the girdle of anointing. Allow nothing to get closer than what God commands in your life. Girdle His will around you.

c. The Breastplate of Righteousness – Greek – thoraz – it covers the chest and the back. Satan can't accuse me in my presence or absence and get away with it because I'm the righteousness of God through Christ Jesus. I have right standing with God. I'm entitled to everything in the covenant from perfect health to eternal life. There's nothing hidden from my reach. Righteousness is what covers the believer's heart. Even when we come up short, the righteous relationship with Christ Jesus is what acts as a covering to protect against accusation. From the heart, life goes through the body. It must be well-protected.

d. My feet shod – Greek – knemides – brazen boots for the feet to cover the front of the leg. A kind of sole was often used to protect the feet from the rocks, thorns and damaging elements with the preparation of the Gospel of peace. While walking into Satan's stronghold with the power of the Gospel message, and setting them free, be prepared to go any and everywhere He sends you to minister the Gospel of peace reclaiming territory, possessions and a sharp shoe to kick some devil's butt.

e. Taking the shield of faith, wherewith ye shield (Greek – thures) to protect the body from blows and cuts. Fiery dart (Greek– belos) dart, or any missile thrown. Satan throws temptation, lust, vain imaginations, ungodly gained money, wine and sexual thoughts our way daily. Some things we can't handle. They must be stopped before they strike us or they may do severe harm. But our shield, which is our faith in Him and His faith in us, can help us win every battle. Faith is the finished works of Jesus from the cradle to the cross, the battle in to leading captivity captive to sitting at the right hand of the Father.

2. How to Use The Weapons–Remember, our weapons are spiritual.

For though we walk in the flesh, we do not war after the flesh: For the weapons of our warfare are not carnal, but mighty through God to the pulling down of strongholds: Casting down imaginations, and every high thing that

exalteth itself against the knowledge of God, and bringing
into captivity every thought to the obedience of Christ
(II Corinthians 10:3-5)

Use these definitions to help understand their purpose:

<u>Mighty</u> – having might, powerful; strong. Also, the very core of manifesting the active will of God in the preachers' life–he shall do mighty exploits... but the people that do know their God shall be strong and do exploits (Daniel 11:23). Get to know your God and Savior.

<u>Might</u> – In order to manifest the power at this level the preacher must get rid of "I". He must submit to the Holy Spirit to do mighty exploits. If not, "I" will exploit him.

<u>Pulling down</u> – destruction, overthrow, demolish to tear down, to degrade, humble. I Peter 2:11 says, *"Dearly beloved, I beseech you as strangers and pilgrims, abstain from fleshly lust, which war against the soul."* The war is in the mind to conquer the soul of man. Every time Satan shoots a dart into your thoughts, he is trying to steal your soul. Pull these destructive thoughts down by submitting your mind to the will of God. Psalms, hymns and worship can help you in this battle. Devils and demons set up strongholds for control of territory. Remember, Satan eats flesh and spits out dirt.

<u>Stronghold</u> – a place having strong defenses; a fortified place–a place where a group has certain views, attitudes, etc. I've found the strongholds in war aren't always the obvious places we tend to look. Sometimes they are hidden right under our noses, draped with pride and arrogance. How many times have we said, "I don't care what any one says, I know God for myself" or "We thought that God should bless us because we did a deed or service here and there." Self-righteousness, pride, idolatry, jealousy, strife and religious back-biting are camouflaged strongholds. Eliminate every possible area that Satan can build a stronghold in your life. Satan is going about seeking whom he may devour. Don't get trapped in a stronghold. It's like quicksand. The more you move, the deeper you're trapped.

Imaginations – the acts or power of forming mental images of what is not actually physically present; a good or foolish notion. There's a great gulf between visions and imaginations, but both come from mental origins. Preachers must spend time with God to get or see a vision. If a preacher spends time away from God, he will mostly get caught up in vain imaginations. A holy vision will increase your faith in God. Vain imagination will tear apart your faith in God. It's dangerous not to know the different between them both. And not to know from whom they're sent. Satan can give you a vision and trick imaginations. They appear to be good and wholesome until you're trapped. Every satanic vision or imagination will be exposed when the Word comes forth. Satan appeals as the pride of life, lust of the eyes and lust of the flesh.

Knowledge – the act, fact or state of knowing, and learning. Knowledge is power. Power is authority. The devil has to respect authority; authority controls the situation and sets order. Knowledge is the difference between you going to heaven and living in hell.

Captivity – the condition or time of being captive, imprisonment. This is the place where those who ignored the stronghold and snares of Satan reside. The preacher who preaches in captivity is different from the preacher who preaches deliverance to the captives. Religious captivity is just as bad as worldly captivity. We must walk in the spirit and not fulfill the lust of the flesh and the lust of tradition.

> *Which things have indeed a show of wisdom in will-worship, and humility, and neglecting of the body; not in any honor to satisfy of the flesh. If ye then be risen with Christ, seek those things which are above, where Christ sitteth on the right hand of God. Set your affections on things above, not on things on the earth.*
>
> (Colossians 2:23;3:2)

We are human, but we don't wage war with human plans and methods; we use God's mighty weapons, not mere worldly weapons to knock down the devil's strongholds. With these weapons we conquer their rebellious ideas and we teach them to obey Christ. We will punish those who remain disobedient after the rest of you became loyal and obedient (II Corinthians 10:3-6 N.L.T).

How do we use these weapons? You must not trust in "I". DO NOT TRUST YOURSELF OR CARNAL-MINDED PROCEDURES TO WAGE WAR AND GET THE VICTORY. God is sovereign and His weapons are superior. The product is a reflection of its Manufacturer. The weapons of God are God's Word, ways and will manifesting His character. The preacher must know God personally. "Seek ye first the Kingdom of God," the role and reign of God. Spend quality time in the Word, listen to the Holy Spirit, preach, teach and prophecy in the lives of others. Accept mentoring and have a teachable spirit. Listen to testimonies of the saints, have fellowship with the anointed, consecrated and sanctified believers. Listen to individuals who fear God and despise the works of Satan.

No one starts out a weapons expert, a sharp shooter or a demolition specialist. You must be trained for the task, and obedient to your superiors. Having good weapons is only a part of our warfare; then there is showing up at the right battleground, being under-equipped or over-equipped. Following orders is important; do as you're told and rely on your training. Don't show up at a gunfight with a pocket knife. That can cost you your life. How to use your weapons is through the directing of the Holy Ghost. Allow God to anoint you with the Holy Ghost and power and you will move forward doing good. When you seek God and He anoints you, the Good News will be preached to the poor, the broken-hearted will be healed, deliverance will be preached to the captives and the recovery of sight to the blind to set at liberty them who are bruised.

Jesus shows us how to use our weapons perfectly. He fasted, prayed and stayed in the Word of God which is the will of God. His purpose was to reveal heaven on earth and destroy the works of Satan. Our weapons don't work on destroying other saints, but help to build and strengthen. It doesn't kill sinners and doom them to hell, but breaks the satanic hold on sinners' lives.

War After The Flesh ... Natural Response Will Fail

If the preacher has no vision or knowledge of warfare, then he will always give a humanistic response to a spiritual situation. He will look at the right things the wrong way.

Just like eve's natural reaction to temptation

And when the woman saw that the tree was good for food and that it was pleasant to the eyes, and a tree to be desired to make one wise, she took of the fruit thereof and did eat and gave also unto her husband with her; and he did eat.

(Genesis 3:6)

Adam and Eve, until now, did the right things, but this was the wrong thing at the wrong time and ungodly reasons controlled by the wrong force. When the woman saw the tree, Satan twisted her imagination. What you see can be deceiving, unless you're seeing a vision from God.

Esau's response:
And Jacob sod pottage: and Esau came from the field, and he was faint: And he said to Jacob, feed me, I pray thee, with the same red pottage; for I am faint: And Jacob said swear to me this day; and he swore unto him: and he sold his birth right unto Jacob.

(Genesis 25:29-33)

Walking after the flesh can cause the preacher to lose his anointing or even his birthright. In desperate times, when your back is up against the wall, what will you compromise or bargain for to get some relief? Will Power, Money or Sex , (P.M.S) soothe your itch?

Solomon's response:
But King Solomon loved many strange women. For it came to pass, when Solomon was old, that his wives turned away his heart after other gods.

(I King 11:1)

Even with the wisdom of Solomon, the flesh with its desires will trap and strip you of your relationship with God. So preacher, don't think you have it all figured out. You can't please the flesh on Saturday and preach on Sunday. It will catch up with you real soon. As smart as Solomon was and the warning he received (read Proverbs 7:5-23; 31:3), the flesh entrapped him. Sin in the flesh will turn your heart away from God, if not today, then tomorrow–Satan is patient.

I remember a time when I thought I needed a certain amount of money to pay some bills. I had prayed, fasted and sought God, but I didn't hear anything at all. Because I didn't get a "yes" or "no" answer I went to borrow the money. The loan officer said they would approve me for a certain amount, but I wondered if this was the way out of a situation. Does God tell us to borrow at high interest rates when walking in the ministry? I didn't think so. I prayed for His perfect will to be done. The agent called back and said "Your credit is great, the collateral is sufficient, but we don't want to deal with a church." Now I believe that's discrimination, but I gave the Christian response and said, "Thank you sir, I'll keep your company in my prayers." I started to praise God for my miracle.

Reaction to Emotion... (Carnal)
When we serve God based on our emotions and ignore truth and revelation, we tend to commit ourselves to a carnal level that will not release the reality of who Christ is. We become attached to the popularity of public opinion. Ministry that is based on emotion can hinder the release of revelation. So don't get caught up with highs and lows of ministry; learn to be content.

And from thence forth Pilate sought to release him: but the Jews cried out, saying, if thou let this man go, thou art not Caesar's friend whosoever maketh himself a king speaketh against Caesar.

(St. John 19:12)

Caesar today is the popular opinion and must be dealt with. The preacher must always be in the position to release Jesus and revelation from God. Lead the crowd, don't follow it. Loving Caesar is the course of the world. You can't be his friend, and be in love with Jesus.

Now he that betrayed him gave them a sign, saying whomsoever I shall kiss, that same is he: Hold him fast. And behold, one of them which were with Jesus stretched out his hand, and drew his sword, and struck a servant of the high priests, and smote off his ear.

(St. Matthew 26:48–51)

In time of confrontation, the preacher must keep his cool. I don't care how wrong the others are, always remember W.W.J.D. (What Would Jesus Do?)–even when another preacher is betraying your faith with a kiss. Keep your sword (Bible) for His (God's) use only.

Our armor and weapons are in the Word of God, the way of God and His will. This authority is given to destroy the works, methods, and ways of the enemy, to bind and defeat him. Now we can choose the weapons of our warfare for we know that they are not carnal, but mighty through God to the pulling down of strongholds. They also are used for the casting down of imaginations, every high thing that exalteth itself against the knowledge of God, and bringing into captivity every thought to the obedience of Christ. The first thing that the military does after you enlist is take you to boot camp. There they strip you, train you to march and teach you how to use your weapons. The enemy is out to destroy every believer. We must be prepared to kick some devil's butt or be defeated.

Power to Kick Butt
And when he had called unto him his twelve disciples, he gave them power against unclean spirits, to cast them out, and to heal all manner of sickness and all manner of disease.

(St. Matthew 10:1)

The first thing that happened here is that Jesus called them. Mister Preacher, Miss Teacher, Brother Sunday School Worker, have you been called or did you just go? Jesus called... and in addition to your call are you chosen or are you just passing by, standing there still looking like a preacher, teacher or Sunday school worker? There is a difference between the sent and the went.

312

"The Sent" are those who waited to be trained and equipped. They are submissive and know how to follow orders. They aren't full of pride and self-centeredness. They know the mission is about Jesus Christ and saving a dying world.

"The Went" is the group who don't think they need boot camp and training. They see how its being done and figure they have just as much intelligence as the next man. They look at the box and don't bother to read the instructions. They're spiritual outlaws and Word criminals.

Next, He gave them power (dynamite). The power Jesus gave them was the right to use authority in His Name. Jesus was able to give because He paid the price through baptism, fasting and the wilderness experience. Thus, the apostles had power to fulfill God's plan. This is a foretaste of Pentecost after the Holy Ghost came upon them. They were being trained to whip the devil, not fear or flee from the enemy. The preacher must rebuke and speak forcefully against unclean spirits to cast them out. This is not patty cake. THIS IS WAR!

The best place for an unclean spirit is in dry places (Matthew 12:43-45). You have the power to cast them out; not to excuse them as sin, they were born that way. They are under-privileged and exploring their sexuality. It is their custom. They're black, white, rich or poor. If they are controlled, possessed, manipulated by an unclean, evil or crossed-up spirit, then cast the demon out. You will be given knowledge and power to heal all manner of sickness and disease.

Jesus told His apostles to heal them, not to accuse, debate or look at the doctor's report. Sometimes it is not good to pray in the church service where the doubter dwells. Go to the pastor's office or take a Sunday School class to pray for healing. Sometimes when healing is taking place there needs to be no distractions. Look at Job 1:6-7. Satan was in a prayer meeting trying to find someone to touch. The devil will do anything he can to stop you from casting him out or reversing the decision of sickness. I say "decision" because many times people may not be conscious but by word, action or ways (lifestyle) but God looks beyond our faults and He sees our needs. He does not care where we have been or what we did when we come with a repentant heart and broken spirit. Jesus said heal them. When there is sickness, disease, sin and death, Jesus has the keys (Authority). The preacher must also prepare for a negative situation. Sometimes people don't want to be delivered. It has been free will choice to get involved in the mess they're in, and they don't want you to help them. Many people don't come to the church to be healed, blessed or freed from sin. Some people enjoy and love what they're doing and will tell the preacher, "Not today Pastor, maybe later."

Reaction and Rejection to Power—Some people don't want what's good or the will of God.

And unto whatsoever city or town ye shall enter, inquire who is worthy; and there abide till ye go thence. And when ye come unto an house, salute it. And the house be worthy let your peace come upon it: but if it be not worthy, let your peace return to you.

(St.Matthew10:11-13)

But if you're rejected, please don't take it personally.

The first thing an unlearned, untrained child does when he gets his first toy is to head for the most dangerous areas of the house. If he gets a bike, he heads for the streets to see how fast it can go. Jesus gave instructions with the power and authority He issued. Power that is well received can be well rejected if it is not controlled properly. There are some people who don't want you to pray for them or set them free.

Remember, Jesus said in Matthew 7:6, *"Give to that which is holy unto the dogs, either cast ye your pearls before swine, lest they trample them under feet and turn again and rend you."*

Everybody don't want what you got. Jesus predicts persecution of Christians in Matthew 23:34-39,

Wherefore behold I send unto you prophets, and wise men, and scribes: and some of them shall kill and crucify; and

some of them shall ye scrounge in your synagogues, and persecute them from city to city: that upon you may come all the righteous blood shed upon the earth, from the blood of the righteous. Abel unto the blood of Zacharias son of Barachias, whom ye slew between the temple and the altar. Verily I say unto you, all these things shall come upon this generation. O Jerusalem, Jerusalem, thou that killeth the prophets, and stones them which are sent unto thee, how often would I have gathered thy children together, even as a hen gathereth her chickens under her wings, and ye would not. Behold our house is left unto you desolate. For I say unto you Ye shall not see me hence forth, till ye shall say, Blessed is he that cometh in the name of the Lord.

Preacher, if you have obeyed God, then there is nothing else that really matters. God is faithful to perform His Word.

The Results of Power
And they went out, and preached that men should repent and they cast out many devils, and anointed with oil many that were sick and healed them.
(St. Mark 6:12-13)

And the apostles gathered themselves together unto Jesus and told him all things, both what they had done, and what they had taught. And he said unto them, come ye yourselves apart into a desert place, and rest a while... and they departed into a desert place by ship privately.
(St. Mark 6:30-31)

The apostles were given power and instruction and they followed them to the letter. Thus, the results were overwhelming, they cast out many devils, demons and unclean spirits, they laid hands and anointed the sick and on the spot miracles were being born. They taught and preached deliverance and the spirits were subject to the power and authority. Revival broke out and excitement was in the air. Jesus called them together after the powerful demonstrations. When a motivated, powerful preacher submits to the will of God, it will scare the hell into Satan.

A Time to Rest

The apostles were told to come aside and rest after the Revival. Jesus knew that the body handling power can be worn out. It is very important to have balance when casting out demons and praying for the sick. It is God's power but your body needs rest to be strengthened. Don't fast all the time you are working in the vineyard, but as you are led by the Spirit of God. Eat right, exercise and rest as much as the Holy Ghost allows. There are times we need a vacation, retreat or to take a cruise. Note: Jesus and the apostles scheduled a cruise vacation (Mark 6:32). Many of us need to sit still and just do nothing. Sometimes, we have gotten stagnated with ministry cares, family cares and world cares (I Corinthians 7:32-33). We need balance, and to listen to our wives and families. It doesn't mean you're compromising when you take quality time off to enjoy creation and vacation.

When Jesus' disciples came to Him and asked about the sign of His coming and the end of the world, Jesus told them many things in Matthew chapter 24:37-38,

> *But as the days of Noe [Noah] were, so shall also the coming of the Son of man be. For as in the days that were before the flood they were eating and drinking.*

This isn't the same as you and your family taking a vacation, enjoying a good meal and riding the ferris wheel. Everyone in the whole world lives for their bellies, and to satisfy the flesh. The lack of spiritual discipline shows up in their appetites. 2 Peter 2:12-17 and Jude 10-13 talk about the spirit of banqueting that manifests itself in out-of-control false prophets, trying to integrate with the righteous. There must be someone in your life who you can take some criticism from when things get cloudy—someone accessible, a mentor, a praying wife, etc...or a good friend to tell you the truth about yourself. We preach hard, eat late at night and rise early for morning prayer, then meet every appointment, balance the church budget, home budget, be a father, husband and keep up with the Jones'. We think that we can't afford the type of vacation we really need. You should take at least three days a month for yourself, three days with your

316

spouse, and three days for your children and three days for fasting and prayer. That's about half of the month and believe me, the ministry won't close or shut down. Heaven won't go bankrupt and God will manage to keep the universe on course.

The Conclusion

EXERCISE

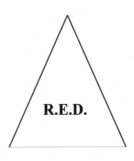

R.E.D.

REST   DIET

We Must Get in the RED

Rest = freedom from work or activity; a silence in music equivalent in duration to a note; something used as a support.

The preacher must rest to get revelation; God will speak to a calm and rested spirit. When we don't rest there's too many forces draining our lives of valuable quality time. God even rested after six days of work and He's a spirit. Spend at least one day a week resting and meditating an hour daily; this will help bring balance.

Exercise = employment, use (of authority); exertion made for the sake of training or physical fitness; a task or problem done to develop skill.

The best body, trained and fit, must maintain an exercise program to stay at the top of the game. Most preachers don't take the time to walk a mile or swim a few laps. I found many times a good 30 to 45 minute walk means time to talk to God. Also it keeps the mind clear. Walk at least 3 days a week, if possible.

Exercise will profit a little dealing with spiritual matters and alot dealing with physical vitality. See your physician for assistance before you start a program and use professional trainers for instruction and tips on how to keep safe without injury. Start out slow, but be persistent. Make this a family outing, turn off the TV, get off the couch and have some sweating fun.

<u>Diet</u> = manner of living; fr. (diaitasthai) ; to lead one's life; food and drink regularly consumed; fare; an allowance of food prescribed for as special reason (as to lose weight).

Fasting should be a key part of our diet. Discipline should control the balance of the rest. When eating, I was told to eat small portions four times a day. Make sure you eat a balanced breakfast and try not to eat a big meal before bed. The best things to eat are what can be eaten naturally with little or no processing. The best foods in the stores are the ones on the outer aisles that need refrigeration and have short expiration dates. Limit the amount of white stuff such as: processed flour, sugar, salt, white rice, milk, white bread, etc. Fry alot less, bake, broil, steam and grill more, do more meal planning and prepare yourself to enjoy the fellowship of breaking bread.

Often you will hear people say, "I'm trying to get out of the RED because it's killing me. I'm stressed out with bills and debts. My outgo is outrunning my income. My income is a distant rich uncle, and my outgo is a constant companion. Lord, please get me out of the RED." One important factor that is often blindly lost when we ask God to get us out of the RED is, if we continue to do the same things, we will get the same result. Most of us build so much of our life on trying to please ourselves with things that we forget how to live and why we were put here. First, we were made to worship and praise God, then to love our fellow man as ourselves. In addition, we were made to enjoy His creation; the land, air, water, trees, animals, and lastly to work and till the grounds. Unfortunately, we work backwards. The 23rd Psalm is a lesson to study while dealing with stress and frustration.

Allow me to share the right side, not the backside of what we need–a different RED. The RED I'm talking about is R–for rest,

E–for exercise, and D–for diet. RED. Preacher, you must die to live and live to die for Him.

The RED may not be the total answer to life's problems (we know Jesus is the Answer), but it sure helps as a deterrent for stress, burnout, bad decisions, haste that makes waste, heart disease, and whatever other things that might hinder your ministry. Study the life of Christ, Paul and others and you'll find a similar pattern of the RED. I adopted the RED pattern in my personal life; I had a wake-up call several years ago (that's right, me, the apostle of God). God placed me in the RED program.

My goal in writing this book is to teach, train and equip believers in the foundations of spiritual warfare. If I have done my job, you should have a sense of the areas in your life where you are in your "comfort zone" and have a desire to change. You should desire a passionate relationship with our Lord Jesus Christ, and understand that obedience to His Word and will in your life leads to fulfillment and blessings—today, and for all eternity.

You should have a desire to be real with God and stop playing religious games. Looking good on the outside to cover up what is inside leads to spiritual death. We must all submit our will to the will of God. His perfect plan never fails. His way is better.

You should have a better understanding of what it is to be a preacher. Your pastor needs your prayers and support. His calling is difficult and it's a constant spiritual battle. Satan would love to take him down.

And finally, stay healthy. Stay in the RED with proper rest, diet and exercise. We must be at the top of our game. Everything we do to prepare ourselves spiritually and physically will help in the end.

Thank you and be blessed. Watch for the next volume–*The Triangle of Faith.*

REFERENCES

Webster Dictionary;
  Springfield: Merriam Webster Incorporated, 1994

Strong, James; *The New Strong's Exhaustive
  Concordance of the Bible*
  Nashville, Thomas Nelson Publishers,1995

Dake, Fenis Jennings; *Dake's Annotated Reference Bible*
  Lawrenceville, Georgia; Dake Bible Sales, Inc., 1963

Vine, W.E. V*ine Dictionary of Bible Words*
  Nashville, Thomas Nelson Publishers,1997.

Willmington's Guide to the Bible
  Tyndale House Publishers, Inc., Wheaton, Illinois 2000

New Living Translation
  Tyndale House Publishers, Inc., Wheaton, Illinois 2000

Beka Book Publications
  Pensacola, FL 1993
  Matthew Henry's Commentary
  Hendrickson Publishers 1994

THE VISION OF OUR MINISTRY

The T.C. Maxwell Ministries (TCM) is composed of committed people who have received a vision from God that Jesus Christ is both Lord and Savior. The word "vision" means God's revelation; to have an insight and understanding as to what God is saying and into what God sees. The revelation that God has given to T.C. Maxwell is found in III John 2 in which God states, "Beloved I wish above all things that thou mayest prosper and be in good health, even as thy soul prospereth."

As we can see from III John 2, God desires for His people to have the very best. However, in order to prosper spiritually, physically and financially, the Church must return to the foundation of the Bible, which is Jesus Christ and His teachings. The vision that God has given to T.C. Maxwell is to teach the Body of Christ how to prosper first spiritually then physically, financially and in all other areas of their lives through the Word of God.

The revelation that we have is not just to build large facilities, a national television program or to develop a center for people to come to from all around the world, but it is to reach the world with the message that God wants His children to obtain the promises and blessings of God. The vision is to see the world obtaining God's best in every dimension of their lives. The commitment is to use every means available to us to fulfill the commission and the vision.

Our prayer is that the Holy Spirit will open the mind and heart to the vision that God has given to the family of TCM as we are reaching the world with a message of commitment, victory and prosperity for God's people.

The purpose of TCM is to seek the Kingdom of God. Most believers who seek the Kingdom of God begin with church attendance, exercise religious duties, or claim that they are helpless sinners totally incapable of reaching Him by our own efforts ("Not by works or righteous which we have done, but according to His mercy he saved us," Titus 3:5). Christ was not being presumptuous when He claimed Himself the only way to God. God left no other alternative. Jesus Christ, God the Son took our sin upon Himself and paid for it by His substitutional death on the cross. Only through trusting Christ alone, through faith, can we possess eternal life in heaven with God (I John 5:13).

TCM is committed to total pursuit. Our prayer is not a word in the ministry is spoken, not a sermon is delivered without the witness of the Holy Ghost that shouts, "The Word of God and its concepts of life as paramount!" So we believe, so we teach.

Knowing Christ as Savior is the beautiful beginning. As children of God, we are to *"grow in grace and in the knowledge of our Lord and Savior, Jesus Christ"* (II Peter 3:18). This pursuit becomes the hot heart of conviction, which is the Apostle Paul's declaration, "For me to live is Christ."

RUN WITH US!!!

Become "The Dynamics of Spiritual Warfare – Monthly Seed" Partner

Did you start a Revival or Riot? We are asked many questions like that and with a name like "The Dynamics of Spiritual Warfare," we've come to expect it. Do we really think that we can Walk in our Authority? I know we can!

Are you a person who will start a Revival or Riot? If the cries of your heart are echoed in the words of this message, would you prayerfully consider "RUNNING WITH US" as a Dynamics of Spiritual Warfare partner? Each seed partner who sows into this ministry a monthly gift of $20 or more will receive a teaching tape of the month. We can never repay you for your support, but it is a small token of our gratitude. Also, by receiving the teaching tape of the month, it will bless you spiritually.

You may become a monthly seed partner by calling or writing to:

email: apostleTCmaxwell@jesusanswers.com
Dr. T.C. Maxwell
P.O. Box 970535
Boca Raton, FL 33497-0535
Phone: 954-779-2593; Fax: 561-558-5002

Thank you for your interest in *"The Dynamics of Spiritual Warfare Teaching Series"*. We look forward to you walking in your authority.

Apostle T.C. Maxwell

enlist NOW for
BOOT CAMP

The boot camp ministry of Apostle Dr. T.C. Maxwell and Prophetess A.R. Maxwell will change your life!

This ministry also conducts seminars for conferences, conventions and local pastors. You may choose a subject that you wish them to minister on. Please contact us at least 60-90 days in advance, the sooner the better.

Boot Camp subjects 2004-2006

	The Anointing–Booklet
	Ignite the Warfare–Book
Warfare:	*The Authority of the Believers–Book*
	The Triangle of Faith–Book (2005)
	School of Five-fold Ministry–Outline
	Intimacy for Men and Women–Outline
Marriage:	Secrets to a Good Marriage–Outline
	Dating, Dollars, and Honey Dew–Outline
	The Scope of God–Booklet

We will supply the following: books, workbooks, t-shirts, pens w/note pads and certificates of completion.

Hosts are responsible for the following: location, registration, and advertisement. There is a minimum of 25 persons per class.

Boot Camp I
Saturday   9:00 a.m-6:00 p.m   Cost: $150/person

Boot Camp II
Wednesday – Friday   9:00 a.m-1:00 p.m   Cost: $150/person

Boot Camp III:
Wednesday – Friday   7:00 p.m – 10:00 p.m   Cost: $150/person

HOW TO CONTACT US:

Via Mail: Dr. T.C. Maxwell Ministry
P.O. Box 970535
Boca Raton, FL 33497-0535

Via Phone: Voicemail: (954) 779-2593
Fax: (561) 558-8002

Via e-mail: apostleTCmaxwell@jesusanswers.com

P.O. Box 970535 Boca Raton, Florida, 33497
954.779.2593

ACKNOWLEDGMENTS

Thank You Lord Jesus Christ for giving me the many ideas for completing this book *The Authority of the Believer.* I pray that the coming workbook will help every ministry, minister and individual in some way. I will continue to move forward in Jesus' Name.

Specials thanks to the workbook committee for all your hard work, time and dedication.

A special thank you for your proofreading:
Pastor Ronny Thompson
Prophetess Z. Thompson
Mother Junia Solomon
Sis. Evadne Maxwell
Min. Tiffany Shannon
Sis. Shetina Maxwell
Mother Bessie Mallory
Min. Tena Grimes
Min. Spencer, Valeria Jones, Lacleshia & Thomas Gregory

Special thanks to my typists:
Evadne, Tiffany & My Pooh Bear (Precious Jewel) daughter.

To the leaders of my past;

- Bishop Mattie Walker, a powerful warrior who presently is with Jesus. I miss you and thank you for believing in me.

- Bishop R. Grisset, a mighty man of valour. Thank you for helping to develope a godly character in me. There's no room for compromise.

Pastor D. Maxwell
Greater Works Ministry
Pompano Beach, FL

Bishop H.C. Moore
Temple of Light
Jacksonville, FL 32209

Bishop Gary Jefferson
Kingdom Dominioners
Orlando, FL 32805

Bishop Ronnie Thompson
Faith Deliverance Tabernacle
Ft. Lauderdale, FL 33311

Pastor A. Morton
Vision of Harvest
Ft. Lauderdale, FL 33311

Pastor L. Bing
North Jacksonville Family Worship Center
Jacksonville, FL

Apostle Willie C. Kellom
One Voice World Changing Ministries
Buford, GA. 30519

Dr. E. Ford
Harvest Time Deliverance
Ocala, FL.

Pastor Peter Butler
Christian Cove Church
Nassau Bahamas

Call now to join in our fellowship. Set your ministry under the Dynamic Teaching and leadership of Apostle T.C. and Prophetess Maxwell.